SOFTWARE ESTIMATION BEST PRACTICES, TOOLS & TECHNIQUES

A Complete Guide for Software Project Estimators

MURALI CHEMUTURI

Printed and bound in the U.S.A. Printed on acid-free paper
10 9 8 7 6 5 4 3 2 1

Library of Congress Cataloging-in-Publication Data

Chemuturi, Murali, 1950-
    Software estimation best practices, tools, & techniques : a complete guide
for software project estimators / by Murali Chemuturi.
        p. cm.
    Includes index.
    ISBN 978-1-60427-024-2 (hardcover : alk. paper)
    1. Computer software—Development. 2. Computer software—Development—
Estimates. I. Title.
    QA76.76.D47C48 2009
    005.1′4—dc22   2009018198

Phone: (954) 727-9333
Fax: (561) 892-0700
Web: www.jrosspub.com

TABLE OF CONTENTS

Foreword xi
Preface xiii
About the Author xvii
Acknowledgments xix
Web Added Value™ xxi

Chapter 1: Software Estimation 1
Background 1
What Is Software Estimation? 2
Why Is Software Estimation Important? 4
When Is Software Estimation Carried Out? 4
Traditional Cost Estimation 5
Summary 8

Chapter 2: Paradoxes of Software Estimation 9
The Paradox of Why Software Estimation Is Performed 10
The Paradox of Software Size 11
The Paradox of Software Productivity 12
The Paradox of Offering Fixed Bids 14
The Paradox of Actual versus Estimated Values 15
The Paradox of Uncertainty 17
Summary 19

Chapter 3: Software Estimation from Scratch 21
Breaking the Project Down into Components and Constructing the
Work Breakdown Structure 22

Complexity of Components 25
Appropriate Software-Sizing Technique 26
Applying the Productivity Figure 26
Uncertainty in Estimation 27
The Impact of Project Execution on Estimation 29
Summary 29

Chapter 4: Software Estimation by Project Type 31
Classification of Software Projects 32
Projects Based on the Software Development Life Cycle 33
      Full Life Cycle Projects 33
      Partial Life Cycle Projects 33
Projects Based on How a Software Solution Is Arrived at 35
      Fresh Development of Entire Software from Scratch 35
      Software Implementation and Customization of a Commercial
      Off-the-Shelf Product 35
      Porting of Software 36
      Migration of Software 37
      Conversion Projects 39
Software Maintenance Projects 39
      Defect Fixing 40
      Operational Support 41
      Fixing Odd Behavior 42
      Software Modification 42
      Functional Expansion 43
Agile Software Development Projects 44
Web Projects 45
Summary 47

Chapter 5: Approaches to Software Estimation 49
Ad Hoc Approach 50
Process-Driven Approach 50
Gross Estimates Approach 51
Detailed Estimates Approach 52
Software Size Estimates 52
Software Development Effort Estimates 53
The Delphi Technique for Software Estimation 54
      Selection of Experts 54
      Briefing the Experts 55

Collation of Estimates Received from the Experts 55
Convergence of Estimates and Finalization 56
Merits and Demerits of the Delphi Technique 56
Analogy-Based Software Estimation 57
Selection of Similar Past Projects 58
Shortlisting of Past Projects 60
Analogy-Based Estimation in Software Maintenance 64
Merits and Demerits of Analogy-Based Estimation 64
Summary 65

Chapter 6: Software Size Estimation 67
Measuring the Size of What, Exactly? 67
Approaches to Software Size Measurement 68
Concerns with Software Size Estimation 70
Lines of Code 71
Merits and Demerits of Lines of Code 73
Function Points 73
External Input 75
External Output 76
External Inquiry 77
Internal Logical File 78
External Interface File 78
Obtaining the Unadjusted Function Point Count 79
Value Adjustment Factor 80
Obtaining the Adjusted Function Point Count 82
Merits and Demerits of Function Points 82
Use Case Points 84
Merits and Demerits of Use Case Points 87
Object Points 88
Merits and Demerits of Object Points 89
Mark II Function Point Analysis 90
Merits and Demerits of Mark II Function Point Analysis 94
Summary 94

Chapter 7: Software Size Units 97
Definition of Software Size Unit 98
Procedure for Software Size Estimation Using Software Size Units 99
Software Development Effort Estimation from Software Size Units 100
How to Obtain Productivity Figures 103

Frequently Asked Questions about Software Size Units Computation 104
Merits and Demerits of Software Size Units 105
Summary 105

Chapter 8: Software Estimation—Complexity or Density? 107
The Paradox of Complexity vis-à-vis Size 108
Density, Not Complexity 112
Summary 113

Chapter 9: Software Development Effort Estimation 115
Effort Estimation Using Software Size 115
    The Present Scenario 115
    The Suggested Scenario 117
Influence of Software Development Methodologies on Software
Estimation 118
Constructive Cost Model (COCOMO) 120
    Basic COCOMO 120
    Intermediate COCOMO 121
    Advanced COCOMO 122
    COCOMO II 123
    Merits and Demerits of COCOMO 123
Task-Based Estimation 124
    Arriving at Software Development Effort Using Task-Based
    Estimation 128
    Merits and Demerits of Task-Based Estimation 133
Summary 133

Chapter 10: Productivity for Software Estimators 135
Productivity 135
Concerns with Productivity 136
Standard Time 137
The Productivity Path 140
Classification of Software Development Activities 142
How Do We Arrive at Productivity? 144
    Empirical Methods 144
    Work Measurement 145
Capacity vis-à-vis Productivity 149
My Recommendation for How to Determine Productivity 150
Summary 150

Chapter 11: Schedule Estimation for Software Development Projects 153
Initial Work Breakdown Structure 154
Work Breakdown Structure with Predecessors Defined 155
Work Breakdown Structure with Initial Dates 157
Work Breakdown Structure with Resource Allocation 159
Scheduling in Practice 161
Graphic Representation of Schedules 161
Summary 162

Chapter 12: Software Development Cost Estimation 165
Pricing Models 165
Cost of Effort 169
Summary 172

Chapter 13: Test Size and Effort Estimation 173
Testing Basics 173
Testing Scenarios 174
    Project Testing/Embedded Testing 174
    Product Testing 175
The "How" of Testing 177
Test Strategy 179
Test Estimation 180
Approaches to Test Effort Estimation 181
    Software-Size-Based Estimation 181
    Test-Case-Enumeration-Based Estimation 183
    Task (Activity)-Based Estimation 184
Issues in Sizing Testing Projects 186
    Who Needs Test Size Estimation? 188
Sizing a Testing Project 189
    Weights 189
    Merits and Demerits of Software Test Unit Estimation 191
Final Words about Test Effort Estimation 192
Summary 193

Chapter 14: Pitfalls and Best Practices in Software Estimation 195
Pitfalls in Software Estimation 196
    Inexperienced Estimators 196
    Lack of Training 197
    Lack of Historical Data 198

Inadequate Duration for Estimation 199
Nonconformance to Reviews 199
Not Measuring the Software Size of the Software Product
Delivered 200
Lack of Causal Analysis of Variances 200
Usage of a Single Productivity Figure 201
Absence of Software Estimation Tools 201
Over- or Underestimation 202
Best Practices in Software Estimation 203
Organizational Support for Software Estimation 204
Software Estimation Process 208
Process 208
Final Words on the Software Estimation Process 213
Presentation of Software Estimates 213
Summary 216

Chapter 15: Criteria for Selecting a Software Estimation Tool 217
Units of Measure for Software Size 217
A Common Unit of Measure for Software Size 218
Software Cost Estimation 218
Scheduling the Software Project 219
Estimation for Partial Life Cycle Projects 220
Usability 220
Usage of Popular Techniques 221
Auditability 221
Reporting Capability 222
Estimator Productivity 222
Summary 222

**Appendix A: Variance Analysis between Actual and Estimated
Values** 225

**Appendix B: Project Types and Suitable Software Estimation
Techniques** 237

Appendix C: Estimation Sheet for Delphi Technique 239

Appendix D: Deriving Productivity from Past Projects 243

Appendix E: Suggested Phases and Tasks for Task-Based Estimation ... 251

Appendix F: Sample Process Definition for Software Estimation 259

Appendix G: Estimation Presentation Template 265

Appendix H: Estimation Request Note Template 269

Appendix I: Quick Reference 273

Appendix J: Abbreviations 281

Index 285

FOREWORD

Almost every software project begins with the utterances "What will this cost?" and "When will this project be done?" Once those words are spoken, project stakeholders begin to wrestle with how to produce an estimate.

There are many methods of estimation, ranging from Delphi to parametric estimation, from sprint or iteration-level estimates to estimates that span years. Each method has its strengths and its weaknesses and its proponents and opponents. Each time frame fits a purpose and has its shortcoming. The common thread in all methods and time frames is to provide an answer to a set of business questions so that all stakeholders in the project process can try to tame the chaos of the future. The problem is that estimates, by their very nature, are inaccurate. Estimates are predictions of the future based on processes that involve humans and therefore are chaotic in the long (and sometimes in the short) run.

Murali Chemuturi's approach to estimation is based on pragmatism, industrial engineering theory, and software engineering. Murali's book begins by laying out definitions of estimation in general and software in particular. Based on these definitions, the four aspects of software estimation—estimation of software size, effort, cost, and schedule—are integrated into a holistic discussion. Examples are provided to illuminate Murali's ideas in a manner that makes his points clear in the reader's mind. The varied techniques for estimation found in the wild, such as task-based estimation, Delphi estimation, analogy-based estimation, and parametric and process-driven software estimation, are detailed in this book. Murali culminates his book with a discussion of productivity and estimation based on software size, including an introduction to the details of the software size unit, which does not adjust the software size based on any factors.

While Murali's view of estimation is pragmatic by nature, he does not shy away from controversy. He challenges those who say that estimation is a waste of time by suggesting they recognize sprint planning as a form of estimation, as well as those who say that there is only one method of estimation.

I first began a dialogue with Murali about estimation on my podcast, *Software Process and Measurement Cast*, in April of 2008. At one point during our discussions, Murali proposed I hypothetically put myself in the position of the person who has to pay for software development. He asked, "How would you feel if told there is no way to know how much the work will cost you, or alternately, there is no way to know what will be accomplished?" Murali and I have not yet finished our discussion on estimation. While I may not always agree with Murali's views, I am always richer for having learned them.

Thomas M. Cagley Jr.
President, International Function Point Users Group
Vice President, David Consulting Group

PREFACE

"Is software estimation necessary?" asked Thomas M. Cagley Jr., president of the International Function Point Users Group, when he interviewed me for a podcast on his Web site (http://www.spamcast.net: SpamCast #s 29 and 32). "Especially in these wonderful days of agile and all that?" he added.

I answered affirmatively. I said that whoever is in the position of approving expenditure demands it. I also gave another explanation.

Software is sometimes developed by software developers for users in other departments within the same organization. In other cases, software is developed to produce a software product to be sold to other organizations, with or without site-specific customization. In still another scenario, organizations specialize in developing software on a contract basis, in accordance with the client's specifications, and deliver it to the client, along with the intellectual property rights to it.

In this book, I have tried to present the topic of software estimation without prejudice to any of the above three flavors of software development by including specific examples of each scenario.

In manufacturing, where profit margins are low, specialists are employed to perform specialist functions. For example, industrial engineers set norms for productivity and estimation, cost accountants perform cost estimation, and a separate quality assurance department takes responsibility for quality and reliability. Standardization and stage inspection are *sine qua non*.

Cut over to software development. Neither a cost accountant nor an industrial engineer is employed—the software engineer performs the functions of these specialties. It is rare to find a software engineer who has remained in the same organization for 15 years, and if you find such a person, he or she is likely managing people. Persons of short tenure do not come to understand the organization well enough to be able to set norms or perform such activities as estimation. Thus, having persons of short tenure in the organization perform estimation, rather than employing specialists to perform it, in essence handicaps these organizations.

I started my career in 1970 and was exposed to the program evaluation and review technique and critical path method in 1971. I switched over to information technology in 1985, initially developing software for in-house applications. I worked for quite a few professional organizations, such as ECIL, TCS, and Metamor and Satyam, among others. In 2001, I began to offer my consultancy to software organizations. Thus, I have been exposed to many organizations through the years, mostly in India and a few in the United States. I had also studied the areas of software project management, software estimation, and software quality extensively. Some of what I learned did not agree with my sense of correctness.

One thing I could not reconcile for myself was the idea that complexity increases the size of software. Complexity, if it is to be considered at all, affects productivity, but certainly not the size of software. When a programmer writes a program on a platform in which he or she is expert, how can that program be considered complex? When a business analyst analyzes requirements in a domain in which he or she is proficient, how can that domain be considered complex? I deal with these aspects at length in this book.

Another thing I could not digest is that many an author has suggested that past data be used for setting productivity norms. This is anathema in manufacturing and other industries, where an industrial engineer sets norms for productivity using the principle of "a fair day's work for a fair day's pay." I have not seen a single instance where it has been suggested that industrial engineering techniques be used to set norms for productivity in the software industry, not even by an author on the subject of software estimation. More on this topic is covered in this book.

One other concept with which I could not agree is the idea of a point being used as a measure of size. In geometry, a "point" is something that does not occupy any space. Points are used in games—they are scored or counted. I am, however, comfortable with the idea of "units" being used for size, as British thermal units are used to measure heat and International Units to measure enzymes such as insulin when administering it to a patient.

Some software size measures require special training to be able to use them properly—so much so that there are standards bodies that offer certification in software estimation using a specific technique. (I have heard the argument that these techniques are not complex at all. If that is the case, then my question is: Why are specialized training and certification needed to use them? Doesn't the fact that training and certification are needed to use these techniques prove that they are complex?) The size measure used ought to be understandable to the person who requests software development, and that person should be able to estimate without the assistance of a certified software estimator. In this book, I introduce such a measure—the software size unit—which, in my opinion, does not require certification of any kind prior to attempting estimation.

A recurring source of confusion I have encountered throughout my years in the software industry is mixing up the terms "productivity" and "capacity," where productivity is used to represent what in reality is capacity. This is addressed in chapter 10 on productivity for software estimators.

There was one question I was asked frequently in the organizations where I provided training or consulting service: How does one arrive at an estimate with little experience in the given domain, when specifications received are sketchy and when there is no one available to offer guidance? I could not find a book that addresses these issues. To date, there is no "Estimation for Dummies." I address that question in this book.

From its beginning, the information technology industry has been eager to define new terms where old ones suffice and to obfuscate simple matters, coming up with a complex explanation where a simple one exists. This book is my attempt to make software estimation simple, straightforward, and usable by persons from other disciplines when asking for software bids, as well as to help practitioners of software engineering.

I would be grateful for your feedback. Please feel free to e-mail me at murali@chemuturi.com. I will try to respond to all e-mails.

Thanks for reading this book. I wish you success in all your endeavors and happiness in life.

Murali Chemuturi

ABOUT THE AUTHOR

Murali Chemuturi is an information technology and software development subject matter expert, author, consultant, and trainer. In 2001, he formed Chemuturi Consultants, an information technology consulting and software development firm that helps software development organizations achieve their quality and value objectives. The firm provides training in several software engineering and project management topics such as software estimation, test effort estimation, function point analysis, software testing, structured systems analysis and design methodology, and software project management, to name a few. The firm also offers a number of products to aid project managers and software development professionals, such as PMPal, a software project management tool; EstimatorPal, FPAPal, UCPPal, TPPal, and SSUPal, a set of software estimation tools; and MRPPal, a full-spectrum material management software package.

Mr. Chemuturi has over 15 years of industrial experience in various engineering and manufacturing management positions, as well as more than 23 years of information technology and software development experience. His most recent position prior to forming his own firm was Vice President of Software Development at Vistaar e-Businesses Pvt., Ltd.

Mr. Chemuturi's undergraduate degrees and diplomas are in electrical and industrial engineering and he holds an MBA and a postgraduate diploma in computer methods and programming. He has several years of academic experience teaching a variety of computer and information technology courses such as COBOL, FORTRAN, BASIC, computer architecture, and database management systems.

In addition to being a widely published author in professional journals, Mr. Chemuturi is an active member of the Institute of Electrical and Electronics Engineers, a senior member of the Computer Society of India, and a Fellow of the Indian Institute of Industrial Engineering.

ACKNOWLEDGMENTS

When I look back, I find that there are so many people to whom I should be grateful. Be it because of their commissions or omissions, they made me a stronger and a better person and both directly and indirectly helped to make this book possible. It would be difficult to acknowledge everyone's contributions here, so to those whose names may not appear, I wish to thank you all just the same. I will have failed in my duty if I did not explicitly and gratefully acknowledge the following persons:

- My parents, Appa Rao and Vijaya Lakshmi, the reason for my existence. Especially my father, a rustic agrarian, who by personal example taught me the virtue of hard work and how sweet the aroma of sweat from the brow can be.
- My family, who stood by me like a rock in difficult times. Especially my wife, Udaya Sundari, who gave me the confidence and the belief that "I can." And my two sons, Dr. Nagendra and Vijay, who provided me the motive to excel.
- My two uncles, Raju and Ramana, who by personal example taught me what integrity and excellence mean.
- Mr. Drew Gierman, Publisher & Vice President of Sales at J. Ross Publishing, for his belief in the content of this book, for his generous allocation of time, and for leading me by the hand through every step of making this book a reality.
- The staff of J. Ross Publishing, all of whom were involved in bringing this book to the public.

- Ms. Sandra Rychel of Montreal, Canada, who pored over every word of this book to ensure that each is the right one. But for her editing genius, this book would not have been as readable as it is now.
- Ms. Sandy Pearlman, who went through the text with a fine-tooth comb to smooth out any rough edges and make it more accurate.

To all of you, I humbly bow my head in respect and salute you in acknowledgment of your contribution.

Murali Chemuturi

Web
Added
Value

*Free value-added materials available from
the Download Resource Center at www.jrosspub.com*

At J. Ross Publishing we are committed to providing today's professional with practical, hands-on tools that enhance the learning experience and give readers an opportunity to apply what they have learned. That is why we offer free ancillary materials available for download on this book and all participating Web Added Value™ publications. These online resources may include interactive versions of material that appears in the book or supplemental templates, worksheets, models, plans, case studies, proposals, spreadsheets and assessment tools, among other things. Whenever you see the WAV™ symbol in any of our publications, it means bonus materials accompany the book and are available from the Web Added Value Download Resource Center at www.jrosspub.com.

Downloads available for *Software Estimation Best Practices, Tools & Techniques: A Complete Guide for Software Project Estimators* consist of a test effort estimation tool (TPPal), a software size unit estimation tool (SSUPal), and a 180-day demo of a comprehensive estimation tool known as EstimatorPal.

Software projects are shelved
Budgets are overshot
When estimation and productivity
Are poorly understood

SOFTWARE ESTIMATION

BACKGROUND

Before IBM launched the personal computer (PC), software as an independent business was not widespread. The computer manufacturer provided the system software and development tool kit to the computer buyers, and the computer buyers developed whatever application software they needed. If someone wanted the programs developed on one computer system to run on another computer system, it was difficult—if not impossible—to achieve. As the industry grew and competition with it, computer manufacturers began to include rudimentary application software packages with their computers, often with source code too. The software in those days was tightly tied to the hardware. Software could not be sold off-the-shelf in stores; software was an appendage to hardware.

Apple Computer, however, was one company that sold software and hardware separately, thus pioneering off-the-shelf software and spawning a hitherto nonexistent commercial off-the-shelf (COTS) software market. In 1982, the IBM PC (and later its clones) took COTS software to a new high, and in doing so, IBM created a huge market for this new area of technology. Soon after, COTS software developers sprouted up and flourished. As software development companies came into existence, the umbilical cord between hardware and software was severed. In time, organizations began to outsource software development work to companies that specialized in this area alone.

While it was unthinkable in the 1970s, before the advent of the IBM PC, that software developers could compel hardware manufacturers to design computers to suit the software, today this is a reality! It may not be an exaggeration to say that for today's computer buyers, the choice of software precedes the choice of hardware. Earlier the question was, "Will the software work with my hardware?" Now the question is, "Will your hardware support the software I selected?"

When a service is subcontracted, mutual acceptance of the service fee by both provider and buyer enters the picture. Traditionally, service providers, like doctors and lawyers, charged by the hour, meaning the fee was determined by how much time was spent on the client assignment. Time and material was the norm providers used to determine their price for software development work outsourced to them, much like doctors charged for their time and for any medicines they provided to the patient.

The time and material method for calculating a service fee put service buyers at a disadvantage: they would not know beforehand how much the service would end up costing them and therefore could not budget for the service. Buyers thus began to ask for fixed bids from service providers, and providers began to offer them. But as close relationships formed between buyers and their preferred providers, buyers began to request that the process for determining the price of the software be more transparent, and providers had to oblige buyers once again.

Thus came about the need for software cost estimation and software effort estimation.

WHAT IS SOFTWARE ESTIMATION?

While it is difficult to define software estimation, the term *estimation* itself is readily defined as follows:

> *Estimation* is the intelligent anticipation of the quantum of work that needs to be performed and the resources (human resources, monetary resources, equipment resources, and time resources) required to perform the work at a future date, in a defined environment, using specified methods.

The key terms and phrases in this definition are

- **Anticipation**—Indicates that estimation precedes performance and that it uses a "best-guess" approach.
- **At a future date**—The work has not yet been performed, but it is planned.
- **In a defined environment**—The environment where the work is going to be performed is known and its characteristics specified. Any variation that occurs to this environment will have an effect on the estimate.
- **Using specified methods**—The methods to perform the work are also defined. Any deviation from these methods will also have an effect on the estimate.

An **estimate** is the result of estimation.

I define *software estimation* as follows:

> **Software estimation** is that estimation of the software size, software development effort, software development cost, and software development schedule for a specified software project in a specified environment, using defined methods, tools, and techniques.

In this definition, the key terms are

- **Estimation**—Defined above
- **Software size**—The amount (quantity) of software that needs to be developed
- **Software development effort**—The amount of effort, in either person-days or person-hours, necessary for developing the software product of an estimated size
- **Software development cost**—The expenses necessary for developing software of a defined size, including the expense of human effort
- **Software development schedule**—The duration, in calendar days or months, that is necessary for developing the defined amount of software

Thus we have the following deliverables from software estimation:

- Components that make up the software, as well as their sizes
- Effort required to develop the software
- Monetary cost of developing the software
- Duration (schedule) required for developing the software

WHY IS SOFTWARE ESTIMATION IMPORTANT?

Software estimation is assuming more importance as a natural consequence of increased outsourcing of software development work. When any work is outsourced, it is necessary to come to an agreement with the supplier on the price to be paid for the assigned work. In an outsourcing scenario, software estimation is needed for the following reasons:

1. To set a budget for the assignment
2. To evaluate proposals received from different vendors for software development
3. To reach an agreement with the selected supplier on the size of the software to be developed and the fee for developing the agreed-upon size of the software

Further, when competition is intense among providers, margins become slim and resources become scarce. Even if a business develops software in-house, estimation is necessary to evaluate competing demands for the software and to apportion the available resources to the highest priority work. For internal software development, software estimation is needed for the following reasons:

1. To allocate a budget
2. To evaluate competing demands for software
3. To monitor the progress of the development work

WHEN IS SOFTWARE ESTIMATION CARRIED OUT?

Software estimation needs to be carried out at least twice within a software development project:

1. **At the time of project acquisition for external projects**—This is in order to provide a basis for the price decision when preparing a

quotation against a request for proposal (RFP). For internal projects, software estimation is carried out at the time of project approval for budgeting purposes.

2. **After the software is developed and delivered**—This is in order to analyze the variance between the software size as estimated at the project acquisition stage and the actual size delivered. Unfortunately, this practice is absent in many organizations. If an organization sincerely wants to improve software estimation, it is necessary to compare the as-built estimate with the original estimate, analyze the variance between the two, and effect necessary improvements.

Software estimation is carried out at these other stages too:

1. During the project planning stage, after the project is acquired, in order to estimate the required resources
2. When the work is allocated to a person, in order to set a target for completion of the allocated work
3. Optionally, after requirements specification is finalized, in order to validate the delivery commitments and, if necessary, to either effect corrections to the delivery commitments or to look for ways to meet the delivery commitments
4. Optionally, after software design is completed, in order to validate the delivery commitments and, if necessary, to either effect corrections to the delivery commitments or to look for ways to meet the delivery commitments
5. In large projects especially, the balance of work to be done is also periodically estimated to ensure that the project is on track and the delivery commitments can be met and to take corrective actions if necessary to meet the delivery commitments

TRADITIONAL COST ESTIMATION

Cost estimation has traditionally been a finance function, specifically of cost accountants, and effort estimation specifically has been an industrial engineering function. All manufacturing and service industries, including airlines, postal services, banks, and so on, use these specialists for costing and effort estimation. The software industry, however, has never employed either of these specialists and does not to this day. The result is that we have an untenable scenario with "holy cows" that cannot be criticized without being condemned.

To the best of my knowledge, the software development industry is the only industry that tries to estimate size first and arrive at effort after. All other industries that use a project-based methodology go by the traditional cost accounting route of cost estimation, outlined as follows:

1. Determine material cost (direct and indirect).
2. Calculate labor cost (direct and indirect).
3. Add factory overhead to the sum of material and labor costs to arrive at the ex-factory cost.
4. Add marketing and distribution costs to arrive at the organizational cost.
5. Add profit to arrive at a price using the cost-plus pricing method, the steps of which are performed by cost accountants.
6. Make a commercial decision on pricing to win the order, a decision that belongs in the marketing and management domains.

Industries that do not use a project-based methodology use any one of the many costing methods, such as standard costing, opportunity costing, marginal costing, incremental costing, product costing, service costing, and so on.

Go to an honest architect and say, "I want to build a deluxe house of 3,000 square feet. Give me a quote that you will stand by. Mind you, I may ask for changes after seeing the house." Most likely, the architect will ask for a host of specifications before offering you a quote.* Go to an honest caterer and say, "I need food for a hundred guests. The food must be good. Give me a fixed bid."

---

* This scenario was described to me by a friend. It is possible that some architects may offer a quote without asking for "a host of specifications." There are some people in every profession who think it wise to offer a low quote up front and then to find reason to either raise the price later or cut costs and thereby quality. A scenario at a car dealership is described in the novel *Wheels* (Arthur Hailey, 1978). The customer points out to the salesman that another dealer is offering a lower price for the same car. The salesman tells the customer that he can also offer such a low price—no problem, but certain accessories would have to be excluded. When the customer asks which accessories, the salesman answers that it depends on the price the customer is willing to pay. If the customer wants $1,000 taken off the price, the engine becomes an accessory. The point is, when a customer makes a demand, there is always someone willing to find a way to meet that demand, either by cutting costs (and thereby quality) or by increasing the price later on. By the way, *Wheels* is an excellent book, and I recommend it.

The caterer will no doubt ask for the number of courses, specifications for each course, and many more details before offering you a quote.

All service providers, apart from those in the software industry, cost the RFP item by item to arrive at the cost, add in their profit, weigh the opportunity, and price the RFP. Their estimate follows the traditional approach to costing and pricing:

1. Calculate direct personnel cost.
2. Calculate indirect personnel cost.
3. Calculate direct material cost.
4. Calculate indirect material cost.
5. Sum the above four costs to arrive at the ex-facility cost.
6. Add organizational overhead to the ex-facility cost to arrive at cost before profit.
7. Add profit to cost before profit to arrive at a minimum price.
8. Add a negotiation margin, if required, to arrive at the final price.
9. Weigh the opportunity and adjust the price upward or downward, to arrive at the final quote.

It is perhaps only in the software industry where RFPs are issued with just one paragraph of specifications that would ultimately take 10 person-years to deliver! The software industry, by and large, is following the method outlined below to arrive at prices for software. Of course, there can be exceptions.

1. Estimate the software size using any of the popular software-sizing techniques.
2. Convert the software size into effort in person-hours (or person-days) using a conversion factor (popularly known as the productivity figure).
3. Convert the effort into money using a conversion factor (person-hour rate or person-day rate).
4. Offer this result as the price, with a provision for billing other expenses at actual cost incurred.

It has not been possible to achieve an undisputed, universally accepted software size measure; such a standard has remained elusive. True, there are some popular size measures, but each has its own set of limitations. This scenario has given rise to some paradoxes in software estimation.

SUMMARY

The introduction of the IBM PC was the harbinger of software development's growth into the specialist activity it is today. The outsourcing of software development has made requesting and offering fixed bids the norm within this new industry, which in turn has necessitated better methods for accurate software estimation. Software estimation is the estimation of the software size, software development effort, software development cost, and software development schedule for a specified software project in a specified environment, using defined methods, tools, and techniques. Software estimation is carried out to set a price for a bid or to evaluate a bid, set a budget, predict the resources required, and make intelligent delivery commitments, in addition to monitoring the project's progress during its execution. However, the software development industry does not follow traditional cost estimation, nor does it employ specialists for this purpose, and this has given rise to some paradoxes.

PARADOXES OF SOFTWARE ESTIMATION

Wikepedia defines paradox as follows:

> A **paradox** is a statement or group of statements that leads to a con-
> tradiction or a situation which defies intuition. . . . Typically, either the
> statements in question do not really imply the contradiction, the puz-
> zling result is not really a contradiction, or the premises themselves are
> not all really true or cannot all be true together. . . . The recognition of
> ambiguities, equivocations, and unstated assumptions underlying known
> paradoxes has led to significant advances in science, philosophy and
> mathematics.

Since the software development industry is still in its nascent stages, the
processes for asking for software development service, offering the service, and
pricing are somewhat haphazard. The software development industry falls under
the umbrella of the services industry, as opposed to the product industry, meaning
it offers a service, not a product. Many parallels can be drawn between the
software development industry and other service industries, but the major difference between the software development industry and other service industries
is that software is much more highly priced and is difficult to comprehend by
nonsoftware professionals. Where there is lack of comprehension and money,
academics step in, research is conducted, jargon is developed, concepts are pro-
pounded, and a new branch of science or engineering comes into being. Software estimation is one such area.

At first glance, there are many paradoxes in software estimation. This chapter discusses some of those paradoxes.

THE PARADOX OF WHY SOFTWARE ESTIMATION IS PERFORMED

To reiterate from chapter 1, software estimation is carried out for the following reasons:

- To price software development and maintenance contracts (for budgeting and approval in the case of internal projects)
- To determine resource requirements
- To arrive at delivery commitments

When we estimate for resource requirements or delivery commitments, we can always do so for each of the activities involved—coding, code walk-through, testing, and so on—to arrive at the requirements for each. By summing up the individual requirements, we can arrive at the resource requirements for the project. The best way to arrive at delivery commitments is through scheduling the project.

Software estimation becomes contentious when we estimate for software pricing. We need to arrive at an estimate that is understood by the client's purchaser, who we cannot assume is well versed in software development and software estimation. Typically, the scenario looks like this:

- There are multiple bidders.
- The capability of the bidders varies, in some cases vastly.
- There will be, in most cases, techno-commercial negotiations, which are mostly commercial in nature, between client and bidder before the contract is awarded.
- The most common question asked by the buyer is something like, "How did you arrive at this price?"
- The answer is expected to be given in nontechnical terms and is expected to facilitate the buyer's comparison with other bids.

It is this scenario that poses the issue, as the negotiators want one universal norm that can be applied across platforms, across organizations, across technologies—across the board. This is the crux of software estimation concerns.

THE PARADOX OF SOFTWARE SIZE

Ample literature exists on how to size software, all of which proposes sizing software in the same way distance or weight is measured, but using a unit of measure for software size that is acceptable to all concerned. Proponents of each size measure claim that their unit of measure is better than other size measures. The result is that we now have many measures of software size: lines of code, function points, use case points, object points, feature points, Internet points, story points, and software test units. All of these measures are in vogue, to my knowledge, and there may be more. True, we use multiple measures for distance (miles and kilometers) and for weight (pounds and kilograms), but one can convert pounds into kilograms and miles into kilometers. Not so for measures of software size. There is no formula which states, for example, that 1 use case point is equal to 1.2 function points!

Now, everyone agrees that some things simply cannot be measured. Take beauty and love, for example. Each person is beautiful in his or her own way, and everyone loves in his or her own way. We don't attempt to measure these attributes in beauty points and love points, do we? Many more examples of things not measurable can be found in industry too. Do we use car points to measure automobiles? Can we say that a BMW has 25 car points and a Toyota Camry has 15 car points, and therefore a BMW is superior to a Toyota Camry by 10 car points? No. We don't have a measure for cars with which such an unbiased comparison can be made.

We don't attempt to measure software products either. What is the size of SQL Server or Oracle? Each is a multi-user relational database management system. When buying one, do we ask to know the size of each to make a fair comparison? We also do not have a fair measure for computer hardware. How do we compare an AS/400 with an RS/6000? Do computer points exist to measure their sizes?

A *point* is not a size measure. Points are counted or scored, but never measured. *Unit* could be a better measure, as in British thermal units or as in a dose of a medicinal enzyme (20 units of insulin). Using a point as a software size measure is a misnomer.

The fact of the matter is that not everything is measurable. For something to be measurable, it must meet the following criteria:

- It must be homogeneous.
- It must be tangible.
- It should be monolithic, not an assembly of multiple parts (physical or metaphysical).

- It should not have any qualitative features.
- It must lend itself to a conversion factor in order to convert its measurement into other units of measure.

Each software size measure mentioned here cannot be converted into the other software size measures.

THE PARADOX OF SOFTWARE PRODUCTIVITY

Productivity is roughly defined as *number of units of output per one unit of time,* and it is generally used with respect to humans. The term *efficiency* normally is used in respect to machines. The definition of standard time (productivity) is this:

> *Standard time is the amount of time taken to accomplish a unit of defined work carried out by a qualified worker after adjustment, using a given method, in specified working conditions, at a pace that can be maintained day after day without any harmful physical effects.*

This definition has been adopted by the American Institute of Industrial Engineers.

Thus, in the manufacturing industry, productivity cannot be stated in a stand-alone mode. It has to be accompanied by specification of the following:

- Defined unit of work
- Work environment
- Working methods
- Tools and technologies used
- Qualified worker, after acclimatization

It is obvious that productivity varies from organization to organization even in terms of well-established measures of productivity. We have universally accepted measures of time: person-hours, person-days, person-months, and person-years. We have yet to agree on a universally accepted unit of measure for software output. Software productivity can be measured as lines of code per person-day, function points per person-day, use case points per person-day, object points per person-day, etc.

In manufacturing or traditional service industries, productivity is measured for one activity at a time—for example, a turning activity, a milling activity, bricklaying, waiting tables, soldering, etc. Productivity of inspection activity and functional testing is measured only in mass and batch production industries; it is not attempted in job order (tailor-made to customer specifications) industries. Productivity measurement of design activity and repair (bug-fixing) activity is not attempted, as they are considered to contain "a creative component."

We have not replicated this manufacturing industry model in the software development industry, and we have not really defined what software productivity is. Therefore, the following questions naturally crop up when attempting to measure software productivity:

- Does productivity refer to coding only, or does it also include code walk-through, independent unit testing, and debugging activities?
- Does productivity include systems analysis and system design work too?
- What about project management and quality assurance overhead? Should these be included when measuring software productivity?

In most cases I have witnessed, software productivity is specified for the entire development life cycle, without any agreement as to what constitutes a development life cycle.

In the manufacturing industry, productivity is specified for an activity, and overall throughput is called *capacity*. Capacity of a plant or an organization takes into account all operations, all departments, and all activities, and it specifies one figure, say 300 cars per day or 1 million tons per year.

Do these sound familiar? *Two days per screen! Fifty lines of code in Visual Basic per person per day!* They ought to, as we frequently hear phrases like these used by software developers. We seem to be confusing capacity with productivity. The software industry has not yet engaged industrial engineers to study and come up with possible measures of software productivity. Productivity is derived from past records or by benchmarking with other similar organizations.

Incidentally, it is the unions that prompted and nudged the manufacturing industry to carry out scientific studies in order to set productivity standards, which led to the concept of *a fair day's work for a fair day's pay*. However, the software development industry is bereft of unions, and therefore no such negotiations occur. Perhaps that is the reason no attempts have been made by the industry to carry out scientific studies in the field of software productivity.

Thus, while there are concerns and issues, there are also solutions, if we do not look for one single measure of productivity for the entire workflow of software development. What needs to be accomplished is the creation of a taxonomy system of software productivity, published as an industry standard. This would greatly facilitate further work on software productivity and a system for units of measure for software size.

THE PARADOX OF OFFERING FIXED BIDS

Many services offer fixed bids; there is nothing peculiar about this. An architect, for example, offers a fixed bid after receiving complete building specs. Businesses in the made-to-order industry offer fixed bids only after receiving complete specifications, and quotes usually include a high-level design drawing too. A caterer would not offer a fixed bid until receiving the menu and the number of guests. A builder offers a fixed bid with an escalation clause after receiving the building plans. In the construction industry, unit rates are offered mostly against a detailed tender document that specifies each of the required items in great detail. The total cost of the building depends on the actual quantity of its components.

Of the above examples, the software industry most closely resembles the construction industry! Take a look at these similarities:

- It is difficult for end users to visualize the final deliverable from the design documents (drawings).
- Users often request changes in the design during the course of project execution.
- Many qualitative aspects (aesthetics) are involved.
- It is very difficult to ascertain the quality of the end product through inspection alone, as destructive testing damages the product and renders it unusable.
- The variety of available components is huge, as are differences in their quality.
- The customer often feels that he or she is being overcharged.
- Acceptance testing is often done in hours or days, though the end product has taken months—even years—to build.
- The end user more often than not feels that a better deliverable was possible for the price paid or a better vendor should have been chosen.

One fundamental difference between the software industry and the construction industry is that while a builder needs full specs, drawings, and a bill of materials to be submitted before offering a fixed bid, a software developer offers a fixed bid after receiving only scanty specifications for the project!

THE PARADOX OF ACTUAL VERSUS ESTIMATED VALUES

Estimation norms in other industries come not from the people who do the job but from industrial engineers who specialize in work measurement and productivity. In the software industry, estimation data is derived from actual historical data that comes from programmers or project managers. Very often, this past data is not subjected to critical examination before it is used! Why do other industries not use historical data for specifying estimation norms? Because the actual amount of time to complete a piece of work varies and depends on these factors:

- The skill level of the person doing the work, with skill levels ranging from super to good, average, fair, and poor
- The level of effort put in by the person, with effort levels ranging from super to good, average, fair, and poor
- The motivation level of the person
- The environment in which the work is carried out
- The methods used to carry out the work
- Clarity of instructions

We can achieve a degree of uniformity in these last four points, but the factors of skill and effort vary even within the same organization.

To my mind, the paradox of actual times best can be described using an analogy to trains:

- Trains run on specially laid tracks, and the issue of unexpected traffic is absent.
- The route and distance remain constant.
- The travel time and halt times at stations are well planned.
- The travel is well controlled by trained professionals.
- Trains are driven by well-trained professionals.

Still, trains either make up or lose time!

The phenomenon of variance between estimated and actual values is understood well by quality control professionals, and they assign a name to variation that occurs: chance variation. Chance variation crops up even in well-controlled environments and under normal conditions. If even the best conditions can still produce variation between estimated and actual values, how can a software project, with its myriad uncertainties, meet estimated times?

Such industries as manufacturing, mining, construction, etc. follow the concept of *a fair day's work for a fair day's pay*. Estimation is thus based on the average effort put in by a person of average skill under specified conditions. Organizations in these industries have carried out work studies and have come up with standard times for most of the activities that take place in their work environments. They have also developed a number of techniques for effort estimation, including time studies, motion studies, work sampling, analytical estimation and synthesis, and so on. If a person happens to be more skilled, puts in more effort, and delivers more than other workers do, that person is paid more money by way of incentive payments. This system of defining work norms and of incentive payments also helps an organization to quantitatively identify "super-performers" and deadwood easily.

Actual time differs from estimated time because of variance in the skill of the person and in the effort put in by the person. This fact is recognized in industries, and estimation norms never change just because actual time shows a variance with estimated time. Estimates and the norms for estimation are changed only when there is a change in the working environment, the tools to do the work, the methods employed to do the work, or the work itself.

The software industry has, to my knowledge, never undertaken a work study for software development, taking umbrage at the assertion that software development is a creative activity. But this is not entirely true. It is obvious that the creative component of software development is in the software design, not in the coding. Besides, the concept of *a fair day's work for a fair day's pay* is never heard in the software development industry. Perhaps this is because software engineers are paid more fairly than their fair day's work deserves.

Presently, the norms for estimation are drawn from earlier projects. Norms are continuously updated, taking their cue from completed projects, and this leads to one of the following three scenarios:

1. **The "eager beaver" project manager**
   a. An estimate is given to the eager beaver project manager.
   b. In order to please the boss, the eager beaver beats the estimate.
   c. The project postmortem concludes that the estimate is an over-estimate, and instead of rewarding the eager beaver, estimation norms are tightened.
   d. The next estimate is made using the new norms.
   e. In this iteration, the eager beaver is frustrated that his or her achievement was not rewarded and either delays the project or resigns and leaves the organization.

2. **The "smart-aleck" project manager**
   a. An estimate is given to the smart-aleck project manager.
   b. The smart-aleck weighs the situation and delays the project until the point of penalty avoidance is reached.
   c. The project postmortem concludes that the estimate is an underestimate, and instead of punishing the smart-aleck, estimation norms are loosened.
   d. The next estimate is made using the new norms.
   e. In this iteration, the smart-aleck knows that he or she was successful in delaying and repeats the same tactic.
   f. The project management office continues to loosen the estimation norms until the marketing team complains of high quotes.
3. **The pragmatic project manager**
   a. An estimate is given to the pragmatic project manager.
   b. The pragmatic project manager plans his or her work such that the estimate is met.
   c. The project postmortem concludes that the estimate is the right estimate, and estimation norms are retained.

In all three scenarios, it is not certain if any of the estimates, in any iteration, is the right one! When estimation norms are continuously updated by retrofitting actual achievements, with the possibility that the actual achievement is one of the above scenarios, it can never be known whether the initial estimation norms were right.

Validation of estimates through comparison with actual achievement and adjusting estimation norms to be in line with actual achievements does not result in the right norms. What needs to be done is this: the actual achievements of the project should be analyzed critically to ascertain the real reasons for variance. The actual achievements should not be adopted for future projects or used to change estimation norms. A framework for such analysis is presented in Appendix A.

THE PARADOX OF UNCERTAINTY

Uncertainty is inherent in any human activity; exceptions are very few. That is why Murphy's Law—*If anything can go wrong, it will*—is so widely accepted as true.

The following are some of the uncertainties a project faces in terms of defining its success:

- In technical terms, was the solution delivered technically appropriate?
- In terms of timeline, was the project delivered on time/schedule?
- In terms of cost/profit/budget, did the project make the predicted profit?
- In terms of quality/reliability, was the solution delivered robust and reliable?
- In terms of repeat business, did execution of the project result in repeat business or did the client switch to a new supplier?

Here are some of the areas in which we face uncertainties while planning a project:

- Completeness of requirements
- Stability of requirements
- Soundness of design
- Reliability of development platform
- Team attrition
- Attrition of key personnel at the client end
- Uncertain achievement of productivity
- Unspecified or underspecified customer expectations

Finally, here are some of the uncertainties we face while estimating effort and duration (schedule):

- Uncertain productivity
- Lack of accepted size measure
- Team skill-level uncertainties
- Team effort-level uncertainties
- The paradox of "average"

How is *average* defined? It is defined as (1) simple average; (2) weighted average, either simple or complex; (3) moving average; (4) statistical mean; (5) statistical mode; or (6) statistical median. How is the probability of success (or risk of failure) computed? Which of the probability distributions should we use: normal, binomial, Poisson, beta, gamma, or t-distribution? The general practice is to use normal or beta distributions, but concerns about their suitability exist.

SUMMARY

The purpose of this chapter is to bring to the surface the key paradoxes that we face regarding software estimation in the software development industry. It is also to focus efforts on how to resolve these paradoxes and bring about industry standards. While there is no silver bullet to address all these issues, and we may have to live with them for some time to come, perhaps the succeeding chapters will throw some light on these aspects and provide some answers.

3

SOFTWARE ESTIMATION FROM SCRATCH

A plethora of literature often comes about when there is a lack of clarity on a subject. More often than not, the books written on the subject compound the confusion rather than clear it up. Having grown from a programmer to a project manager, and as a developer of software estimation tools, a consultant, and a trainer on the subject, I have often been confronted with this confusion: most software estimators know one or more software-sizing techniques, with a reasonable understanding of function point analysis or use case point estimation techniques, but are stymied when it comes to making a real-life software estimate.

The issue is that most times software developers are asked to prepare an effort estimate based on scanty specifications. In many cases, the request for proposal (RFP) contains not more than a paragraph about the functionality needed. In other cases, the software developer asked to prepare the estimate has not worked in the application domain before, and he or she has no idea what components make up the system described in the RFP.

The most frequent question about software estimation that was asked of me in my training programs was, "How do we break the application into its constituent components? Once we know the components, we can estimate. Is there any tool that can do it for us?" I had to respond that there is no tool that takes the RFP specifications as input and breaks them down into their components automatically. This is something that a person with knowledge of the domain has to do.

What if the estimator is not knowledgeable in the domain for which software needs to be developed? I attempt to answer that question in this chapter.

Software estimation is carried out more than once during the life of a software development project. The project acquisition stage is where the detail available to the estimator is at a minimum, so it is at this stage that confusion over estimation arises. All other stages progressively increase the detail and hence reduce uncertainty (and confusion) in estimation. Therefore, I will try to shed some light on software estimation as attempted at the project acquisition stage (or for internal projects, at the project approval stage).

What most people either do not know or do not have a clear understanding of is how to apply software size estimation techniques to a real-life situation, such as when the boss or marketing department asks for a software estimate against an RFP or a project initiation note. The following are the most common questions estimators ask, beginner and experienced alike:

- How do I arrive at all the components that need to be included in the estimate, before the design is completed?
- How do I arrive at the complexities for each of the components?
- What about effort to be spent on quality assurance activities? How do I treat them in the estimation? Should they be included or not?
- What about overhead activities—time spent on various committees, progress-tracking meetings, assistance to other organizational wings like human resources, marketing, etc.? How do I treat them? Should they be included or not?
- What about the time lost due to fragmentation when the duration of the activity is not finished at the end of the workday? Say, for example, somebody completes the work an hour before closing and starts working on the next allocation the next day. How do I account for such eventualities in the estimate?

I will address these questions in the following sections.

BREAKING THE PROJECT DOWN INTO COMPONENTS AND CONSTRUCTING THE WORK BREAKDOWN STRUCTURE

Sometimes detailed specifications are received for a project that needs software estimation. This is an excellent scenario, as breaking the project down becomes easier. The other end of the specification-detail continuum is that the specifications are limited to a small paragraph in an e-mail message requesting a fixed bid. In this case, project breakdown is most difficult. Somewhere in between these two ends of the spectrum are the real-life scenarios. How do we go about breaking a project down? I will address this question using some typical worst-case scenarios as a basis.

Here are four examples of a request for an estimate that gives few to no specifications:

1. A company needs an estimate for developing a simple material management system.
2. A business that wants to get on the Internet needs an estimate for a no-frills Web site that is functional, mainly to allow customers to browse through catalogs and place orders and to track the status of those orders. Management reports are needed as well.
3. A business is presently using One-Write (or QuickBooks, Tally, etc.), and as its operations have grown, it is looking to upgrade to the next level. The ability to use the software over the Internet is desirable.
4. A nonprofit organization is looking to upgrade its existing operations to a collaborative environment. It is flexible on the technology to be used, but Internet usage needs to be built in. The organization is presently using Microsoft Office for its human resources and finance activities and also to bring in its client interfacing activities into the ambit of the new system.

The list could go on and on. So, how do we go about it? First, read carefully, and ignore all adjectives:

1. In the first example, the company wants a material management system. It does not specify any exceptions, so assume that all necessary functionalities are expected to be included.
2. In the second, the business wants a fully functional e-commerce Web site. "No frills" generally means no frills in a proposal; the business expects your lowest quote.
3. In the third request, the business wants a Web-based accounting system.
4. In the last example, "nonprofit" means "not making any profit," so the organization is expecting a lower quote. The system requirements are specified in Excel spreadsheets all over the organization. You need to collect them, study them, and develop the software.

It takes a bit of experience to accurately "read" what an organization is asking for in an RFP. If you are a beginner, it is best to work under the guidance of a senior person.

Now that the scope of the project is known, the project needs to be broken down into its constituent components. Adopting a top-down approach is most effective, following these steps:

1. Break down the project by one level into modules:
   a. Material management breaks down into purchasing, warehousing, and inventory analysis.
   b. E-commerce Web site breaks down into loading catalogs, browsing catalogs, shopping cart, order processing with payment processing, management information system, and so on.
2. Then break down each module into its constituent functions.
3. Continue to break down, from one level to the next, until no further breakdown is possible. Remember to list each level down in an Excel spreadsheet or a similar spreadsheet.
4. Next, break down each function into inputs, outputs, and storage requirements.
5. Then determine the process of taking inputs and converting them to outputs, as well as storage for longer term needs.

That constitutes the list of components. However, the catch is that you need to be knowledgeable about the domain in question to be able to accomplish the successive breaking down of levels. If you have such knowledge, excellent, but what if you are not well versed in the area? Where do you get the information you need to carry out this breakdown process?

Here are some alternative sources from which you can learn about detailed functionality:

- If you worked on a similar project in the past, you can take the knowledge you acquired from it and apply it to the current project.
- Ask a software developer who is knowledgeable about the domain to teach you more about it.
- Try asking your boss. He or she may not be able to debug your program, but amazingly, bosses are knowledgeable in such matters as achieving an accurate and complete breakdown or where to find the required information on how to do so. Sometimes bosses might even have the particular domain knowledge themselves.

- Ask a functional expert in your organization (surely your organization has a finance manager, a human resources manager, a marketing manager, etc.) or an outside expert for advice and guidance. Go back to this person after you have completed the breakdown and ask him or her to check it for completeness.
- The Internet is amazing. It possesses a wealth of information and demo software for virtually anything. Use your favorite search engine to look up the application in question, and download a few demos to try them out. It will make you knowledgeable enough to break down the project into its constituent components.

Now you know how to break down a project into its constituent components, and you have a list. This list is usually referred to as the work breakdown structure.

COMPLEXITY OF COMPONENTS

Almost all software size estimation techniques necessitate rating the complexity of the component (or transaction, as some techniques prefer to call it). These techniques specify rules for a complexity rating in great detail, sometimes even down to the micro level, to controls on the screen or number of data elements in a file or a table. It is easy to comply with these rules once an application is developed and available to retrofit the estimate. However, when you are estimating at the time of project acquisition  (when you have no guarantee that the project will be awarded to you, and as a result, your objective is to spend as little time as possible on preparing the estimate), using these complexity rating rules is impractical. Here is what I suggest in this case:

1. Use your programming experience and best judgment, and rate the complexity of each of the components in the work breakdown structure.
2. Review each of the complexities, critically examining all of them and modifying them as you deem fit and proper.
3. Have a senior person (someone with at least two or more years of experience than you) review the complexities.
4. Remember that a login screen is of average complexity in some size estimation techniques and some applications!

While I agree that this method of deciding component complexity may not appear foolproof, I suggest it just the same, in view of the detail available and the effort and resources that can be committed to this activity during the project acquisition stage.

Now fit this work breakdown structure into the chosen software-sizing technique.

APPROPRIATE SOFTWARE-SIZING TECHNIQUE

Which technique should you select? Here are some guidelines to help you decide:

- Use your organization's standardized technique.
- Use the technique with which you are most familiar and comfortable. If you are not familiar with any of the techniques, consider the following:
  - ☐ Try using function points. This technique is by far the most popular and most widely used, but first you need to learn it. Many free, downloadable resources are available on the Internet for self-teaching.
  - ☐ Use task-based estimation. This is simply estimating the effort required for each of the components in the work breakdown structure to arrive at the total effort needed for the project. This technique is explained in subsequent chapters.
- Use the technique your customer has requested or is familiar with.
- Use the technique for which you have reliable (to the extent possible) productivity data.
- Use the technique your boss suggests.

APPLYING THE PRODUCTIVITY FIGURE

Once you have the software size, apply the productivity figure—meaning the person-hours per unit of software size—and obtain the effort required for the project. Where do you get this productivity figure? Here are some sources:

- Your organizational data, which is available from any of the following: the quality assurance department, software engineering process group, knowledge repository, or project management office.

- Industry benchmarks, such as the International Function Point Users Group, the International Software Benchmarking Standards Group, the nearest Software Process Improvement Network, or the Software Project Managers Network. These groups are all likely to have this type of data on hand for a variety of applications and development platforms.
- Search the Internet. This data may be available on a Web site.
- Ask your boss or people in the marketing department in your organization. An experienced marketing person usually has an uncanny knack for being able to arrive at the duration and effort required to execute a project.
- If all else is out of your reach, use your best hunch.

My recommendation for converting size into effort is as follows:

1. Do not use a single figure to convert size into effort. Rather, use a minimum of four productivity figures, namely:
   a. One for requirements analysis
   b. One for carrying out design
   c. One for construction (coding and self unit testing)
   d. One for testing (for a minimum of three types of testing: integration, system, and acceptance testing)
2. Compute the total effort, then add a percentage to allow for a safety factor against unforeseen occurrences, such as changes requested by the customer, technical issues, etc. This percentage is to be based on:
   a. Duration, with longer durations requiring a higher percentage
   b. Confidence in the technology being used
   c. Expected changes and issues from the customer
   d. Confidence in the team to produce error-free work
   e. The development environment and tools proposed to be used

UNCERTAINTY IN ESTIMATION

The word *estimation* suggests that it precedes actual accomplishment. Therefore, there is uncertainty in estimation. Though uncertainty cannot be eliminated, the suggestions listed here help to minimize it:

1. Always give three estimates: best-case (optimistic), normal-case (most likely), and worst-case (pessimistic) scenarios. Best case is 90 percent

of your estimate and worst case is 110 percent of your estimate, with normal case being your original estimate. You may use percentages other than the suggested ones for best-case and worst-case scenarios depending on your organization's norms and your confidence in the opportunity in question.

2. When converting software size by applying a productivity figure to effort, again apply the same three values:

    a. To the worst-case software size, apply the worst-case productivity figure, which is 110 percent of the normal productivity figure (for example, 10 person-hours per unit size becomes 11 person-hours per unit size).

    b. To the best-case software size, apply the best-case productivity figure, which is 90 percent of the normal productivity figure (for example, 10 person-hours per unit size becomes 9 person-hours per unit size).

    c. To the normal software size, apply the normal productivity figure.

3. Thus, you have three scenarios:

    a. Worst-case scenario—when the software size is highest and productivity is lowest.

    b. Best-case scenario—when the software size is lowest and productivity is highest.

    c. Normal-case scenario—when the software size and productivity are normal.

4. Give these figures to the requester of the estimate.

What you are communicating precisely is

1. The project is likely to be executed in the normal-case scenario.
2. If everything proceeds as expected, the project could be executed in the best-case scenario.
3. If everything goes wrong, the project could be executed in the worst-case scenario.

Remember that pricing the project and committing to a delivery schedule are commercial decisions dictated more by the client requirements and, to some extent, by the competition. It is possible that marketing commits to a best-case scenario, but in reality the project is executed according to the worst-case scenario! Nevertheless, we need to plan to ensure that we meet the commitments made to the client by infusing more resources or better methodologies.

THE IMPACT OF PROJECT EXECUTION ON ESTIMATION

Project execution plays a crucial role in ensuring that estimates are met. What needs to be achieved by software estimation during the project acquisition stage is a realistic estimate and the best- and worst-case scenarios, so that marketing can price accurately and the project execution team can meet its delivery commitments made to the client. The methodology discussed here should ensure that. Sloppy project execution may result in overshooting the effort estimate. A tight, well-controlled project execution may result in undershooting the effort estimate.

Whether the actual effort overshoots or undershoots the effort estimate, it should not be interpreted as meaning that the estimate is in error. When the actual effort varies from the estimated effort by more than chance variation (that is, by more than 10 percent), the following could be the reasons:

- The actual size of the software produced varies from the estimated software size.
- While the estimate assumes average skill and average effort, the allocation of manpower could result in predominantly poorly skilled (or super-skilled) manpower for the project execution.
- Project execution could be sloppy (or excellent).
- Estimation norms could be wrong.

Therefore, the variation must be analyzed (causal analysis). That may involve questioning the estimator and the project executor, but this should not be construed as doubting the integrity of these persons. Corrective action should depend on the results of the analysis.

Quality assurance activities, to the extent specified here, are included in the productivity figure. Add additional effort if special testing or other quality assurance activities are needed by the client or are foreseen by you.

Overhead and unproductive activities, such as attending meetings, are also part of the productivity figure. If they are likely to be excessive and additional effort needs to be included, you can have the marketing department assist you in including additional effort toward these activities.

SUMMARY

The purpose of this chapter is to guide the beginner in software estimation so that he or she can make reasonably accurate software estimates. Sources available for acquiring domain knowledge are also mentioned. Some information is also provided to enable the selection of an appropriate software size measure for the estimation. How to convert the software size to development effort using a productivity figure is also explained. All in all, this chapter provides guidance for preparing software estimation from scratch—something like "Software Estimation for Dummies."

SOFTWARE ESTIMATION BY PROJECT TYPE

Software development projects are not homogeneous; they come in various hues. Consider these scenarios:

- An organization wants to shift some of its business processes from manual information processing to computer-based information processing. It entrusts the software developers with the work of studying the user requirements and carrying out all the activities necessary to implement the computer-based system.
- An organization wants to shift some of its business processes from manual information processing to computer-based information processing. It does not want software to be developed from scratch. Rather, it wants to implement a commercial off-the-shelf (COTS) software product and customize it to suit its needs.
- An organization has a computer-based system that needs to be shifted to another computer system, as the existing system has become obsolete and support is no longer available to keep it in working condition.
- An organization has a computer-based system and wants to shift it from a flat file system to a relational database management system.

- An organization uses a computer-based information-processing system and needs to either effect modifications to the software or add functionality. It has entrusted this work to a third party.
- An organization has developed a computer-based information-processing system and wants the system thoroughly tested by an independent organization. It entrusts the testing to a third party.

As you can see, these scenarios are essentially software projects, but the work involved in each varies vastly from the others. This chapter looks at the classification of software projects and suggests the estimation methodologies suitable for each class.

CLASSIFICATION OF SOFTWARE PROJECTS

There are five classes of software projects, several of which are divided into subclasses:

1. Projects based on the software development life cycle:
   a. Full life cycle projects
   b. Partial life cycle projects
2. Projects based on how a software solution is arrived at:
   a. Fresh development of the entire software from scratch
   b. Software implementation and customization of a COTS product
   c. Porting of software
   d. Migration of software
   e. Conversion of existing software to suit changed conditions, such as Y2K and euro conversion projects
3. Software maintenance projects:
   a. Defect fixing
   b. Operational support
   c. Fixing odd behavior
   d. Software modification
   e. Functional expansion
4. Agile software development projects
5. Web projects

Let us now discuss each one in greater detail.

PROJECTS BASED ON THE SOFTWARE DEVELOPMENT LIFE CYCLE

Full Life Cycle Projects

Some confusion exists about what constitutes the software development life cycle. It is generally agreed that user requirements analysis, software requirements analysis, software design, construction, and testing are all universally accepted parts of the software development life cycle. Confusion lies, however, in the following areas:

- Feasibility studies, which determine whether the project is worthwhile
- Special testing
- System implementation, including installation of hardware, system software, application software, etc.
- System commissioning, including the creation of master data files, user training, pilot runs, parallel runs, etc.

When the end product is used within the same organization, some consider these four steps part of the software development life cycle too. For those organizations that specialize in software development and that develop software for use by a different organization, these four steps are considered outside the scope of the software development life cycle. From the standpoint of software development only, these areas can be left out of software development projects.

A full life cycle project starts with user requirements and ends with delivery of the software. All postdelivery activities and preuser requirement activities are outside the scope of the software development life cycle. All software-sizing techniques, including function points, use case points, object points, Mark II function point analysis, and software size units, are appropriate for these projects. Therefore, software size can be made applicable for all full life cycle projects. In addition, Delphi estimation, analogy-based estimation, and task-based estimation are also applicable for this class of projects. (Delphi and analogy-based estimation are detailed in chapter 5, and task-based estimation is detailed in chapter 9.)

Partial Life Cycle Projects

Partial life cycle projects are those that execute only a portion of the software development life cycle. Such projects include the following:

- **Testing projects**—The scope of work involves conducting the specified or necessary software tests on the software product in order to certify that product. Unit testing and code walk-through are normally not included in this type of project.
- **Independent verification and validation projects**—These projects go beyond mere testing; they include code walk-through to determine the efficiency of coding.
- **Multi-vendor projects**—The project is divided among two or more vendors to benefit from the advantages of each vendor's specialty and best practices. Areas of specialization include:
  - □ Requirements analysis and software design
  - □ Software construction
  - □ Testing

None of the above project types can make use of software size measures in a direct manner. For independent verification and validation projects and the three types of multi-vendor projects listed, Delphi estimation, analogy-based estimation, and task-based estimation methodologies can be used. For testing projects, four test effort estimation techniques are suitable, namely:

- Software test units estimation
- Deriving software test units from software size
- Test-case-enumeration-based estimation
- Task-based estimation

These test effort estimation techniques are described in greater detail in chapter 13.

The software size can, however, be used in an indirect manner for other partial life cycle projects. First, estimate the software size using any software size measure which has been selected. Next, using past project records, derive a relationship that can convert software size into testing effort for each phase of the project, such as:

- Number of person-hours to carry out software design per unit of size measure
- Number of person-hours to carry out software construction per unit of size measure
- Number of test cases per unit of size measure and number of test cases that can be executed per person-hour

- Number of person-hours to conduct unit (integration, system, acceptance, etc.) testing per unit of size measure

Meticulous records need to be kept in order to derive these relationships to make use of the software size measure in full as well as partial life cycle projects. Alternatively, industrial engineers can organize work studies to develop such norms.

PROJECTS BASED ON HOW A SOFTWARE SOLUTION IS ARRIVED AT

Fresh Development of Entire Software from Scratch

These projects are identical to full life cycle development projects. Refer to that section above.

Software Implementation and Customization of a Commercial Off-the-Shelf Product

Numerous popular COTS software products are available in the market, and they serve customers very well. Implementation of such systems as enterprise resource planning, customer relationship management, supply chain management, enterprise application integration, and data warehousing software falls under this category. The typical phases of these projects include the following:

1. Study the present system.
2. Compare and contrast the present system against the COTS product by carrying out a gap analysis.
3. Discuss with the customer the desired levels of customization in the system and in the project.
4. Prepare a statement of work for customization of the COTS product.
5. Carry out the necessary software design.
6. Carry out the construction.
7. Carry out the testing.
8. Integrate the custom code with the COTS product. In some cases, this may mean building a layer over the COTS product, and in other cases, it may mean integrating the custom-developed code with the source code of the COTS product.

9. Modify the source code of the COTS product, if necessary.
10. Implement the software and custom code.
11. Train the users on the system, including troubleshooting, operations, and maintenance of the system.
12. Deliver the final customized system.

There is a degree of variation to these phases in a project that involves altering one COTS product and another COTS product or one application domain and another application domain. For such products, if the customization involves the development of a fresh software layer over the COTS product, then the software layer's size can be estimated. On the other hand, if it involves correction of the source code of the COTS product, then sizing is not possible.

The methods of estimation that can be used for preparing the software effort estimates for this class of projects include task-based estimation, Delphi estimation, analogy-based estimation, and custom effort estimation models tailored to suit the implementation and customization of the COTS product. Custom effort estimation models are specific to the COTS product and need to be built exclusively for each product.

Porting of Software

These projects deal with the porting of software from one hardware platform to another hardware platform. Typical characteristics of these projects include:

- The programming language is normally the same on both platforms.
- There are slight differences between implementations of the programming language.
- Most of the time, a software tool is inadequate and manual intervention is needed to make the existing software work properly on the new hardware, without any defects.

Project execution involves the following steps:

1. Document the known and understood differences between the two versions of the programming language, the result of which is a differences map document.
2. Develop a software tool to make corrections in the code as detailed in the differences map document. Sometimes the vendors of programming languages supply such tools.

3. Run the software porting tool on all programs, to have the tool make all the corrections it possibly can.
4. Manually go through all the code to make the corrections that could not be accomplished by the tool.
5. Conduct the necessary or specified software tests.
6. Modify the software engineering documents to reflect changes made in the software.
7. Conduct acceptance testing.
8. Deliver the software.

While it is possible to size the existing software, it would not be practical to size the work that needs to be done. It is the same as fixing defects. This type of project can be estimated using the Delphi estimation, analogy-based estimation, and task-based estimation methodologies.

Migration of Software

New versions of programming languages or databases are released regularly. Visual Basic has gone through six versions. Similarly, Oracle has reached version 11. Operating systems such as Microsoft Windows are also upgraded: MS-DOS, Windows, Windows 2, Windows 3, then Windows 95, Windows 98, Windows 2000, XP, and now Vista. When such upgrades are released, it may become necessary to upgrade software for one of three reasons:

1. To take advantage of the new features and facilities provided in the new version
2. To add additional hardware or system software when an older version is no longer available and the existing software does not function well with the new software (By the way, in these days of multitier Web-based software architectures, an upgrade of any tier necessitates migration!)
3. To remove the existing software's current limitations, as the new release does not have the limitations that the older version has

Of course, if the configuration of the hardware and software remains exactly the same and the existing software is meeting the organization's needs, there is no reason to upgrade. However, given the ever-changing and increasing needs of most organizations, upgrading the existing software is often necessary.

It is possible to measure the size of the existing software, but the work is not dependent on its present size. Rather, the work involved depends on the differences between the two versions. The new version contains features and facilities totally absent in the older version. Therefore, a software tool cannot be used to make the necessary changes in the software to make the software workable. In order to take advantage of the new features and facilities available in the newer version, those changes must be manually implemented, which involves the following steps:

1. Study the new version.
2. Decide which new features are desirable and need to be implemented.
3. Develop a functional expansion design document, detailing the new features to be implemented in the existing software.
4. Run the upgrade tool, if provided by the vendor, to upgrade the software.
5. Implement the functional expansion design in the software coding and incorporate necessary software changes. This may include correcting the existing code.
6. Conduct all tests necessary to ensure the software delivers all the functionality it was supposed to before migration and all the functionality it is designed to deliver for the new software, without any defects.
7. Conduct acceptance testing.
8. Deliver the software.
9. If data migration is also included in the scope of work, additional steps include:
   a. Map the old database schema to the new database schema.
   b. Develop software and locate the tools, if any are provided with the new database, to migrate data from the old database to the new database.
   c. Run the tools to migrate data from the old database to the new database.
   d. Arrange for any additional data entry that may be needed to populate the newly added fields, if any.
   e. Test the database for known test cases using the software, comparing the results with the desired results and making any necessary corrections so that the new database runs properly with the application.
   f. Integrate the database with the software.

Specific migration projects may have different activities from those described here. Porting and migration projects look similar, and there is no strict distinction between the two. Sometimes the terms "porting" and "migration" are used interchangeably.

Software sizing is not appropriate for this class of projects. Yes, we can size the existing project, but it would not help us to determine the migration work. Therefore, Delphi estimation, analogy-based estimation, and task-based estimation are the right methodologies for this class of projects.

Conversion Projects

Y2K and euro conversion projects are excellent examples of conversion projects. In Y2K projects, all programs had to be verified, and any necessary modifications had to be incorporated to make these programs compliant with Y2K. In euro conversion projects, countries that did not use decimals in their financial software had to incorporate decimals, and all countries had to provide for using the euro currency symbol.

Activities typical of a conversion project are as follows:

1. Study the existing software and the specifications for the necessary conversion.
2. Prepare a conversion guidelines document, detailing the procedure for incorporating the required modifications in the software.
3. Develop a tool, if feasible, to automatically incorporate the modifications in the software.
4. Run the tool.
5. Perform a manual walk-through for each program to locate the remaining required modifications, and implement these modifications.
6. Conduct unit testing and other tests as specified or as necessary.
7. Conduct acceptance testing.
8. Deliver the software.

In these projects too, the size of the existing software can be measured, but it would not be useful to predict the amount of corrections necessary. Therefore, the software estimation methodologies best suited for this type of project are Delphi estimation, analogy-based estimation, and task-based estimation.

SOFTWARE MAINTENANCE PROJECTS

Software maintenance projects are major money-earners for software development organizations. Generally, a contract is signed between the parties, setting out general terms and conditions for the entire project for a given time period, say one or two years. The contract continues to be extended as long as both parties are satisfied with the results of the project. This general contract specifies the following points:

- Billing rates
- Mode of requesting work
- Service level agreement
- Persons authorized to raise work requests, accept deliveries, and give clarifications
- Escalation mechanisms for issue resolution
- Billing cycles and payment schedules
- Any other points specific to the parties involved or to the project

Normally, a maintenance work request, sometimes referred to as a program modification request, a program change request, a defect report, or a software change request, triggers software maintenance work. A maintenance work request must be raised with proper authorization for the maintenance work to be started. However, for immediate needs, a telephone call, a fax, or an e-mail suffices, although it must be formalized later on through a formal maintenance work request.

The work included in software maintenance projects is classified into five types.

Defect Fixing

The work involves fixing a reported defect. A defect may be classified as:

- Critical (a showstopper)
- Major (interferes with the smooth functioning of work)
- Minor (a nuisance really; the work is hardly affected)

Defect fixing requires a service level agreement, which typically defines the turnaround time (that is, the time from when a defect is reported to the time it is fixed, a regression test completed, and the corrected software delivered back to the production environment) for each class of defect, based on priority. Sometimes the turnaround time is as little as two hours. The maximum turnaround time for fixing a defect in most cases is about two days. Follow-up on the progress of fixing a defect should be frequent.

The steps for fixing defects are as follows:

1. Study the defect report.
2. Replicate the defect scenario in the development environment.
3. Study the code.
4. Locate the defect.
5. Fix the defect, in conformance with the code change guidelines.
6. Arrange for a peer review and implement feedback, if any.
7. Arrange for independent regression testing and implement feedback, if any.
8. Deliver the fixed code to the production environment for implementation in the production system.
9. Close the request.

Defect fixing is usually performed fairly quickly, so unless the duration allowed for is more than one calendar week, it really makes no sense to attempt estimation. If defect fixing is expected to take more than a week, then Delphi estimation and analogy-based estimation are the methodologies to use.

Operational Support

Similar to defect fixing, operational support needs to be attended to immediately. Activities include:

- Running periodic jobs (end of day/week/month)
- Making backups
- Restoring data from backups
- Performing user management (including creating, deleting, and suspending user accounts; changing access privileges; etc.)
- Providing one-on-one assistance at specific workstations
- Extracting data and producing ad hoc reports on an urgent basis
- Providing a temporary patch to enable operations to continue
- Investigating operational complaints

As with defect fixing, these activities require a service level agreement, and turnaround times are generally of a short duration, ranging from one hour to one business day. In such cases, there is no point in performing estimation, as it would take about the same time as the work itself would take to be completed. For longer durations, Delphi estimation, analogy-based estimation, and task-based estimation can be used.

Fixing Odd Behavior

In large, complex software systems as well as in older systems, sometimes defects randomly crop up and become difficult to replicate in the development environment. If a defect occurs in the field, the person at the workstation where it occurred will not have noted the chain of events that led to the defect. Until the same defect crops up at different workstations at different times, the problem is handled by an operational support activity, and it will not be recognized as a defect. Such puzzling defects are placed in this category of software maintenance. Fixing odd behavior may take longer than a week, since it requires research because it involves the unpredictable occurrence of a defect. The cause could be the application software, the system software, the client workstation, a virus, network security, or any combination of these.

The steps for fixing odd behavior are as follows:

1. Study the odd-behavior reports.
2. Try to replicate the behavior in the development environment.
3. Study the code.
4. List all possible reasons for the reported behavior.
5. Review the code for each alternative to find opportunities to improve the code.
6. Repeat the above steps, eliminating all the causes one by one.
7. Unearth all opportunities to improve the code (code that may cause defects) and modify the code as necessary.
8. Arrange for a peer review of the improved code and implement feedback, if any.
9. Arrange for independent regression testing.
10. Deliver the software to the production environment for implementation of the improved code into the production system.
11. Wait for another report of identical odd behavior, and repeat the above steps.
12. Keep the request open until production requests its closure.

Software size estimation is not possible for this type of work. However, Delphi estimation, analogy-based estimation, and task-based estimation can be used for estimating the effort required to fix odd behaviors.

Software Modification

This type of work perhaps forms the bulk of software maintenance work. Modification of working software may be necessary because of:

- Changes in requirements due to passage of time
- Changes in business processing logic
- A need to make the software more convenient for users
- Changes in statutory requirements

Typical modifications include report changes and screen changes (moving data fields around, adding or deleting a data field or two, etc.).

The steps for software modification are as follows:

1. Study the software modification request.
2. Analyze the existing software to identify components where modification is requested.
3. Prepare a design modification document and obtain approval from the appropriate executives.
4. Implement the approved design modification in the code.
5. Arrange for a peer review of the modified code and implement feedback, if any.
6. Arrange for independent functional testing of the modified functionality, in conformance with the approved design document, and implement feedback, if any.
7. Arrange for independent regression testing and implement feedback, if any.
8. Deliver the modified software to the production environment for implementation into the production system.
9. Close the request.

Software size estimation is not possible for this type of work. However, Delphi estimation, analogy-based estimation, and task-based estimation can be used for estimating the effort required for software modification.

Functional Expansion

When additional functionality is required in existing software, functional expansion is implemented. This type of work is generally of a longer duration, exceeding one calendar week. The work of functional expansion includes:

- Adding a new screen or report
- Adding additional processing functionality, such as quarterly, half-yearly, or yearly processing
- Adding a new module to the software
- Integrating with other software

- Building interfaces with other software
- Adding new hardware and building an interface to that hardware from the software

Functional expansion generally fits the full software development life cycle model. It undergoes a full software engineering and project management process, and it can be treated as an independent project if the duration is relatively long. Some organizations treat functional expansion with a duration of 1 person-month of effort or more as an independent project.

Therefore, what is required first is to estimate the effort to determine if the work can be spun off as a separate project. If the estimated effort justifies a new project, then it undergoes all the activities expected of a project. Delphi estimation, analogy-based estimation, and task-based estimation can be used for estimating the effort required. Since this type of project permits software sizing, it is normal practice to estimate the software size along with effort, cost, and schedule. Estimating software size facilitates computation of productivity.

AGILE SOFTWARE DEVELOPMENT PROJECTS

Agile projects play down the importance of documentation and place significant emphasis on satisfying the customer. Agile project advocates suggest using experienced and motivated software developers, giving them freedom and placing trust in them. As an alternative to documentation, they suggest "co-location" of the customer or end user and the development team. Agile is a new philosophy that has spawned a new set of methodologies. As agile methodologies put more emphasis on coding, shorter delivery cycles (four weeks or less) per iteration, and a number of iterations to complete the software development, software estimation seems superfluous.

Now, the question is, when following agile methodologies, do we really need to estimate? The Agile Manifesto does not cover this subject, so there is no official answer. Some, perhaps, may say that software estimation is not required for agile methodologies; I have met a couple of such persons who lump software estimation in with superfluous documentation. They say it goes against the grain of the agile philosophy. But I say yes, we do need to estimate. Without software estimation, how do we know how many persons are needed to complete the current iteration? And how do we know how many iterations will be needed to complete the project?

Put yourself in the shoes of the person sanctioning the money for a project. Suppose the person in charge of software development comes to you and says,

"I do not have any idea how much the total project will cost. But I can tell you how much the current iteration, which will last four weeks, costs."

Would you sanction the money? Not very likely. You would probably tell that person, "I need more information than that to sanction the money. You see, I need to set a budget and to get that budget approved. Please come back to me with a rough estimate of the total cost and a more accurate estimate for the current iteration."

Any project in today's organizations needs a budget for starting the project and for sanctioning resources to execute the project. Whoever is in the position of sanctioning resources (even a die-hard agile advocate) needs estimates before sanctioning them.

It is not that estimation is total anathema to agile methodologies. Agile methodologies use story points as the main software size measure for estimating software size. Unfortunately, however, there is no universally accepted definition of what constitutes a story point. There is also no defined methodology to which software estimators can refer when estimating in story points.

In addition, there are no set phases or tasks in agile-based software development. This means that different software projects may require different sets of tasks. Suffice it to say that agile methodologies allow the developers absolute freedom, with the end result and customer satisfaction as the most significant considerations.

However, software size does not alter whether or not documents (requirements or design, for example) are used. Therefore, I advocate estimating the size of software using any software size measure convenient to the team for the entire software, not just for the software that is being developed in the current iteration. For each iteration, though, I do advocate estimating the software development effort, as effort forms the basis for developing a schedule and assessment of resources needed for completing the iteration.

Therefore, I suggest that task-based estimation is the most suitable methodology for estimating effort for iterations of all agile projects and for estimating software size for the entire software intended to be developed over several iterations.

WEB PROJECTS

Web projects, or Web-based application development projects, differ from other projects in that they involve more than two tiers. Some of these tiers are (1) a presentation tier, (2) a database server tier, (3) an app server tier, (4) a Web server tier, and (5) a security server. There could be several others.

When it comes to artifacts, a Web application consists of:

- HTML pages that include graphics to enhance the look and feel of the Web pages
- Back-end programs for data manipulation
- Middleware programs for application server or rules engines
- Middleware programs for security management
- Other application-specific artifacts

Another notable feature of Web projects is that back-end programming and middleware programming may be in different programming languages, and a project may need persons of different skill sets to handle each language. Another feature that is asked for in these projects is independence from databases and Web browsers. This necessitates coding routines that are not oriented toward functionality. Also, a Web application needs to be developed such that it facilitates an easy change of code. Environmental changes, such as a new security threat, release of a new browser, or upgrade of an existing browser, can trigger software maintenance in a Web application even though the functionality remains unaltered.

Software size for a Web application is not a single size. One size is needed for HTML pages with graphics, and one size is needed for each type of programming language used. In other words, one size is needed for each tier. Once this is understood, software estimation becomes manageable:

1. Use any software size measure that is standardized in your organization, or use the one with which you are comfortable.
2. Estimate the size of the software to be developed at each tier.
3. Convert size into software development effort using the procedure for converting software size to effort.
4. Estimate graphics separately using task-based estimation and based on the skill of the graphic artist.
5. Sum the efforts of all the above to arrive at the overall effort requirement for the project.

The above procedure may be adopted for estimation of Web projects.

Graphics still fall in the creative arena, but the person producing the graphics should be able to give an estimate.

SUMMARY

In this chapter, different categories of software development projects are enumerated. Categories include projects based on the software development life cycle, projects based on the software development methodology used to arrive at the software solution, and software maintenance projects. Each of these categories is divided into subcategories. For each subcategory of projects, appropriate software estimation methodologies, which are detailed in subsequent chapters, are recommended. Appendix B is a table that summarizes the discussions in this chapter, listing project type and the corresponding software estimation methodologies.

5

APPROACHES TO SOFTWARE ESTIMATION

Software estimation has four aspects to it, namely:

1. Software size estimation
2. Software development effort estimation
3. Software development cost estimation
4. Software development schedule estimation

Cost estimation and schedule estimation flow from the project's estimated effort. Effort can either flow from software size or be estimated independently.

There are multiple approaches to software estimation, which can be classified into two categories. The first category has to do with management's attitude toward software estimation, which can be broken down into the following two distinct approaches:

1. Ad hoc approach
2. Process-driven approach

The second category of software estimation approaches concerns details, meaning how much detail is included in the estimate. Here again, we find two distinct approaches:

1. Gross estimates
2. Detailed estimates

Let us now discuss these four approaches.

AD HOC APPROACH

Quite a few organizations take this approach to software estimation. They do not perceive the process of estimation as an important activity, as it is the "opportunity" pricing model (as opposed to the cost-plus pricing model) that enables businesses to win orders. In cases where differences in currency exchange rates allow for ample profits (as is the case of Indian software companies), it does not make sense to focus attention and resources on an uncertain activity like software estimation. The following describes the scenario typical of the ad hoc approach:

1. A request for proposal is received by the organization.
2. Marketing (or whoever is fronting the project acquisition) approaches the head of the technical department (sometimes called the delivery head) for estimation.
3. The technical head assigns the task to an estimator—not necessarily the most appropriate one, but rather the one who happens to be available at the moment.
4. The estimator carries out the estimation to the best of his or her ability and turns in the estimate to its requester.
5. No formal causal analysis is carried out to determine the variance between actual values and estimated values. Why not? Because this would involve the expense of more effort and resources, and the results may not yield valuable information. In some cases, results of the analysis may even produce information that is contrary to management's policies, or the analysis may suggest that process-driven software estimation should have been used. Often, an organization's reason for not performing a formal causal analysis goes something like this: "Everybody knows the reasons for variances. No point in spending more resources on what we already know."

Software estimation is carried out using these four steps for every new request for proposal the organization receives.

PROCESS-DRIVEN APPROACH

Using this approach, the organization has a well-defined process in place for how to carry out the activities of software estimation, from requesting an estimate, to delivering the estimate, to variance analysis. This approach is discussed in greater detail in chapter 14.

GROSS ESTIMATES APPROACH

The gross estimates approach derives the estimate in one of three ways:

1. **Delphi estimation**—This method involves having experts in the application domain and in software development make a "best-guess" estimate of software size or software development effort, or both, based on their expertise and experience. Estimates are then converged, either by using a statistical method or by iterating the estimates between experts until a satisfactory convergence is achieved.
2. **Analogy-based estimation**—Here, a similar past project is used as the basis from which to extrapolate and derive the estimate for the current project. The estimate is based on actual values achieved in the past project, and adjustments are made in the estimate by the estimator for the differences between the selected past project and current project.
3. **Parametric estimation**—This method came about from Dr. Barry Boehm's constructive cost models (COCOMO I and COCOMO II), wherein a set of equations gives the software effort estimation.

   In the **basic COCOMO** model, the estimator selects the project type, and the equations do the rest of the calculations, including those for development effort and duration. The **intermediate COCOMO** model combines project size in lines of code, the project type, and a set of cost drivers. Using a formula, the model gives the software development effort in person-months. **Advanced COCOMO** and **COCOMO II** are more involved and for the purposes of this book will not be discussed.

   Using parametric models is becoming a profitable method of estimation among the following project types:
   a. Implementation of enterprise resource planning (ERP) packages (such as SAP, PeopleSoft, JD Edwards, and BaaN), supply chain management (SCM) software packages (such as Tradematrix and Manugistics), and customer relationship management (CRM) packages—These projects are fairly homogeneous, with linear scalability in terms of number of modules, number of locations,

number of users, and so on. Once you have figures for actual effort, cost, and duration for a few projects, you can apply a set of formulas to the effort for past projects and arrive at the estimates for the current project.

b. Infrastructure projects such as implementing Web sites, with both hardware and software—These projects are also fairly homogeneous in that mathematical relationships can be built for estimation based on past projects.

One advantage of the gross estimates approach is that it offers a starting point, especially for organizations that are either young or are new to software estimation. Another advantage is that estimates can be derived very quickly. However, one key disadvantage of this approach is that it is not amenable to reviews and audits.

DETAILED ESTIMATES APPROACH

Detailed estimates are further classified by the process through which they are derived:

1. The size of the software to be developed is estimated first, and the other estimates (effort, cost, and schedule) are derived from this estimated software size.
2. The size of the software to be developed is not estimated, but the software development effort is estimated directly, with cost and schedule derived from this effort estimate.

SOFTWARE SIZE ESTIMATES

Lines of code (LOC) was the first unit of measure used for software size. In the third-generation-language era, LOC worked well despite some disagreement among estimators about what constitutes a line of code. For example, is LOC logical or physical? How should commenting lines be treated? Other such questions were often raised. Then came function points from IBM. Other software size measures followed soon after: object points, use case points, feature points, Internet points, story points, test points, Mark II function point analysis, and software size units.

Of all these units of measure, function points has the largest following, and the International Function Point Users Group (IFPUG) champions its use. The IFPUG certifies persons in function point counting by administering its Certified Function Point Specialist (CFPS) examination. The organization has released its *Counting Practices Manual* and periodically updates it.

In all these methods, software size is converted into software development effort using a productivity figure, such as 10 person-hours per function point, for example. The cost and schedule are then derived from effort.

However, there is no universal agreement on what unit of measure should be used for software sizing. No standards body—not the American National Standards Institute, the Institute of Electrical and Electronics Engineers, the Deutsches Institut für Normung, or the British Standards Institute, to name a few—has accepted and standardized the use of any one unit of measure for software sizing.

The advantage to estimating size is that we can come to an agreement with the customer on the quantity of software being developed. Size and effort, put together, allow us to compute the productivity (rate of achievement) of software development and facilitate benchmarking with other projects or organizations. The problem is, however, that there is no universally agreed-upon definition of software size, and no set relationship between existing units of measure, such as between miles and kilometers, pounds and kilograms, etc., has been established.

SOFTWARE DEVELOPMENT EFFORT ESTIMATES

The following estimation methods skip software size and estimate the software development effort directly:

1. **Task-based estimation**—In this method, the total work is broken down into phases, and phases are further broken down into tasks. The effort needed to perform those tasks is then estimated. Total effort is derived as the sum of the effort of all tasks.

2. **Analogy-based estimation**—In this method, a past project that is similar in application domain to the present project is selected, and its actual achievements are extrapolated to make estimates for the current project.

The estimate for software development effort, derived from either of these methods, is then used to derive the cost estimate and schedule estimate.

THE DELPHI TECHNIQUE FOR SOFTWARE ESTIMATION

Delphi is a city in Greece. In ancient times, it was considered a place where the power of prediction could be conferred upon a person. A temple was built there, and virgin girls were appointed to answer questions about the future; these girls were called Oracles. The Oracles' prophecies were considered wise counsel. Taking its cue from this legend, the Delphi technique involves the drawing of wise counsel from senior and experienced software developers (Oracles) for preparing estimates for software development projects.

Using this method of software estimation, the project specifications are given to a minimum of three experts in order to collate their opinions. With at least three experts, a range of values will be offered, which will allow convergence of the estimates.

The Delphi technique entails the following steps:

1. Selection of experts
2. Briefing of the experts
3. Collation of estimates from the experts
4. Convergence of estimates and finalization

Selection of Experts

The experts selected must have software development experience as well as experience and knowledge in the project's specific application domain. Although a minimum of three experts is required when using the Delphi technique, the actual number of experts selected depends upon the following factors:

- Complexity of the project—The more complex the project, the more experts needed.
- Availability of experts who have the domain knowledge
- The nature of the organization's competition and the reasons the organization wants to acquire the proposed project (perhaps for the prestige associated with the project or to penetrate a new market opportunity, for example)—If the competition is perceived to be stiff and margins are expected to be low, more expert advice is needed.

Delphi estimation is widely used in software maintenance projects for estimating the effort required for short-duration work requests. In such cases, only one expert is needed. When multiple experts are used, the Delphi estimation is referred to as *wideband Delphi estimation.*

Briefing the Experts

The experts selected need to be briefed about the project. This can be done either independently in a one-on-one conversation or in a group meeting. The following aspects of the project need to be communicated:

- Objectives of the estimation
- Explanation of the project scope
- Competition and its nature in the project bidding
- Timelines for completing the estimate and the deliverables expected from the experts
- Any clarification requested by the experts

After the briefing, the experts are ready to work on the estimates. How much time the experts should be allowed to arrive at their estimates depends on the requirements of the project and the willingness of the experts. I advocate a minimum of one calendar day so that the experts have time to mull over the project and arrive at accurate estimates.

Collation of Estimates Received from the Experts

The experts are expected to offer one figure only for software development effort and, optionally, for software size. This figure is their best guess or hunch. Each of these Oracles (experts) offers his or her opinion, and the opinions of all the experts are then tabulated, as shown in table 5.1.

Table 5.1. Compilation of expert opinions

Name of expert	Size estimate	Effort estimate
Expert 1	A	X
Expert 2	B	Y
Expert 3	C	Z
Expert *n*	K	L

Convergence of Estimates and Finalization

Once the experts' estimates have been collated, they are converged. Convergence can be achieved in two ways:

1. The software estimate for the project is derived using either the arithmetic mean (average) or statistical mode from the opinions offered by the experts.
2. The extreme estimates (the highest figure estimate and the lowest figure estimate) are interchanged:
   a. The highest estimate is given to the expert who gave the lowest figure estimate.
   b. The lowest estimate is given to the expert who gave the highest figure estimate.
   c. The experts are asked to review the estimate, give their opinion on it, and, if necessary, revise their original estimate.
   d. If this process leads to convergence between the extremes, then the software estimate for the project is derived using either the arithmetic average or statistical mode from the opinions offered by the experts.

This estimate (after achieving convergence or deriving the average) is the final figure needed to proceed with the project. A sample Delphi estimation sheet can be found in Appendix C. You may use it as is, modify it to suit your organization, or develop a new template to match your specific needs.

Merits and Demerits of the Delphi Technique

Merits of the Delphi technique include the following:

- It is very useful when the organization does not have any in-house experts with the domain knowledge or the development platform experience to offer a quick estimate.
- It derives an estimate very quickly.
- It is simple to administer and use.
- If appropriate experts are chosen carefully, the results can be surprisingly accurate.

These are the demerits of the Delphi technique:

- It can be too simplistic.
- It may be difficult to locate the right experts.
- It may be difficult to locate an adequate number of experts willing to participate in the estimation.
- The derived estimate is not auditable.
- It is not possible to determine the causes of variance between the estimated values and the actual values.
- Only size and effort estimation are possible. A schedule cannot be prepared using this method.

ANALOGY-BASED SOFTWARE ESTIMATION

Analogy-based software estimation centers on the principle that *actual values achieved within the organization in an earlier and similar project are more accurate predictors of a future project's performance than an estimate developed from scratch.* This method facilitates bringing the organizational experience to bear on a new project.

To use this technique profitably, certain prerequisites are required:

- The organization should have executed a number of projects in the past.
- The organization should be keeping meticulous records of past projects.
- The organization must conduct a project postmortem for every project, and causes of variances must be identified using meticulous methods. Actual values achieved by a project are validated depending on the causes identified. The data from validated actual values is then included in the organization's estimates repository (or knowledge repository) and made available for future reference. Care must be taken to prevent erroneous data from influencing future projects. Appendix A shows the methodology for conducting variance analysis for variances between actual and estimated values.
- The organization should have a well-organized and well-maintained knowledge repository from which it is feasible to locate similar past projects and extract the validated project data.
- The estimators should be trained in drawing analogies accurately, as well as in accessing the knowledge repository and extracting validated data to extrapolate from it for future projects.

Selection of Similar Past Projects

This is a crucial step in analogy-based software estimation, and care must be taken when shortlisting similar projects. The first step in shortlisting is, of course, defining the project type:

- **Full life cycle software development project**—Normally referred to as a development project
- **Software implementation project**—Implementing such software systems as ERP, SCM, CRM, etc.
- **Conversion project**—Converting an application to make it usable in new circumstances (Y2K projects, euro conversion projects, etc.)
- **Porting projects**—Porting from one software platform to another, such as from one version of Unix to another version of Unix (Sun Solaris to HP UX)
- **Migration projects**—Migrating an application from one hardware platform to another (Data General to IBM mainframe, for example)

The most crucial aspect for the success of analogy-based estimation is selection of the right set of past projects. The following parameters need to be considered:

- **Application domain**—This is perhaps the single most important feature to be considered. It would not make sense to draw an analogy between two projects in different application domains. Would it make sense to select a marketing information project to draw an analogy for a material management information project? Of course not.
- **Organization size of the prospective client**—The extent of functionality would differ between organizations of different sizes even if the domain is the same. The functionality of material management, for example, in a medium-size organization would significantly differ from that in a large organization. A past project that is comparable in size to the current project should be selected.
- **Number of locations of the prospective client**—The functionality in a single-location organization would be vastly different from the functionality in a multi-location organization. Therefore, a past project should be selected that is similar to the current project in number of locations of the client organization.

■ **Nature of modules in the application**—The majority of the modules in the past project must be similar to those in the current project. Adjustments and extrapolation can be done for an extra module or two, but not more than that.

The following parameters from the development platform need to be considered:

■ **Number of application tiers**—A two-tier application project would significantly differ from a three-tier application project.

■ **Back end**—Today, almost all applications are built with a relational database management system (RDBMS) for data storage and retrieval. As long as the back end in both the past and the current project is an RDBMS, they can be considered similar. However, if the back end of one project is flat files and the other is RDBMS, then the difference between the two projects is too significant.

■ **Web server**—Different Web servers cause different amounts of software development work. It may be necessary to extrapolate based on the Web servers used. This would be applicable in Web-based application development.

■ **Middleware**—The middleware used has different impacts on the amount of effort required.

■ **Rules engine**—If the proposed project uses a rules engine, it is best to select a past project that also used a rules engine. Also significant is the fact that different rules engines have different impacts on the amount of effort required for software development.

■ **Programming language**—The amount of work is influenced to a large extent by the language in which programs are developed. If the past project used a different programming language than the present project will, it may be necessary to adjust the estimate for the difference in programming language.

■ **Development environment**—The type of tools used for editing the programs, debugging, compiling, etc. has a large impact on the productivity of programmers. Therefore, it is important to select past projects that have similar software development environments.

■ **Software development process used**—It is important to select past projects that are similar in the manner of developing software. Past projects should conform to the process that is likely to be used in the current project.

■ **Location of development**—The development location can be either
   in-house or at the client's location. It is better to select a past project
   that was executed in a similar type of development location.

Shortlisting of Past Projects

The overriding criterion for selection of projects is similarity of the application
domain. It is futile to shortlist projects that are in different application domains.
Therefore, it is essential to make this the first criterion for shortlisting of projects.
Then the projects can be shortlisted in a table such as table 5.2.

Shortlisting projects can perhaps be accomplished through an automated
process that narrows down the selection to two or three projects. However, the
estimator should be the person who selects the one project from the automatically generated shortlisted projects to be the base estimate for the present project.
Automating this step is not recommended. Here, human judgment is necessary
to select the project that:

■ Is closest to the present project in terms of the parameters listed
■ Needs the least possible extrapolation to arrive at the new estimate

Once a past project is selected, the following steps can be performed to arrive
at the new estimate:

1. Make a comparative analysis of all parameters between the past project
   and the present project.
2. Make adjustments for differences as necessary. There are two possi-
   bilities:
   a. If detailed estimates are available for the past project, the old
      estimates can be tailored to fit the new project.
   b. If only gross estimates are available, adjustments need to be made
      to the gross estimates.
3. Finalize the new estimate, have it reviewed by a peer, and implement
   feedback, if any.
4. Arrange for a managerial review and implement feedback, if any.
5. Present the estimate to the requester, using the standard formats from
   the organizational estimation process.

When a detailed estimate is available for the past project selected, the following steps can be performed to arrive at the new estimate:

Table 5.2. Compilation of candidate projects

Criteria	Current project	Project 1	Project 2	Project 3	Project *n*
Type of project	Development	Development	Development	Development	Development
Application domain	CRM	CRM	CRM	CRM	CRM
Organization size	Medium	Large	Large	Medium	Small
Number of locations	2	6	8	3	1
Modules	■ Purchasing ■ Warehouse ■ Inventory control	■ Purchasing ■ Warehouse ■ Inventory control ■ Shipping ■ MRP	■ Purchasing ■ Warehouse ■ Inventory control ■ Shipping ■ MRP	■ Purchasing ■ Warehouse ■ Inventory control ■ MRP	■ Purchasing ■ Warehouse ■ MRP
Application tiers	3	4	4	2	1
Back end	RDBMS	RDBMS	RDBMS	RDBMS	Flat files
Web server	IIS	WebSphere	WebSphere	NA	NA
Middleware	Nil	WebLogic	WebLogic	NA	NA
Rules engine	Nil	Ilog	Ilog	Nil	Nil
Programming language	J2EE	DotNet 03	DotNet 05	Visual Basic 6	COBOL
Development environment	J2EE	DotNet 03	DotNet 05	Visual Basic 6	COBOL
Development process	CMMI® 5	CMMI® 3	CMM® 5	CMM® 3	ISO 9000
Development location	In-house	In-house	In-house	Client	Client

1. Save the old estimate as the new estimate.
2. Examine each detail of the old estimate.
   a. If a detail is identical to the current project, retain it.
   b. If a detail is completely out of scope for the current project, delete it.
   c. If a detail is partially applicable to the current project, adjust the detail to reflect the reality of the current project.
   d. Carry out the above three steps for every detail of the old estimate to arrive at the new estimate.
3. Examine the details and determine if any of them are pertinent to the current project but are totally missing from the old estimate. Include these details in the estimate to make it comprehensive in terms of estimate details.
4. Examine the environmental aspects, such as the development platform, programming language, number of application tiers, development location, middleware, etc., and make appropriate adjustments to the estimate.
5. Now that the estimate is ready, arrange for a peer review and implement feedback, if any.
6. Arrange for a managerial review, implement feedback, if any, and obtain approval.
7. Submit the estimate to the requester, using the standard formats from the organizational estimation process.

If only gross estimates are available:

1. Examine each parameter of the new project against the old project.
2. Assign a weight to each parameter:
   a. A weight of 0 indicates that a parameter is not applicable at all to the current project.
   b. A weight of 1 indicates that a parameter is identical to the new project.
   c. A weight of more than 0 but less than 1 indicates that a parameter is applicable, but at less than 100 percent.
   d. A weight of more than 1 indicates that a parameter is applicable, at more than 100 percent.
3. Sum all the weights and derive the arithmetic average to obtain the composite weight factor (CWF).
4. Multiply the gross estimates of the past project by the CWF to obtain the new estimate.

5. Now that the estimate is ready, arrange for a peer review and implement feedback, if any.
6. Arrange for a managerial review and obtain approval.
7. Submit the estimate to the requester, using the standard formats from the organizational estimation process.

Table 5.3 illustrates this procedure.

Let us assume the past project selected has:

1. A size of 500 function points
2. A development effort of 5,000 person-hours

In table 5.3, the CWF is 1.16. The past project values are multiplied by this CWF to arrive at the following new estimate values:

Table 5.3. CWF computation for analogy-based estimation

Criteria	Current project	Selected project	Weight
Type of project	Development	Development	1.0
Application domain	CRM	CRM	1.0
Organization size	Medium	Large	0.4
Number of locations	2	6	0.4
Modules	■ Purchasing ■ Warehouse ■ Inventory control	■ Purchasing ■ Warehouse ■ Inventory control ■ Shipping ■ MRP	0.4
Application tiers	3	4	7.0
Back end	RDBMS	RDBMS	1.0
Web server	IIS	WebSphere	0.8
Middleware	Nil	WebLogic	0.0
Rules engine	Nil	Ilog	0.0
Programming language	J2EE	DotNet 03	1.0
Development environment	J2EE	DotNet 03	1.0
Development process	CMMI® 5	CMMI® 3	1.2
Development location	In-house	In-house	1.0
CWF			1.16

1. Size = 500 × 1.16, which results in 580 function points
2. Development effort = 5,000 × 1.16, which results in 5,800 person-hours

Analogy-Based Estimation in Software Maintenance

Because software maintenance deals with short-duration work requests, estimating software size may not be practical. In such cases, analogy-based estimation is used. However, the formal methodology described here is not used; analogy is drawn from a similar work request executed earlier.

Merits and Demerits of Analogy-Based Estimation

Merits of analogy-based software estimation include the following:

- It is based on actual values achieved within the organization for an earlier project, and therefore is more reliable than other methods of estimation.
- It is easy to learn, and an accurate estimate can be arrived at quickly.
- New organizations can purchase estimation data from such standards bodies as the International Software Benchmarking Standards Group and readily use this technique. While these estimates are not from within the organization, they provide a starting point and a variety of estimates from which to choose.
- It facilitates the use of organizational expertise and experience, brought to bear upon the current project like no other software estimation technique possibly can.

These are the demerits of analogy-based software estimation:

- The shortlisting of past projects and selection of the final project require meticulous record-keeping and software tool support. Any laxity in this step will render the estimate inaccurate and unreliable.
- An organization needs to maintain a well-designed knowledge repository that conforms to a meticulous process.
- There might not be any past projects relevant to the current project upon which the organization can draw.
- It cannot be implemented in a new organization.

SUMMARY

Organizations can take several approaches to software estimation, largely depending on the organization carrying out the software estimation activity. An ad hoc approach generally does not give software estimation activity its due importance, whereas a process-driven approach helps an organization to capture its experts' experience and facilitates improvement in software estimation. One classification of software estimation is based on the detail included in the software estimate. The gross estimation methods—the Delphi technique and the analogy-based technique—do not provide much detail and therefore do not lend themselves to peer review and audit, but they are a quick way to derive software estimates of acceptable accuracy. Detailed software estimation includes estimating the software size and from the software size deriving effort, cost, and schedules.

SOFTWARE SIZE ESTIMATION

In a contract with the client, the size of the software that is to be developed needs to be specified as "number of units of software." When the software is delivered to the client, this size specification confirms that the agreed-upon amount of software was in fact developed and delivered for the agreed-upon price. This may sound simple—if not obvious, but in reality, this practice is not easy to execute.

MEASURING THE SIZE OF WHAT, EXACTLY?

This is the first question that needs to be answered before proceeding with a discussion about measuring the size of the software that is to be developed. The answer seems obvious: we are measuring the size of a software product. But what constitutes a software product? To answer this question, we must first define what a product is specifically. Here are a few common definitions of a product:

- A bundle of benefits to its customer, according to a definition
- Something for which one or more customers are willing to pay money
- Something that fulfills some need

These definitions of a product are based on a customer's standpoint. Software developers, however, do not look at a product from the standpoint of a customer, but rather see it from the standpoint of delivery. As such, what, then, do software developers deliver as a product? Perhaps it is easier to explain what it is that they do *not* deliver through the following example scenarios. When you buy a car, a DVD player, or a calculator, you get a car, a DVD player, or a calculator, and with each of these comes a user manual and perhaps a few spare parts. These items, however, are consumer products, and contract software development is not comparable to consumer products. It is more akin to contract manufacturing.

If you are setting up a large power station and you order a generator, the manufacturer supplies not just the generator and a user manual but also the as-built drawings, installation instructions, a troubleshooting manual, and bills of material. Contract software development is akin to this scenario. Software development organizations supply not just software and user documentation but requirements specification documents and design documents as well. Even though requirements specification documents are delivered, we have to keep in mind that they are a precursor to the software design documents and therefore do not form part of the product.

Thus, in contract software development (project-based development), the software product includes the following:

- Software source code and software executable code
- User documentation, including a user manual, a troubleshooting guide, an operations manual, test logs, etc.
- Software design documents

The paradox that software developers face is this: Should the size of all the above be measured or only the size of the software source code? Taking the example of a power station, the logical argument is that when ordering a power station to be built, the as-built drawings and bills of material are considered as appendages of the main product and therefore are not included when measuring the size of the product. When ordering a huge generator, the drawings and other documents are still appendages; measurement is limited to the generator. Therefore, it is safe to conclude that software developers ought to measure the size of software only, meaning the source code only.

The next question that needs to be addressed is whether software developers should measure size from the user's point of view or from the developer's point of view.

APPROACHES TO SOFTWARE SIZE MEASUREMENT

There are two schools of thought on this aspect of measuring software size. One school of thought is directed at *functional measurement,* meaning *from the stand-*

point of the customer or end user, and the other is *artifact measurement,* meaning *from the standpoint of the developer.*

Functional measurement forms the backbone of such size measures as function points, Mark II function point analysis, and use case points. Artifact measurement forms the backbone of the size measures lines of code, object points, and software size units. Each of these units of measure is explained in greater detail throughout this chapter and the next.

Which approach is correct? The software development industry seems divided on this question, although such confusion is absent in other industries. This is how an estimation transaction in most other industries flows (usually):

1. The customer gives user specifications for the product to the supplier.
2. On the supplier side:
    a. Management considers its capacity, in terms of technical capability and the load in its production facility, to meet the timelines to deliver the product.
    b. The designer converts the user specifications into preliminary drawings to be used for cost estimation.
    c. The estimator considers the productivity specific to each workstation.
3. Estimation (of cost, effort, and delivery schedule) is carried out based on what is going into the product, not from the customer standpoint.

Consider a scenario where a customer is ordering a bus. The customer gives such specifications as the number of seats, a 1,000-mile nonstop run, air-conditioning, a lavatory, space for two drivers, and so on. To estimate the cost of producing the bus, the estimator lists out all the materials and labor, overhead, and the profit margin. The estimate would not contain elements of customer specifications directly.

This is an example of artifact-measurement-based estimation. Almost every industry, including the construction industry, manufacturing industry, and services industry, uses the artifact measurement approach. It has lent predictability to estimation and has served these particular industries very well. There is no confusion at all in these industries with respect to measurement, yet confusion and disagreement abound in the software development industry. The concept of functional measurement originated in the software industry only in the late 1970s, with the introduction of the function point. The confusion with software estimation is now mainly due to this concept. We have developed an inappropriate concept, and we are defending it with all our might, which has resulted in software estimation being considered a black art.

Therefore, it is my opinion that artifact-measurement-based software estimation is the right approach to software size measurement.

CONCERNS WITH SOFTWARE SIZE ESTIMATION

Is software size estimation really necessary? The answer is yes and no! Strictly speaking, software size estimation is not necessary for the management of software projects. There are age-old effort estimation techniques, such as task-based estimation, Delphi estimation, and analogy-based estimation, with which software development effort can be estimated and from that software development cost and schedule derived. The tools Microsoft Project and Primavera, for example, allow us to achieve these objectives conveniently.

If achieving the end result is the only objective of the project, without restrictions on efficiency and effectiveness of resource use, then yes, effort estimation alone is adequate and size estimation is not required. This is so in research projects, as there is uncertainty and uncharted areas in such endeavors.

One drawback of estimating effort directly is that we are not able to derive the rate of achievement (or productivity) of software development. *Productivity* enables software development organizations to achieve the following:

- Benchmark their achievement against other organizations to compare and contrast and to know where they stand in terms of economy, efficiency, and effectiveness in how they perform their work.
- Improve performance. Productivity allows software development organizations to set targets for such improvement and then to achieve those targets.
- Judge whether the performance or achievement of the organization and the software engineers is right performance, underperformance, or overachievement. Without productivity and benchmarking, software development organizations have no means of knowing where their software engineers stand in terms of performance.
- Differentiate more easily between performers and nonperformers and between super-performers and average performers. In essence, productivity facilitates fair dispensation of positive rewards and negative rewards based on real performance.
- Discover opportunities for improvement.

To compute productivity, software size must be estimated. Chapter 10 discusses the concept of productivity in greater detail. True, it is not possible to estimate software size in all cases, especially in software maintenance, software implementation, and customization projects. However, in all other project types, wherever it is feasible, software size has to be estimated.

Having said that, we need to note the real and practical concerns associated with estimating software size. As stated previously in this book, the first and primary concern about software estimation is that no universal unit of measure has been agreed upon and established within the industry. Thus, we have multiple units of measure for measuring software size; to reiterate, these units of measure are function points, use case points, object points, Mark II function point analysis, and lines of code, to name the most common ones. Furthermore, there is currently no accepted way of converting software size from one measure to another. Each of the size estimation techniques listed here is described in greater detail throughout this chapter.

One odd aspect of these measures is that the size is adjusted (increased or decreased) according to such factors as complexity. Size is something that does not change. For example, a pound of cheese is not altered if the person weighing it is less or more experienced in weighing items or if the scale used is either a mechanical scale or an electronic one (assuming that both are accurate). A distance of one mile remains one mile whether a teenager is walking it or an old man is walking it or whether the mile is a rural street or a busy city street. In the second example, the only difference is rate of achievement: the old man will likely take longer to complete walking the mile than the teenager, and a person can move more quickly on a empty street than on a busy street. Chapter 8 discusses the issue of complexity in greater detail.

Each unit of measure discussed here comes with a detailed set of documentation that contains clear-cut definitions and detailed explanations. It is beyond the scope of this book to delve into all of this detail. I have included a brief overview of the methodology for each of these software size measures for the sake of information. However, the reader can research individual documentation, freely available on the Internet, for more information on each of them.

LINES OF CODE

Lines of code (LOC) was the first software size measure attempted in software size estimation. Program size was measured in the number of LOC needed to achieve the functionality. As soon as software developers began using this unit of measure, questions cropped up. The most frequent questions concerned definition, meaning exactly what is a line of code:

- Is a line of code a physical line? If so, some lines comprise 10 characters, some constitute 72, and some now 255 characters. Is there no distinction between short lines and longer lines?
- Is a line of code a statement? If so, some statements take one physical line and some statements take multiple physical lines. What is the distinction between longer statements and shorter statements?
- Should in-line documentation (comments) be counted?
- Should variables be declared one per line or should numerous variables be declared in one line? How should they be counted?
- Should library code be counted?

These questions have never been answered satisfactorily. However, this software estimation size measure was used for submitting bids to customers during the third-generation-language (3GL) era. Today, organizations use it for allocating work and to set targets for programmers. Its use for submitting bids is more or less extinct. LOC as a size measure has been used by COCOMO I to arrive at effort in person-months. It was also the primary measure of software size in the 3GL era. LOC estimation is carried out in the manner shown in table 6.1.

Based on table 6.1, the average is arrived at using the formula

$$\text{Expected LOC} = \frac{(4 \times \text{likely LOC}) + \text{minimum LOC} + \text{maximum LOC}}{6}$$

Some people use only minimum and maximum LOC to arrive at a simple average.

Table 6.1. LOC estimation

Module name	Program	Functionality	Minimum LOC	Maximum LOC	Likely LOC	Expected LOC
Module 1						
Module 1.1	Program 1	ABC	100	150	125	140
Module 1.2	Program 2	XYZ	95	120	105	105
Module 2						
Module 2.1	Program 1	PQR	200	300	250	250
Module 2.2	Program 2	STV	150	200	175	175
Total LOC						670

Merits and Demerits of Lines of Code

Merits of LOC include the following:

- Since the ultimate product in software development is source code—that is, written lines, it makes sense that "written" LOC are the size measure for the amount of software produced.
- It is easy to measure. No matter who counts the LOC, the count is the same. There is no ambiguity.
- It is a straightforward method in that it is simple to understand and use.

Demerits of LOC include several ambiguities, among which there is no universal agreement on the following:

- What constitutes a line of code has not been established, nor has which of the following two types of code needs to be counted:
  - *Physical*—A line that ends with a carriage return. In this case, some programming languages allow only 80 characters per line; others allow up to 255 characters per line. How should these differences be treated?
  - *Logical line*—The statement. Statements such as "if" may stretch across multiple physical lines for clarity and readability.
- Whether in-line documentation, such as commenting lines, should be counted has not been agreed upon within the industry.
- It is unclear how the counting of variable declarations should be handled and whether they should be counted in multiple declarations per line or as one line for every variable.

FUNCTION POINTS

The function point (FP) is by far the most popular size measure used to date, as it is accepted as the standard by more organizations than any other software size measure. The unit of measure was developed in the late 1970s by Allan J. Albrecht at IBM. The International Function Point Users Group (IFPUG), mentioned previously in chapter 5, oversees the use of the FP and upgrades FP methodology by including newer developments in software development technology. While the FP was developed based on a character user interface during the

3GL era, the unit of measure has now been upgraded to facilitate estimation of fourth-generation languages and graphical user interface (GUI) technologies.

An ***FP*** *is a rough estimate of a unit of delivered functionality of a software project.* The FP analysis technique involves counting three types of transactions:

1. External inputs
2. External outputs
3. External inquiries (queries)

It also involves two types of data files:

1. Internal logical files
2. External interface files

Here is an explanation of each:

- **External input (EI)**—An elementary process that provides distinct application-oriented data to the software
- **External output (EO)**—An elementary process that provides distinct application-oriented information to the user
- **External inquiry (EQ)**—An elementary process that accepts an on-line input that results in the generation of some immediate software response in the form of an on-line output
- **Internal logical file (ILF)**—Refers to all logical data files maintained ("create," "read," "update," and "delete," or CRUD) by the system being developed
- **External interface file (EIF)**—Refers to any machine-readable interfaces, including data files that are maintained by another system

EO and EQ may seem similar, but the distinction is that EQ generates unprocessed data, while EO generates processed data.

Each of the above transactions and file types is classified into three complexity levels: low, average, and high. Complexity of an FP is based on the number of file types referenced (FTRs), record element types (RETs), and data element types (DETs) referenced.

- **FTR**—A data file. In the present era of relational database management systems (RDBMS), a table or a view (join) is an FTR. An FTR contains RETs.
- **RET**—Can be visualized as a record in a flat file scenario. In an RDBMS scenario, it may be viewed as a table record.

- **DET**—A dynamic data element. In an RDBMS, this is a field in the table. It could also be a variable in the program. Hard-coded values (constants) are not treated as DETs. A specific numerical value is assigned to each transaction and file counted, based on the complexity level.

Once all transactions are counted, the total count is multiplied by a value adjustment factor, which ranges between 0.65 and 1.35. Deriving the value adjustment factor is based on 14 general system characteristics. This gives the FP count for a project.

Let us now go into a bit more detail.

External Input

The following aspects should be kept in mind when identifying EIs:

- An EI is a transaction type of FP. Each transaction must be an elementary process, that is, the smallest unit of activity that is meaningful to the *end user.*
- An EI is an elementary process for which the system receives input from outside.
- The input may be received from the user either through input screens or from another application.
- The input data must be used by the system to maintain a data file.
- In a flat file scenario, an EI would have been a screen, but in a GUI scenario, it is not so straightforward. GUI is discussed later in this chapter.

Complexity Rating for External Inputs

The complexity rating (or level) of EIs is based on the number of FTRs and the DETs referenced. Table 6.2 illustrates the threshold levels. The number in pa-

Table 6.2. Complexity of EIs

FTRs	DETs		
	1 to 4	**5 to 15**	**More than 15**
Less than 2	Low (3)	Low (3)	Average (4)
2	Low (3)	Average (4)	High (6)
Greater than 2	Average (4)	High (6)	High (6)

rentheses indicates the number of FP for that EI. That is, a simple (or low complexity level) EI results in 3 FP, an average EI results in 4 FP, and a high-complexity EI results in 6 FP.

Graphical User Interface and External Input

A GUI screen may consist of several transaction types, and the following GUI elements are counted as DETs:

- Set of radio buttons
- Check boxes
- Command buttons
- Icons and graphic images
- Sound bytes
- Photographs or other graphic images
- Error messages and confirmation messages

Command buttons can be used to spawn an entire process in itself. In such cases, they have to be treated on a case-by-case basis.

The following GUI elements are to be treated as EQs:

- Combo boxes
- List boxes
- List views
- Drop-downs

The IFPUG's *Counting Practices Manual* offers much more detail about the rules for identifying GUI elements. The reader who would like to use the FP approach in depth is advised to get certified by the IFPUG.

External Output

An EO is a transaction-type FP. An EO could be on the screen or hard copy. An EO is an elementary process in which derived data is provided by the system to the external world. An EO may update an ILF.

Complexity Rating for External Outputs

Table 6.3 gives the complexity rating for EOs. The number in parentheses indicates the number of FP for a specific EO. That is, a simple EO results in 4 FP, an average EO results in 5 FP, and a high-complexity EO results in 7 FP.

Table 6.3. Complexity of EOs

FTRs	DETs		
	1 to 5	**6 to 19**	**More than 19**
Less than 2	Low (4)	Low (4)	Average (5)
2 or 3	Low (4)	Average (5)	High (7)
Greater than 3	Average (5)	High (7)	High (7)

Graphical User Interface and External Output

For GUI and EO, note the following:

- Selection of an item in a list box or combo box may cause a list view to fill up, because it contains derived data. Such cases may be treated as EOs.
- Some notification messages may contain derived data. Such cases also need to be considered as EOs.
- If a report is displayed on the screen with a facility to produce hard-copy output, it must be counted as two EOs.
- Each graph needs to be counted as an EO.

The IFPUG's *Counting Practices Manual* offers much more detail about rules for identifying EOs. The reader who would like to use the FP approach in depth is advised to get certified by the IFPUG.

External Inquiry

An EQ is an elementary process, with both input and output parts that result in retrieving data from one or more ILFs and EIFs. Usually the input part is one or two key values that facilitate data retrieval and do not cause an ILF to be updated. The retrieved data does not contain any derived data.

Complexity Rating for External Inquiries

Table 6.4 gives the complexity ratings for EQs. The number in parentheses indicates the number of FP for that EQ. That is, a simple EQ results in 3 FP, an average EQ results in 4 FP, and a high-complexity EQ results in 6 FP.

Input can involve a click of the mouse, search values, confirmation buttons, selection of an item in a list, and so on. The resulting output could be a change of color or font, a display of values retrieved from a file, messages, etc.

Table 6.4. Complexity of EQs

FTRs	DETs		
	1 to 5	**6 to 19**	**More than 19**
Less than 2	Low (3)	Low (3)	Average (4)
2 or 3	Low (3)	Average (4)	High (6)
Greater than 3	Average (4)	High (6)	High (6)

Internal Logical File

An ILF is a data file that is maintained, meaning it is created, updated, or deleted by the present application. It has at least one EI associated with it. It may also be associated with one or more EOs and EQs. In an RDBMS scenario, it is a table or a view (join) that is maintained by the application being counted.

Table 6.5 gives the complexity ratings for ILFs. The number in parentheses indicates the number of FP for that ILF. That is, a simple ILF results in 7 FP, an average ILF results in 10 FP, and a high-complexity ILF results in 15 FP.

External Interface File

An EIF is a data file that is not maintained by the present application. An EIF has a minimum of one transaction (EI, EO, or EQ) associated with it.

Table 6.6 gives the complexity ratings for EIFs. The number in parentheses indicates the number of FP for that EIF. That is, a simple EIF results in 5 FP, an average EIF results in 7 FP, and a high-complexity EIF results in 10 FP.

Note that we need to consider only those DETs that are used by the present system, even though the EIF may be comprised of more DETs. Similarly, even if the EIF consists of more RETs, we need to consider only those RETs that are used by the present application.

Table 6.5. Complexity of ILFs

RETs	DETs		
	1 to 19	**20 to 50**	**More than 50**
1	Low (7)	Low (7)	Average (10)
2 to 5	Low (7)	Average (10)	High (15)
Greater than 5	Average (10)	High (15)	High (15)

Table 6.6. Complexity of EIFs

RETs	DETs		
	1 to 19	20 to 50	More than 50
1	Low (5)	Low (5)	Average (7)
2 to 5	Low (5)	Average (7)	High (10)
Greater than 5	Average (7)	High (10)	High (10)

Obtaining the Unadjusted Function Point Count

Enumerate all the transactions and files in the present system. Then consolidate them in a table similar to table 6.7.

Let us assume a count of 5 for each transaction or file in table 6.7. The results are shown in table 6.8. The total unadjusted FP count is 480 for the system.

Table 6.7. Unadjusted FP count

FP type	Simple	Average	High	Total
EI	count × 3	count × 4	count × 6	Total FP due to EI
EO	count × 4	count × 5	count × 7	Total FP due to EO
EQ	count × 3	count × 4	count × 6	Total FP due to EQ
ILF	count × 7	count × 10	count × 15	Total FP due to ILF
EIF	count × 5	count × 7	count × 10	Total FP due to EIF
Total unadjusted FP				Sum of all the above in this column

Table 6.8. Unadjusted FP count example

FP type	Simple	Average	High	Total
EI	5 × 3	5 × 4	5 × 6	65
EO	5 × 4	5 × 5	5 × 7	80
EQ	5 × 3	5 × 4	5 × 6	65
ILF	5 × 7	5 × 10	5 × 15	160
EIF	5 × 5	5 × 7	5 × 10	110
Total unadjusted FP				480

Value Adjustment Factor

As stated previously, the value adjustment factor (VAF) is based on 14 general system characteristics (GSCs). GSCs describe the environment in which the application is deployed and the influence that it may have on the development work. Each GSC can have a value ranging from 0 (no influence at all) to a maximum of 5 (full influence):

0 = no influence at all
1 = incidental influence
2 = moderate influence
3 = average influence
4 = significant influence
5 = strong influence

The 14 GSCs are listed in table 6.9. I have deviated slightly from the descriptions given by the IFPUG for the GSCs. While they are technically accurate, I have found that beginners in FP usage have difficulty understanding them initially.

Each of the GSCs is rated, all ratings are summed, and the VAF is computed using the following formula:

$$VAF = 0.65 + \left(\frac{\text{sum of GSC ratings}}{100} \right)$$

Thus, you can see that if all the GSCs were rated at 0, then the VAF would be 0.65. If all the GSCs were rated at 5, the VAF would be 1.35. The IFPUG's *Counting Practices Manual* offers a more detailed description and assistance in rating the GSCs.

Consider the ratings for the GSCs shown in table 6.10. The sum of the ratings is 44. The VAF would be

$$VAF = 0.65 + \left(\frac{44}{100} \right)$$

resulting in 1.09.

Table 6.9. GSCs

Ref. no.	GSC	Brief description
1	Data communications	Would the system being developed need to handle data communication aspects?
2	Distributed data processing	Would the system being developed need to provide for distributed data processing?
3	Performance	How critical are the turnaround times?
4	Heavily used configuration	Would the system being developed need to optimize hardware usage?
5	Transaction rate	Is the system expected to be transaction heavy?
6	On-line data entry	Would all the data be entered on-line by users?
7	End-user efficiency	Would the system being developed need to be designed to achieve efficiency for end users?
8	On-line update	How many ILFs would be updated on-line by the system?
9	Complex processing	Would the system need to handle complex mathematical equations or logic?
10	Reusability	Would the system being developed need to be designed in such a way that it can fulfill needs of disparate users?
11	Installation ease	Would the application being developed need to be designed so that installation is easier?
12	Operational ease	Would the application contain modules to make it easier for operations staff?
13	Multiple sites	Is it expected that the system would be installed at multiple sites?
14	Facilitate change	Would it be necessary to keep maintainability of software in mind while developing the application?

Table 6.10. GSC rating example

Ref. no.	GSC	Rating
1	Data communications	2
2	Distributed data processing	3
3	Performance	4
4	Heavily used configuration	5
5	Transaction rate	1
6	On-line data entry	2
7	End-user efficiency	3
8	On-line update	4
9	Complex processing	5
10	Reusability	1
11	Installation ease	2
12	Operational ease	3
13	Multiple sites	4
14	Facilitate change	5

Obtaining the Adjusted Function Point Count

The unadjusted FP count (obtained by counting the transactions and the files) is multiplied by the VAF to obtain the adjusted FP count:

$$\text{Adjusted FP count for the system} = (\text{unadjusted FP count}) \times \text{VAF}$$

Let us use the figures arrived at above and look at the results:

$$\text{Adjusted FP count} = 480 \times 1.09$$

resulting in 523.2 or, say, 523 FP. The adjusted FP count is normally referred to as the FP count.

Merits and Demerits of Function Points

Merits of the FP approach include the following:

- It provides a unit of measure for measuring software size, which has the largest following of any unit of measure for software size.
- A certification body exists for the method, and certified persons are available to carry out FP estimation.
- The methodology is so well documented that if two certified persons count FP for the same application, they are likely to achieve counts that are very close, with only a slight margin of error or variance.

- It can be used to come to agreement with the customer on the quantity of software to be delivered and to confirm that quantity at the time of delivery.
- It can be used to benchmark two software products and compare them.
- It facilitates computation of software development productivity and measuring performance of software developers.
- It facilitates deriving software quality (as FP per defect) and benchmarking project quality with other organizations, as well as between different software engineers or between different projects within an organization.
- It facilitates process improvement, as relative values for such aspects as productivity and quality can be derived more effectively from FP.
- It is used as the de facto method for mainframe applications.

These are the demerits of the FP approach:

- Originally, it was a user-identifiable, distinct function. ILF and EIF are not user-identifiable functions, especially at the estimation stage.
- It was developed during the batch-processing COBOL days, and it does not address GUI and Web applications satisfactorily. GUI is largely event oriented compared to batch processing. There is no agreement among estimation experts regarding the treatment of GUI controls.
- In the flat file days, the functions "add," "modify," "delete," and "inquire" needed different programs and were therefore counted as four FP transactions. Now, with improvements in programming languages and RDBMS technology, all four are made possible through a single piece of code. Should these functions still be counted as four FP transactions?
- Complexity is not relevant. The idea that complexity increases size is untenable—size remains constant. Chapter 8 discusses this matter in more detail.
- It does not classify certain events properly. Take a login screen as an example: it receives three inputs (user ID, password, and "OK" button), but it does not store the information, nor does it give any information back. It simply allows entry into the system. As another example, consider the uploading of files to a Web site: when the "upload" button is clicked, the upload event takes place; it does not store or retrieve information, nor does it provide any output. These transactions cannot be classified as an EI, an EO, or an EQ!

- The GSCs used to derive the VAF need to be updated for today's environment. Again, the concept of the VAF increasing the size of the software is untenable, though it certainly does affect the productivity.
- FP analysis is complex. Why else would it need certification? Software size measurement should not be so tough that a person needs certification to use it. One need only look at the IFPUG bulletin board, where the heated discussions among certified estimators give an indication of the complexity inherent in the interpretation of the IFPUG's *Counting Practices Manual.*

The IFPUG's *Counting Practices Manual* offers much more detail about FP counting. The reader who would like to use the FP approach in depth is advised to get certified by the IFPUG.

USE CASE POINTS

The use case points (UCP) method of software estimation was developed by Gustav Karner of Objectory Systems (later Rational Software and now IBM) in 1993. The UCP method is similar to the Mark II FP analysis method of software estimation. It was developed for those software developers using Unified Modeling Language (UML) and Rational Unified Process (RUP) for software engineering and development. With the UCP method, the use cases in the proposed system are enumerated.

Each use case falls into one of three classes based on complexity. Each of these three classes categorizes use cases in one of two ways, either by number of transactions or by number of classes:

1. **Simple use case**—1 to 3 transactions or 5 or fewer classes in the software; carries a weight of 5
2. **Average use case**—4 to 7 transactions or 6 to 10 classes in the software; carries a weight of 10
3. **Complex use case**—8 or more transactions or 11 or more classes in the software; carries a weight of 15

Each use case is comprised of actors. Each actor is classified into one of three levels based on complexity:

1. **Simple actor**—A system interface; carries a weight of 1
2. **Average actor**—A protocol-driven interface; carries a weight of 2
3. **Complex actor**—A GUI; carries a weight of 3

Table 6.11. UUCP example

	Simple	Average	Complex	UUCP
Use cases	3 × 5	4 × 10	5 × 15	130
Actors	20 × 1	25 × 2	30 × 3	160
Total AUCP				290

Once all use cases are enumerated, along with their actors, the results are summarized in a table, as shown in table 6.11.

I have again deviated slightly from the standard terminology. The sum of weights resulting from use cases is referred to as the *unadjusted use case weight*, and the sum of weights resulting from actors is referred to as the *unadjusted actor weight*. I prefer the simpler *unadjusted use case points (UUCP)*.

Now these UUCP are adjusted with two types of factors:

1. Technical complexity factor (TCF)
2. Environmental complexity factor (ECF)

Each of these factors is rated from 0 to 5, where 0 means the factor is irrelevant and 5 means the factor is most important. Each factor has a predetermined weight. The final value for each of the factors is the value obtained by multiplying the assigned value by its predetermined weight.

Computation of the technical factor (TF) is shown in table 6.12. As you have perhaps noted, there are 13 factors in all, and they are very similar to the GSCs of the FP approach. The values in the "assigned value" column are the values assigned based on the applicability of the factor to the project in question.

TCF is computed using the following formula:

$$TCF = 0.6 + \left(\frac{TF}{100} \right)$$

That is,

$$0.6 + \left(\frac{42.5}{100} \right) = 1.025$$

Table 6.13 shows the computation of the environmental factor (EF). Notice that there are only eight factors. The values in the "assigned value" column are the values assigned based on the applicability of the factor to the project in question.

Table 6.12. Computation of TCF example

Factor	Description	Weight	Assigned value	Computed factor weight x assigned value
T1	Distributed system	2.0	0.0	0.0
T2	Response time	1.0	2.0	2.0
T3	End-user efficiency	1.0	5.0	5.0
T4	Complex processing	1.0	3.0	3.0
T5	Reusable code	1.0	4.0	4.0
T6	Easy to install	0.5	3.0	1.5
T7	Easy to use	0.5	4.0	2.0
T8	Portable	2.0	5.0	10.0
T9	Easy to change	1.0	2.0	2.0
T10	Concurrent	1.0	2.0	2.0
T11	Security features	1.0	5.0	5.0
T12	Access for third parties	1.0	3.0	3.0
T13	Special training	1.0	3.0	3.0
	Total TF			42.5

Table 6.13. Computation of ECF example

Factor	Description	Weight	Assigned value	Computed factor weight x assigned value
E1	Familiarity with the project model used	1.5	2.0	3.0
E2	Application experience	0.5	4.0	2.0
E3	Object-oriented experience of the team	1.0	3.0	3.0
E4	Lead analyst capability	0.5	4.0	2.0
E5	Motivation of the team	1.0	3.0	3.0
E6	Stability of requirements	2.0	3.0	6.0
E7	Part-time staff	−1.0	4.0	−4.0
E8	Difficult programming language	−1.0	1.0	−1.0
	Total EF			14.0

ECF is computed using the following formula:

$$ECF = 0.4 + (-0.03 \times EF)$$

That is,

$$1.4 + (-0.03 \times 14) = 1.4 - 0.42 = 0.98$$

Now we can compute the adjusted use case points (AUCP) using the following formula:

$$AUCP = UUCP \times TCF \times ECF$$

Using actual values, we compute the AUCP as

$$AUCP = 290 \times 1.025 \times 0.98$$

The resulting AUCP is

$$AUCP = 291.305$$

AUCP is generally referred to as UCP for the project.

Merits and Demerits of Use Case Points

Merits of the UCP approach include the following:

- It assumes that UML is the software development methodology, which is the most frequently used methodology for Web application development.
- It is backed by Rational Software (now owned by IBM) and is supposed to be the result of a study of a large number of projects.
- It is fairly simple, except for deciding the three complexity levels for use cases.
- It is does not need certification to be used.

These are the demerits of the UCP approach:

- Use cases vary vastly in size. It simply is not practical to classify them into three convenient complexity levels.
- As use cases differ vastly in size, it is not practical to arrive at an accurate UCP estimate that reflects the real scenario.
- Classification of actors does not appear to be correct. In this methodology, all GUI actors are to be classified as complex actors, but realistically, how accurate is it to classify a login screen as a complex actor?
- It adheres to the untenable argument that "complexity increases software size."
- It has 21 factors that adjust the software size. Again, these factors may affect the productivity (rate of achievement), but software size ought to remain the same.

OBJECT POINTS

The object points (OP) method is used in COCOMO II as the size measure for a proposed software product. This technique's terminology suggests that it was developed with client-server technology in mind. Due to its simplicity, the OP method seems most useful for all present-day projects, including Web-based projects.

With the OP method, the software artifacts (screens, reports, and 3GL components) are enumerated. Each of these objects is rated on a complexity level as simple, medium, or difficult. The rules for classifying screens into different levels of complexity are shown in table 6.14. The rules for classifying reports into different levels of complexity are shown in table 6.15. "Server" indicates tables on the server. "Client" indicates tables on the client machine. 3GL components have only one level of complexity, and that is the "difficult" level.

These objects are given a weight that depends on the complexity level, as shown in table 6.16. Then all the objects are enumerated and summarized in a table, as shown in table 6.17.

If there is a possibility of reusing existing code, the percentage of reused software is deducted from the OP count to obtain the number of new object

Table 6.14. Complexity levels for screens

Number of views contained	Number and source of data tables		
	Total <4 (1 server, 1 or 2 clients)	Total between 4 and 8 (2 or 3 servers, 3 to 5 clients)	Total >8 (>3 servers, >5 clients)
2 or less	Simple	Simple	Medium
3 to 7	Simple	Medium	Difficult
8 or more	Medium	Difficult	Difficult

Table 6.15. Complexity levels for reports

Number of sections contained	Number and source of data tables		
	Total <4 (1 server, 1 or 2 clients)	Total between 4 and 8 (2 or 3 servers, 3 to 5 clients)	Total >8 (>3 servers, >5 clients)
1	Simple	Simple	Medium
2 or 3	Simple	Medium	Difficult
4 or more	Medium	Difficult	Difficult

Table 6.16. Weights for objects

Object	Weight based on complexity level		
	Simple	Medium	Difficult
Screen	1	2	3
Report	2	5	8
3GL component	NA	NA	10

Table 6.17. OP example

Object	Simple	Medium	Difficult	Total OP
Screens	10 × 1	15 × 2	8 × 3	64
Reports	8 × 2	5 × 5	10 × 8	121
3GL components			4 × 10	40
Total OP				225

points (NOP) to be developed. For example, let us assume 20 percent reuse. Thus:

$$NOP = OP - reuse$$

Using actual values, we compute NOP as:

$$NOP = 225 - (225 \times 20 \text{ percent})$$

The resulting NOP are

$$NOP = 225 - 45$$

$$= 180$$

OP do not make use of any complexity factors to adjust the final size, as FP and UCP do.

Merits and Demerits of Object Points

Merits of the OP approach include the following:

- While it is used as part of the COCOMO II methodology, it can be used independently.
- End users can easily identify the components of OP.

- This is the way software is developed—as screens, reports, or program routines. It is easy to identify software development work with OP.
- It is extremely easy to learn and use. The risk of error is the lowest when estimates are given by different estimators.
- It can also be used with COCOMO II methodology, which is based on the study of a significantly large number of software development projects and is supposed to be accurate.
- It does not make use of any dubious factors to adjust the size of software.
- It acknowledges the fact that there is scope for reuse of earlier software components, which is the practice in many present-day organizations. It also provides for the same in estimation.

These are the demerits of the OP approach:

- It uses complexity to increase size, which, as explained elsewhere in this book, is untenable.

I think that this is one of the simplest and most straightforward methods for estimating software size. With the exception that it uses complexity to increase software size, I cannot see any other demerits of this approach, and I am somewhat surprised that this size measure has not become universal.

MARK II FUNCTION POINT ANALYSIS

Mark II function point analysis (MK II FPA) is championed by the U.K. Software Metrics Association (UKSMA). It was defined by Charles Symons in *Software Sizing and Estimating: MK II FPA*, published in 1991. After development within KPMG from 1985 to 1986, with the protected status of a proprietary method, it is now in the public domain. The Metrics Practices Committee of UKSMA is now the design authority for MK II FPA and is responsible for its continuing development.

UKSMA defines MK II FPA as

> *a method for the quantitative analysis and measurement of information processing applications. It quantifies the information processing requirements specified by the user to provide a figure that expresses a size of*

the resulting software product. This size is suitable for the purposes of performance measurement and estimating in relation to the activity associated with the software product.

Size is expressed as MK II FP or MK II FP index. MK II FPA uses logical transactions to estimate software size. The following are aspects of a logical transaction:

1. It is the lowest level of a self-consistent process.
2. It consists of three components:
   a. Input from users (human beings, machines, or other applications)
   b. Processing of the inputs, which involves storing data for future use and deriving data (computation, classification, ordering, and reporting) for delivery as output
   c. Output to users (human beings, machines, or other applications)
3. It consists of processing components (which consist of inputs and outputs) and entities.
4. DETs pass into the logical transaction as inputs and pass out as outputs.

UKSMA defines a logical transaction as follows:

Each logical transaction is triggered by a unique event of interest in the external world, or a request for information and, when wholly complete, leaves the application in a self-consistent state in relation to the unique event.

An entity is the same as the one used in data modeling. It is taken as the primary entity, meaning a full third normal form is not required. The functional size of a logical transaction is the weighted sum of its input, processing, and output components. The weights of each are given in table 6.18, where We is the weight of all entities, Wi is the weight of the input DETs, and Wo is the weight of the output DETs.

Table 6.18. Weights

Ref. no.	Element	Weight
1	Entity	1.66 (We)
2	Input DETs	0.58 (Wi)
3	Output DETs	0.26 (Wo)

The four steps in MK II FP estimation are as follows:

1. Identify all logical transactions in the system.
2. Count the number of entity types referred to by the logical transaction (Ne).
3. Count the number of input DETs (Ni) for each logical transaction.
4. Count the number of output DETs (No) for each logical transaction.

Now we are ready to compute the functional size FP index (FPI), using the following formula:

$$FPI = (Wi \times \Sigma Ni) + (We \times \Sigma Ne) + (Wo \times \Sigma No)$$

where FPI is the functional size, Wi is the weight of the input DETs, We is the weight of all entities, Wo is the weight of the output DETs, ΣNi is the number of all input DETs, ΣNe is the number of all entities, and ΣNo is the number of all output DETs. Normally a table such as table 6.19 is used to enumerate all logical transactions needed to make an estimate.

Using actual values, we can compute the FPI as:

$$FPI = (0.58 \times 140) + (1.66 \times 10) + (0.26 \times 179)$$

The resulting FPI is

$$FPI = 81.2 + 16.6 + 46.54$$

$$= 144.34$$

Table 6.19. MK II FPA example

Ref. no.	Logical transaction description	Entities referred	Input DETs	Output DETs
1	Patient registration	■ Patient record ■ Wards record	50	55
2	Patient examination	■ Patient record ■ Examination record ■ Billing record	25	32
3	Patient discharge	■ Patient record ■ Examination record ■ Billing record ■ Receipts record ■ Receivables record	65	92
Total		10	140	179

Table 6.20. Technical complexity factors

Ref. no.	Factor	Assigned value for the DI
1	Data communications	0
2	Distributed data processing	3
3	Performance	4
4	Transaction rate	5
5	Heavily used configuration	2
6	On-line data entry	1
7	Design for end-user efficiency	3
8	On-line update	4
9	Complex processing	3
10	Reusability	5
11	Installation ease	2
12	Operations ease	4
13	Multiple sites	2
14	Facilitates change	5
15	Requirements of other applications	2
16	Features of confidentiality and security	3
17	Specific user training needs	1
18	Direct use by third parties	0
19	Documentation	2
20	User-defined characteristics	5
	Total DI	56

This functional size needs to be adjusted for technical complexity. There are 20 technical complexity factors, as shown in table 6.20. Each of these factors needs to be assigned a degree of influence (DI) that it exercises on the application. The assigned value can range between 0 (the factor has no influence on the application) and 5 (the factor has significant influence on the application).

Now the technical complexity adjustment factor (TCAF) can be computed using the formula

$$TCAF = 0.65 + (\text{sum of DI} \times 0.005)$$

Using actual values, we can compute the TCAF as:

$$TCAF = 0.65 + (56 \times 0.005)$$

The resulting TCAF is

$$TCAF = 0.65 + 0.28$$

$$= 0.93$$

Now we can obtain the adjusted FPI (AFPI) using the FPI obtained above with the formula

$$AFPI = FPI \times TCAF$$

Using actual values, we can compute the AFPI as:

$$AFPI = 144.34 \times 0.93$$

$$= 134.24$$

Serious practitioners of MK II FPA should obtain material from UKSMA, which provides much more detail about the MK II FPA method for sizing software.

Merits and Demerits of Mark II Function Point Analysis

Merits of MK II FPA include the following:

- It sizes the transaction instead of counting inputs, outputs, and processes, which is more easily understood by the end user. MK II FPA truly reflects functionality in such a way that a noncomputer-savvy person can understand software size more easily than with any other software size measure.
- It is fairly easy to learn and use.
- A professional body stands behind it to improve upon the methodology when necessary.

These are the demerits of MK II FPA:

- It uses factors to influence the software size, which is untenable—factors do affect productivity, but not the software size.

SUMMARY

This chapter discusses software size estimation. Software size estimation is important as it enables computation of productivity, thus allowing software development organizations and software development engineers to benchmark their work with other organizations and software engineers. Productivity measurement also allows for rewards and punishments to be dispensed fairly. A brief overview of software size measures—LOC, FP, UCP, OP, and MK II FPA—is presented, along with the methodology for their computation. Merits and demerits of each size measure are also discussed to enable the reader to choose the appropriate size measure for his or her applications. Discussion of detailed methodology is beyond the scope of this book, and the reader is advised to refer to the original sources.

SOFTWARE SIZE UNITS

My major concern about all the software size measures described in Chapter 6 is that they use points to signify software size. In geometry, a point is something that does not occupy space. Points are used in games; they are scored or counted, and complexity does not affect them. A point never becomes more than a point, no matter what complex maneuvers it takes to score a point. No factor—wind, sun, humidity—affects points. Only in the software industry is it believed that complexity and other factors affect points.

Where there are no universally accepted units of measure, the unwritten convention has been to use "units" as the measure. For example, the unit of measure for heat is the British thermal unit. In medicine, enzymes are measured in International Units or simply in units. Insulin is administered to diabetics in number of units per day. "Unit" is used in this context to mean a unit of measure for something.

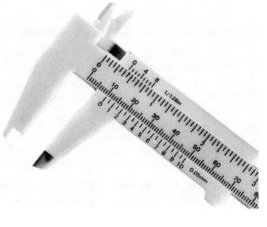

Software size has come to be measured in points. From the time the function point was introduced for software size estimation, all other units of measure have followed suit. Perhaps the reasoning is that points are scored, so functions are counted (scored). Enzymes, measured in units, catalyze an action.

Heat, measured in British thermal units, catalyzes an action. In software too, a unit catalyzes development action.

Therefore, taking inspiration from the above, I propose the software size unit for measuring software size.

DEFINITION OF SOFTWARE SIZE UNIT

What comprises a software system? It basically consists of two types of elements:

1. **Data elements**—The data that enters the system, is processed, and is either stored for future use or given as output
2. **Process elements**—The software routines that process data elements and achieve the desired functionality

A data element is an input to the system. It may enter the system through user input, be read from a data file or table, or be received from another system. It could be a constant (when used as a parameter for the software system) or a variable. Data elements are classified into three types:

1. **Numeric data elements (NDEs)**—Consist of the digits 0 to 9, one decimal point, and a positive or negative sign. An NDE transforms and is transformed in the system. The whole system revolves around this data element. It can be either a dynamic or a static data element.
2. **Alphanumeric data elements (ADEs)**—Consist of all humanly readable characters, including the space character. An ADE passes through the system. When it enters, validation checks are performed to ensure its type and length. It can be either a dynamic or a static data element.
3. **Control data elements (CDEs)**—Trigger some process within the system. Links on a Web site and command buttons on a screen are examples of CDEs.

Process elements act on data elements and transform input to desired outputs. Process elements are classified into three types:

1. **Input process elements (IPEs)**—Receive data elements into the system from the external environment, such as through a keyboard, from a file or a table, from a device such as a scanner, or from a

network. An IPE stores (that is, inserts or updates) the input data elements in a secondary storage device.

2. **Output process elements (OPEs)**—Send data elements from the system (including from secondary storage and from the screen) to the external environment, such as to a screen, a report, a device such as a printer, or a network. The data that is sent out may be processed or unprocessed and may consist of static and dynamic data elements.

3. **Associate process elements (APEs)**—Process elements that either help IPEs or OPEs or assist in maintaining certain system functions, the results of which are sometimes not seen by users. Some examples of APEs are

   a. A software routine that helps to generate data for a report, where the report is generated by a reporting tool like Crystal Reports

   b. A software routine that manages the session in a Web application

   c. A software routine that manages or interfaces with any of the network layers

   d. A software routine that manages or interfaces with any of the application tiers

*A **system** is software that fulfills some need and performs a set of defined functions. It can consist of screens, reports, program routines, and so on. The size of a software system is derived from the data elements and process elements that comprise the system. A software size unit is an input process element that has five numeric data elements.*

PROCEDURE FOR SOFTWARE SIZE ESTIMATION USING SOFTWARE SIZE UNITS

A software tool for estimating software testing project size, effort, cost, and schedule is available from the Web Added Value™ Download Resource Center at www.jrosspub.com.

Delivered software size is measured in software size units (SSU), and it is used to come to an agreement between the customer and the vendor. Delivered software size is also used for estimating the effort required to develop software. The effort required to deliver software is the sum of the effort required for requirements analysis, software design, construction, and testing. Here is a concrete example to explain:

- An NDE has a weight of 1, an ADE has a weight of 0.35, and a CDE has a weight of 0.75. These weights are used for normalizing the data elements when estimating software size.
- An IPE has a weight of 1, an OPE has a weight of 0.75, and an APE has a weight of 1.25. These weights are used for normalizing the process elements when estimating software size.

Now we are ready to calculate the delivered software size:

1. Enumerate the process elements (IPEs, OPEs, and APEs) that comprise the system.
2. For each process element, count the data elements (NDEs, ADEs, and CDEs).
3. For each process element, compute the equivalent total data elements (TDE) using the formula

$$TDE = NDE + (ADE \times 0.35) + (CDE \times 0.75)$$

4. Compute the SSU for each process element using the formula

$$SSU = \left(\frac{TDE}{5}\right) \times \text{process element weight}$$

5. Sum the SSU of each process element to obtain the SSU for the project, before adding a contingency allowance.
6. Add to the total SSU a contingency allowance of 10 percent for possible requirement changes to obtain a size estimate for the project.

Table 7.1 illustrates the procedure for a warehouse management system software development project.

Then the software size is rounded up to the next multiple of 5 units. Thus the estimated size of the software development project for the warehouse management system in Table 7.1 is 65 SSU.

SOFTWARE DEVELOPMENT EFFORT ESTIMATION FROM SOFTWARE SIZE UNITS

Having estimated the size of the software to be developed, we have to estimate the software development effort. Since the work carried out at various stages

Table 7.1. Example of a software estimate using SSU

Ref. no.	Process element	Nature of process element	NDE	ADE	CDE	TDE	Equivalent SSU
1	Material master definition	Input	4.00	3.00	0.00	5.05	1.01
2	Supplier master definition	Input	1.00	12.00	0.00	5.20	1.04
3	Material categories definition	Input	1.00	1.00	0.00	1.35	0.27
4	Units definition	Input	1.00	1.00	0.00	1.35	0.27
5	Category—supplier mapping	Input	1.00	1.00	0.00	1.35	0.27
6	Administration—user definition	Input	0.00	4.00	0.00	1.40	0.28
7	Material availability inquiry	Input	1.00	4.00	0.00	2.40	0.48
8	Material inquiry search routine	Associated	1.00	4.00	0.00	2.40	0.48
9	Purchase order entry	Input	11.00	12.00	2.00	16.70	3.34
10	Material receipts entry	Input	9.00	12.00	1.00	13.95	2.79
11	Material issues	Input	3.00	8.00	0.00	5.80	1.16
12	Material returns	Input	1.00	8.00	0.00	3.80	0.76
13	Reports	Input	6.00	2.00	0.00	6.70	1.34
14	Issues costing routine	Associated	3.00	12.00	0.00	7.20	1.44
15	Balances costing routine	Associated	6.00	20.00	0.00	13.00	2.60
16	Below reorder level report	Output	4.00	12.00	0.00	8.20	1.64
17	Category-wise report	Output	6.00	15.00	0.00	11.25	2.25
18	Consumption report for a period	Output	2.00	18.00	0.00	8.30	1.66
19	Goods receipts register for a period	Output	7.00	11.00	0.00	10.85	2.17
20	HML report	Output	2.00	7.00	0.00	4.45	0.89
21	Material category report	Output	3.00	8.00	0.00	5.80	1.16
22	Material category summary	Output	2.00	8.00	0.00	4.80	0.96
23	Material code consumption for a period	Output	5.00	9.00	0.00	8.15	1.63
24	Material issues register	Output	4.00	14.00	0.00	8.90	1.78
25	Nonmoving items register	Output	5.00	9.00	0.00	8.15	1.63
26	Purchase order receipts for a period	Output	6.00	14.00	0.00	10.90	2.18
27	Priced stores ledger for a period	Output	18.00	15.00	0.00	23.25	4.65
28	Priced stores ledger summary for a period	Output	18.00	15.00	0.00	23.25	4.65
29	Project consumption	Output	4.00	8.00	0.00	6.80	1.36
30	Source-wise report	Output	3.00	7.00	0.00	5.45	1.09
31	Stock report as on a date	Output	4.00	8.00	0.00	6.80	1.36
32	Vital, essential, desirable report	Output	4.00	8.00	0.00	6.80	1.36
33	Vendor-wise receipts report	Output	8.00	15.00	0.00	13.25	2.65
34	On-line help	Output	0.00	40.00	0.00	14.00	2.80
	Totals		154.00	345.00	3.00	277.00	55.40
	Contingency allowance 10 percent		15.40	34.50	0.30	27.70	5.54
	Estimated SSU for the project		169.40	379.50	3.30	304.70	60.94

of the software development life cycle requires persons of different skill sets, it is necessary to have different productivity figures for each of the skill sets, namely:

- **Requirements analysis effort**—SSU is used to estimate the effort required to carry out requirements analysis, which includes eliciting user requirements, developing software requirements, preparing the necessary documentation to capture requirements, arranging for a peer review of the documentation, and fixing defects, if any. To convert SSU into effort needed for requirements analysis, productivity of requirements analysis is used (for example, 6 hours per SSU rounded up to the next multiple of 8, that is, to a person-day).

  For clarification, when the total effort is in multiple days, any effort in a fragment of a day, in reality, is wasted. For example, when the effort is 22.6 days, in reality it takes 23 days. That is the reason for advocating rounding up to the next multiple of 8, especially for large projects. If a project is small in terms of effort, fractions of days may be retained.

- **Software design effort**—SSU is used to estimate the effort required to carry out software design, including database design, architecture design, user interface design, report design, program design, preparation of necessary documentation, test planning, peer review of design, and fixing defects, if any. To convert SSU into effort needed for software design, productivity of software design is used (for example, 8 hours per SSU rounded up to the next multiple of 8—a person-day—to avoid fragmentation of the day).

- **Construction effort**—SSU is used to estimate the effort required for construction activity, which includes coding, independent verification, independent unit testing, and fixing defects, if any. To convert SSU into effort needed for construction, productivity of construction is used (for example, 10 hours per SSU rounded up to the next multiple of 8—a person-day—to avoid fragmentation of the day).

- **Testing effort**—SSU is used to estimate the effort required to carry out independent software testing. Software testing includes integration testing, system testing, and acceptance testing. To convert SSU into effort needed for testing, productivity of testing is used (for example, 4 hours per SSU rounded up to the next multiple of 8—a person-day—to avoid fragmentation of the day).

Table 7.2. Effort estimation using SSU

Ref. no.	Stage	SSU size	Productivity in person-hours per SSU	Total effort in person-hours	Total effort rounded up to next multiple of 8
1	Requirements analysis	65	6	390	392
2	Software design	65	8	520	520
3	Construction	65	10	650	656
4	Testing	65	4	260	264
	Total effort				1,832

Rounding up to the next multiple of 8 ensures that the result is in full person-days. Estimates can be in fragments of a person-day, but in reality, any fragment of a day would be wasted during execution. It may be ideal to assume that a person who completes a task at 4:00 p.m. would start the next task immediately, putting in an hour of diligent effort until the end of the day, but real life is different—that hour would be wasted.

Table 7.2 shows how to arrive at the effort required for a software development project. The effort is 1,832 person-days. The person-days required for administrative activities such as project initiation, project planning, project closure, and project management overhead, if necessary, are added to this figure. This value can be used to schedule the project and arrive at the final effort for computing the cost of the project.

HOW TO OBTAIN PRODUCTIVITY FIGURES

The productivity figure is unique to an organization, due to the specific environment and unique processes that are used therein. Therefore, the best way to determine this figure is to conduct a productivity study using the work-sampling method (a work measurement technique). This task is best accomplished by a qualified industrial engineer. The local chapter of an industrial engineering organization would be glad to oblige your request for a work-sampling study and to develop the productivity norms for your organization. I suggest such a study be carried out whenever major changes in an organization's development environment, methods (development processes), or organizational structure occur.

Appendix D offers a methodology for deriving productivity from past projects. This methodology may also be used for deriving necessary productivity figures.

FREQUENTLY ASKED QUESTIONS ABOUT SOFTWARE SIZE UNITS COMPUTATION

Q: *Can a screen be equated to an IPE?*
A: If a screen takes inputs only from the user, then it can be equated to an IPE. In many cases, however, a screen captures some information, derives it, and displays some information to assist the user in the entry process. In such cases, the screen needs to be considered as more than one IPE. It may contain other IPEs as well as OPEs and APEs.

Q: *Does that mean that one screen can have multiple IPEs, OPEs, and APEs?*
A: Yes.

Q: *How are inquiry screens treated?*
A: An inquiry screen is comprised of one or more input data elements and a set of output data elements. Therefore, the input data capture portion can be treated as an IPE and the output portion of the screen can be treated as an OPE. One suggestion: treat all screens as "screens"; do not classify them as "input screens," "inquiry screens," or "output screens."

Q: *How is a combo box treated?*
A: A combo box has two elements: one is a data element, as it provides data to the software, and the other is an APE to fill the combo box with selectable values. Therefore, each event in a combo box, such as "click," "double-click," etc., has to be treated as an APE. Thus, a combo box can be treated as a set of data elements and a set of process elements.

Q: *How is a list box treated?*
A: A list box has two elements: one is a set of data elements, as it provides data to the software, and the other is an APE to fill the list box with selectable values. Therefore, each event in a list box, such as "click," "double-click," etc., has to be treated as an APE. Thus, a list box can be treated as a set of data elements and a set of process elements.

Q: *How is a list view treated?*
A: A list view has two elements: one is a set of data elements, as it provides data to the software, and the other is an APE to fill the list box with selectable values.

Each event, such as "click," "double-click," etc., has to be treated as an APE. Thus, a list view can be treated as a set of data elements and a set of process elements.

Q: *Are the weights for data elements and process elements to be used as they are or can they be customized?*
A: If one thing characterizes software development, it is diversity. If you feel that different weights are justified in view of the unique nature of your project, you may certainly customize them.

MERITS AND DEMERITS OF SOFTWARE SIZE UNITS

Merits of the SSU approach include the following:

- It is free of subjective aspects, such as environmental and technical factors.
- It is free of the untenable argument that "complexity influences software size."
- It uses "density" and derives an analog measure that is in continuous and fractional numbers, not just in integers.
- Its straightforward methodology is easy to master and use. Certification is not needed.
- It is in the public domain, free to be adapted to the unique needs of an organization.
- Free software tools are available.

These are the demerits of the SSU approach:

- Because its introduction into the software development industry is relatively recent, a satisfactory amount of feedback from the field is not yet available.

SUMMARY

"Point" as a unit of measure for software size is a misnomer. The unwritten convention regarding size measurement, where a universally accepted unit of measure is absent, has been to use "units," as British thermal units is used for heat measurement and International Units for enzymes such as insulin. SSU uses this convention for software size measurement. SSU is a unit of software size measure that is not influenced by such factors as complexity—neither for a transaction nor for environmental or technical complexity of an application. Size is computed using the density of information being packed into the application. This chapter discusses the definition of SSU and the methodology to estimate software size using SSU. A free software tool is available from the Web Added Value™ Download Resource Center at www.jrosspub.com for your use to estimate software size in SSU.

8

SOFTWARE ESTIMATION— COMPLEXITY OR DENSITY?

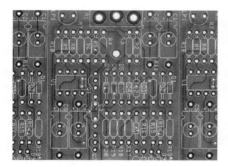 

I feel that this paradox deserves a special chapter in and of itself. Every software size estimation technique adjusts the ultimate software size using a "complexity" measure of its own. I am of a different opinion altogether on the issue of complexity as it is applied to software estimation. Most software size estimation techniques, whether function point analysis, use case points, object points, etc., adjust the size of software using *complexity factors*. The names of these complexity factors may differ, but they all serve one purpose—to adjust software size based on a common principle.

I have often felt that the term "complexity" is a misnomer in software estimation. Let me present my views.

THE PARADOX OF COMPLEXITY VIS-À-VIS SIZE

Everything is simpler than you think and at the same time more complex than you imagine.

—Johann Wolfgang von Goethe

What is complexity? Perhaps it will come as no surprise that in the software development industry there is no universally accepted definition of complexity! To quote Dr. Sam Vaknin from his paper *The Complexity of Simplicity* (http://www.samvak.tripod.com):

A straight line can be described with three symbols (A, B, and the distance between them), or with three billion symbols (a subset of the discrete points which make up the line and their inter-relatedness, their function). But whatever the number of symbols we choose to employ, however complex our level of description, it has nothing to do with the straight line or with its "real world" traits. The straight line is not rendered more (or less) complex or orderly by our choice of level of (meta) description and language elements.

This implies that it is up to us to make something complex or simple by our choice of words or symbols to describe it.

The following are a few interpretations of the word "complex" as it pertains to general understanding:

- We do not fully comprehend the work. Therefore we say that it is "complex."
- A path is uncharted and there are unforeseen "hurdles" throughout. We are not sure how many hurdles there are or how to get across them, so we say that the path is "complex."
- The work is "delicate." That is, if we are not careful, some part of the work may break or fail or cause severe damage. Therefore we label it as "complex."
- There may not be adequate room to maneuver or manipulate the work, so we label it as "complex."
- There is danger inherent in the work, so we label it as "complex."
- Limitations are imposed on how to achieve a result, such as certain methods are excluded, certain tools cannot be used, certain facilities are not available, and so on. We thus say the work is "complex."

Often, we label something as complex if we do not understand it or if we lack the capability to either understand or do it. Here are a few examples of such cases:

- For a homeowner, repairing a plumbing problem is a complex activity, but for a professional plumber, it is a normal task.
- For an orthopedic surgeon, who can construct a joint in the human body, carpentry (which is far simpler than repairing bones and joints) is complex.
- For a plumber, electrical work is complex.
- By extension of these examples, COBOL is complex for a Java programmer, graphical user interface programming is complex for a character user interface programmer, Java is complex for a Visual Basic programmer, and so on.

Simple activities often become complex when we impose limitations on them. Take, for example, the classic puzzle of joining nine dots in a straight line, shown here. The complexity is brought about by imposing limitations, namely: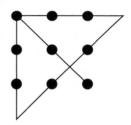

1. Only four straight lines are to be used.
2. The pencil should not be lifted from the paper while drawing the lines.

In the early days of software estimation, this phenomenon led to complexity. The aspects of limited random access memory (RAM) and limits on the number of data files that could be opened simultaneously (limited by the number of tape drives available) caused programming to be a complex activity. Today, these limitations no longer apply, as we now have adequate RAM and the limitation on the number of files that can be opened has been removed due to abundant disk capacity.

I am sure you catch my drift: I am implying that we find an activity complex when we are either not trained to do it or are handicapped in doing it or when limitations are imposed.

It is a fact that in organizations we do not allow a person to do a job at which he or she is not adept (skilled). A novice in the manufacturing industry is never allowed to handle tasks independently unless a senior worker is closely supervising. Since we do not assign a task to an unskilled person, is it proper to add such a measure of complexity to software development? Surely we would not allow a Visual Basic programmer to write Java programs and vice versa!

A programmer who is assigned the task of coding an artifact (such as a screen or a report, for example) may take more time or less time to complete the task depending on the number of controls that need to be handled or the number of lines he or she has to code. The programmer is qualified and trained to do the work—work that is certainly not complex, but is time consuming.

Therefore, is it proper to label a component (function point, object point, use case point, etc.) as simple, average, or high in complexity? What we surely can say is that a component is small, medium, or large in size.

This brings us to the next incongruity in the aspect of complexity: Does complexity come in three convenient steps in nature? No. Complexity is a continuum; it is analog in nature. It cannot be restricted to three levels only. By dividing complexity into three levels, anyone—including an expert—can have a different perception of what falls into which level, especially in borderline cases.

Another incongruity of complexity as it is applied to software estimation is the idea that size needs to be adjusted according to degrees of complexity. Consider the following dialogue between two people:

> A: "How many miles did you walk today?"
> B: "Today I walked on an even-surfaced sidewalk, so I'd say 3 miles."

> A: "Why do you mention the quality of the surface [complexity] you walked on? What possible bearing does it have on the answer to my question?"
> B: "I adjust the distance by the type of surface on which I walk. Yesterday, I walked indoors on my treadmill, so that means 3.9 miles. The day before, I walked on a mountain trail, so that means 6 miles."

> A: "Wow! How did you arrive at these figures?"
> B: "I walk for 45 minutes. I adjust the distance I walk based on the quality of the surface [complexity] I walk on. On an even-surfaced sidewalk, the multiplication factor is 1. Indoors on a treadmill, the multiplication factor is 1.3. And on a mountain trail, the multiplication factor is 2."

Would you silently accept B's explanation? Not likely. You would feel compelled to say that the distance does not change because of the quality of the surface walked on (complexity), but rather the *rate* of walking (productivity) changes.

Here's another scenario:

> A: "How many steps are there on the staircase in your office building?"
>
> B: "That depends on the climber."
>
> A: "What do you mean?"
>
> B: "I will explain. I adjust the count of the stairs [points] based on the climber's [programmer's] capability to climb the stairs.
>
> If the person is between 3 and 5 years old, I multiply the count of stairs by a factor of 10. If the person is between 6 and 12 years old, I multiply the count of stairs by a factor of 1.2. If the person is between 13 and 18 years old, I multiply the count of stairs by a factor of 0.9. If the person is between 19 and 35 years old, I multiply the count of stairs by a factor of 1.0. If the person is between 36 and 45 years old, I multiply the count of stairs by a factor of 1.35. If the person is between 46 and 55 years old, I multiply the count of stairs by a factor of 3. If the person is between 56 and 65 years old, I multiply the count of stairs by a factor of 5. If the person is over 65 years old, I multiply the count of stairs by a factor of 20."

Would you agree with B's explanation? No. You are likely to say, "Look, you should know that the count of stairs does not change. It remains the same. What changes is the rate of climbing [productivity] the stairs based on a person's age. Where did you learn that size changes because of a person's capability?"

Thus, it is clear that size remains constant irrespective of complexity and personal expertise. What changes is the rate (productivity) at which the work is accomplished. Thus, when complexity increases, productivity decreases—the size of the work does not change! When the level of personal expertise is low, productivity is low, but the size of the work remains the same. In both cases, the size of the task to be completed does not change! Here is another analogy: Mount Everest remains at an altitude of 29,000 feet (8,848 meters or 29,028 feet, to be precise) regardless of who tries to climb it, when they climb it, or the time they take to climb it.

Then why do all present software size estimation techniques adjust the size due to complexity, programmer capability, or other similar factors? The answer is that perhaps because in the days when the function point software size estimation technique was developed, computers imposed many restrictions on the programmer. RAM was limited (512 kilobytes was a luxury!) and peripheral devices were few and slow. Opening another file meant starting another tape drive, and the hardware restricted how many files could be opened concurrently. The onus was on the programmer to optimize the computer resources. Declaration of variables had to have a purpose, and a programmer could not declare variables as he or she liked. If more functionality was to be achieved by a program, the complexity of writing a program increased because of limited computer resources, namely RAM and other peripherals.

Computer programming was truly complex in those days. A programmer had to keep in mind not only the functional aspect but also the hardware and system software limitations. The programmer had to know how much RAM was needed to open another data file. A line of code was limited to 80 characters, and a longer statement had to be broken into a number of lines. In those days, the term "complexity," and using it to justify increasing software size, was appropriate.

Today, no such limitations exist. One gigabyte of RAM is the norm for a laptop. The programmer is now free from managing computer hardware resources. Opening another file (table) does not mean starting another tape drive, as any number of files can be opened concurrently. Hardware restrictions are a thing of the past. A line of code can have 255 characters now. Today, a programmer need not worry about hardware limitations; he or she needs to concentrate on achieving the functionality only. Nowadays, how many programmers really know (or care) how much RAM it takes to open one more table?

What I mean to say is that factoring in "complexity" to determine size was applicable some time back, but not anymore.

DENSITY, NOT COMPLEXITY

In the current age of software development and software estimation, the term we should perhaps use for what increases software size is, in my opinion, *density*.

If you have the same volume of two liquids of different densities, the liquid with greater density is heavier than the liquid of lesser density. The same principle applies to solids as well: a solid with greater density is heavier than a solid of equal volume but lesser density. Another example is the classic question we ask youngsters: "Which is heavier, a pound of feathers or a pound of gold?" A pound of gold is the usual answer.

Engineering drawings can be likened to software programs, as both have a creative component and preparation of both depends on a design document. In engineering, drawings normally come in five sizes:

1. A0—measures 1 square meter
2. A1—measures ½ a square meter
3. A2—measures ¼ of a square meter
4. A3—measures ⅛ of a square meter
5. A4—measures ¹⁄₁₆ of a square meter

Ask any engineering draftsperson how much time it will take to prepare an A0 size drawing. He or she will tell you that it depends on the *density* of the lines and pictures packed into the drawing. Here we have a parallel for software development. The time it takes to develop a screen, even when it is developed in the same development platform, depends on the density of controls to be placed on the screen. Similarly, a report takes varying amounts of time to develop based on the density of data packed into it.

To illustrate this point further, let's take an example related to computers. An integrated chip that has more transistors packed into it takes more time to develop than an integrated chip that has fewer transistors. The chipmakers use the term density, not complexity, to describe their chips. They might say, for example, that they are now packing a million transistors per square inch compared to the 100,000 transistors they packed earlier.

Thus, functionality achieved with fewer lines of code has less density than functionality achieved with more lines of code, assuming that both cases use the minimum possible lines of code.

As you can see, I propose that we use "density" in place of "complexity" to adjust software size when it comes to software estimation. This is the principle used in the software size units method for measuring software size.

SUMMARY

This chapter discusses the issue of using complexity to increase software size. It defines the term "complexity" as well as illustrates its meaning. It challenges the belief that complexity affects the size of software and, through various examples and analogies, demonstrates that this notion is untenable—that size does not change due to complexity.

Further, this chapter introduces the concept that density affects the size of software and illustrates how the density of the information packed into a program influences software size. The chapter thus advocates the consideration of information density, in place of complexity, in software size estimation.

9

SOFTWARE DEVELOPMENT EFFORT ESTIMATION

There are two routes to estimating software development effort for a project:

1. Estimate the software size and arrive at the effort required to develop the software for the project using this software size estimate.
2. Directly arrive at the effort required to develop software for the project.

EFFORT ESTIMATION USING SOFTWARE SIZE

The Present Scenario

To arrive at an effort estimate from a size estimate, we use a productivity figure. A *productivity figure* expresses the rate of achievement. The rate of achievement can be expressed as person-hours per unit of software size or as software size per person-day. Here are a few examples:

- 10 person-hours per function point or, conversely, 0.7 function point per person-day
- 15 person-hours per use case point or 0.45 use case point per person-day

- 10 person-minutes per line of code or 50 lines of code per person-day
- 10 person-hours per Mark II function point index or 0.7 Mark II function point index per person-day

Either manner of specifying a productivity figure is acceptable, but it is recommended that the same manner be used consistently throughout the organization.

To convert software size into effort, apply the productivity figure as shown in the following examples:

1. **Person-hours per unit of software size**—If the software size is 100 function points, productivity is 10 person-hours, calculated as

$$\text{Effort} = 100 \times 10$$

$$= 1,000 \text{ person-hours}$$

2. **Units of software size per person-day**—If the software size is 100 function points, productivity is 0.7 function point per person-day, calculated as

$$\text{Effort} = \frac{100}{0.7}$$

$$= 142.86 \text{ person-days}$$

Thus, we arrive at software development effort from the software size. I have one suggestion though—use three productivity figures:

1. **Best-case (optimistic) scenario**—If all things go right during the project, this will be the maximum possible output per unit of time.
2. **Worst-case (pessimistic) scenario**—If everything goes wrong during the project, this will be the minimum possible output per unit of time.
3. **Normal-case scenario**—If some things go wrong and other things go right during the project, this will be the normal output per unit of time.

Compute the best-case effort estimate and the worst-case effort estimate for the project. Even if you use an average of best-case and worst-case effort estimates, communicate both estimates to the decision makers so that they understand the limits of the effort estimates, as well as the range of effort the project is likely to consume.

There is another way to arrive at software development effort using software size and that is the COCOMO method, touched upon previously in chapter 5.

The Suggested Scenario

Productivity for software estimators is explained in greater detail in chapter 10, but one basic principle is best introduced at this point, which is that it would be disadvantageous to apply a single figure of productivity to compute effort. I suggest the following:

1. Determine the software size.
2. Estimate the effort required for each of the skill sets that the project needs, using the productivity for each of the skill sets.
3. Determine the number of people that can deliver each skill set necessary.
4. Distribute the effort among the allocable persons and round each allocation up to the next person-day.
5. Sum all the efforts to arrive at the total effort required to execute the project.
6. Add a contingency allowance to allow for possible changes during project execution. A normal contingency allowance is 10 percent of the estimated effort.
7. Carry out this exercise twice—once for the best-case scenario and again for the worst-case scenario, and compute the average.
8. Provide these three estimates to the requester of the estimate.

Arguments for Applying One Productivity Figure to Convert Software Size to Effort

- It is easy to maintain organizational norms. The law of averages works out overall.
- It is feasible to benchmark against other organizations, and it facilitates process improvement.
- It is easy to implement in the organization.
- Best-case and worst-case scenarios can always be worked out by adding and subtracting 10 percent from the one productivity figure.
- It is the way the software development world is working!

Arguments for Applying Multiple Productivity Figures to Convert Software Size to Effort

- All software development work is not carried out by one class of persons, so how can we apply one productivity figure?
- Applying more than one productivity figure is not so complex that it can confuse software engineers.
- Closer insights into the organization's productivity can be revealed, and opportunities for improvement can be identified more easily.
- It is the right way!

INFLUENCE OF SOFTWARE DEVELOPMENT METHODOLOGIES ON SOFTWARE ESTIMATION

While software development is ultimately the activity of programming—that is, writing source code, compiling and linking with libraries, and building the executable code, there are multiple paths that lead to this stage. These paths are usually referred to as software development methodologies.

The first flow of software development was as follows:

1. Define requirements and obtain approval.
2. Carry out software design and obtain approval.
3. Develop programs and test the software.
4. Perform acceptance test and deliver the final software product.

This flow is called the waterfall model, as the development cascades from one stage to another in a finish-to-start relationship between predecessor and successor activities. This model was modified later with the introduction of a start-to-start relationship between predecessor and successor activities. Requirements collection and software design were carried out using the structured systems analysis and design method.

Later, object-oriented analysis and design methods stepped in for requirements analysis and software design activities, and object-oriented programming languages also came into being, bringing a paradigm shift from the waterfall model to object-oriented methodologies in software development. Then came graphical user interface and event-driven programming, and these were followed by multi-tier architectures.

The major methods of managing software development projects can be summarized as follows:

1. Waterfall and modified waterfall models
2. Object-oriented methodologies
3. Iterative models, including incremental development and spiral models
4. Rapid Application Development (RAD) and Joint Application Development (JAD)
5. Agile methods, such as Extreme Programming, SCRUM, dynamic systems development method, clear case, feature-driven development, test-driven development, and RUP, all of which follow iterative development
6. A mix of all the above

All these methodologies differ from one another in some way, but they do so especially with respect to documentation and how requirements analysis and software design are carried out. The waterfall model and its variants put emphasis on "getting it right the first time," and they aim to achieve this by rigorous documentation and approvals. Agile methodologies put more emphasis on delivering a quality product and less emphasis on documentation. They aim to achieve this mainly through co-location of the customer and end users with the development team. To avoid any possible issues as a result of not using documentation, agile methods advocate developing the software in short iterations (called sprints) of four weeks or so per iteration. RAD and JAD are also somewhat akin to the agile methodologies in the sense that they aim to reduce dependence on documentation.

One thing is certain though: the method used to develop the software does not alter the size of the software. Size remains the same whether a waterfall model or an agile method is used. What changes is the effort, the cost, and the schedule to develop the software.

Software development effort is affected by productivity, which does change from method to method. In a waterfall methodology, the code is produced in one iteration, whereas in other methodologies, the same amount of code is achieved in multiple iterations. The same is true for testing and debugging, as well as requirements analysis and software design. However, by not documenting the requirements and design and by not obtaining formal approvals, a certain amount of time certainly is saved. Therefore, productivity is higher for requirements analysis and software design when using agile methodologies.

Thus, to summarize the influence of software development methodologies on software estimation, we can be certain of three things:

1. The size of the software to be produced is not affected by the type of method used to develop it.

2. Productivity for construction and testing is not affected by the type of method used.
3. Productivity for requirements analysis and software design is higher when using agile methods, due to this type of methodology's non-documentation philosophy.

In carrying out software estimation, it is important to bear these facts in mind when applying productivity figures to convert software size into software development effort. Application of multiple productivity figures to derive development effort from software size ensures that the impact of software development methodologies is considered and included.

CONSTRUCTIVE COST MODEL (COCOMO)

COCOMO was originally developed by Dr. Barry Boehm after he studied a very large number of software projects of different sizes and from different domains. COCOMO has a large following in the software development industry. The original COCOMO had three varieties: basic, intermediate, and advanced. Then COCOMO II was released.

COCOMO classifies projects into three modes:

1. **Organic**—A simple project with small teams working with an informal set of requirements and constraints
2. **Semi-detached**—A project with mixed teams working with a mix of rigid and less rigid sets of requirements and constraints
3. **Embedded**—A project that must operate within a tight set of constraints

Basic COCOMO

Basic COCOMO computes software development effort as a function of software size in thousand lines of code (KLOC). The equation for basic COCOMO is

$$E = a \times \text{size}^b$$

where E is the effort required to develop the software in person-months, size is the software size in KLOC, and a and b are constants, whose values are shown in table 9.1.

Table 9.1. Values of constants in basic COCOMO

Mode	a	b
Organic	2.4	1.05
Semi-detached	3.0	1.12
Embedded	3.6	1.20

Intermediate COCOMO

Intermediate COCOMO makes use of 15 cost drivers in addition to an equation. The equation for intermediate COCOMO is

$$E = a \times size^b \times EAF$$

where E is the effort required to develop the software in person-months, size is the software size in KLOC, EAF is the effort adjustment factor derived from the 15 cost drivers, and a and b are constants, whose values are shown in table 9.2.

There are four categories of cost drivers, listed here and shown in table 9.3:

1. Product attributes
2. Hardware attributes
3. Personnel attributes
4. Project attributes

Each cost driver is rated on a scale from "very low" to "extra high," based on the value of its importance to the project. The rating indicates the weight of the corresponding cost driver. "NA" indicates that the respective cost driver is not to be rated for that level.

EAF is obtained by multiplying all the cost driver ratings. In other words, the product of all multipliers (values of the cost drivers) is the EAF.

Table 9.2. Constants for a and b

Mode	a	b
Organic	3.2	1.05
Semi-detached	3.0	1.12
Embedded	2.8	1.20

Table 9.3. Cost drivers for intermediate COCOMO

	Rating					
Cost driver	Very low	Low	Nominal	High	Very high	Extra high
Product attributes						
Required software reliability	0.75	0.88	1.00	1.15	1.40	NA
Size of application database	NA	0.94	1.00	1.08	1.16	NA
Complexity of the product	0.70	0.85	1.00	1.15	1.30	1.65
Hardware attributes						
Run-time performance constraints	NA	NA	1.10	1.11	1.30	1.66
Memory constraints	NA	NA	1.00	1.06	1.21	1.56
Volatility of virtual machine environment	NA	0.87	1.00	1.15	1.30	NA
Required turnaround time	NA	0.87	1.00	1.07	1.15	NA
Personnel attributes						
Analyst capability	1.46	1.19	1.00	0.86	0.71	NA
Software engineer capability	1.29	1.13	1.00	0.91	0.82	NA
Applications experience	1.42	1.17	1.00	0.86	0.70	NA
Virtual machine experience	1.21	1.10	1.00	1.90	NA	NA
Programming language experience	1.14	1.07	1.00	0.95	NA	NA
Project attributes						
Use of software tools	1.24	1.10	1.00	0.91	0.82	NA
Application of software engineering methods	1.24	1.10	1.00	0.91	0.83	NA
Required development schedule	1.23	1.08	1.00	1.04	1.10	NA

Advanced COCOMO

The advanced COCOMO model (sometimes called detailed COCOMO) applies the intermediate model at the component level, and then a phase-based approach is used to consolidate the estimate.

Advanced COCOMO defines six project phases:

1. Requirements phase
2. Product design phase
3. Detailed design phase
4. Code and unit test phase
5. Integrate and test phase
6. Maintenance phase

The maintenance phase falls outside the scope of the software development life cycle, though it certainly forms part of the software life cycle. Advanced COCOMO breaks down cost drivers into each of these phases for all 15 cost drivers.

Deeper discussion of advanced COCOMO is beyond the scope of this book. The interested reader is advised to refer to the original material by Dr. Barry Boehm.

COCOMO II

It would not serve the reader's interest to explain the COCOMO II model briefly. COCOMO II is a very involved model, and I suggest referring to Dr. Boehm's *COCOMO Model Definition Manual* in its entirety for more information and for mastering the technique.

Merits and Demerits of COCOMO

Merits of COCOMO include the following:

- It is based on the study of a large number of software development projects and therefore is a reliable method. The law of averages should work out at the very least.
- The technique is easy to master and to implement.
- It facilitates comparing and contrasting actual values with estimated values; there are fewer variables with which to contend.
- It is completely person independent; all estimators performing the estimation will arrive at the same values.

These are the demerits of COCOMO:

- It is not conducive to detailed review and it is not auditable.
- Due to lack of detail, a causal analysis of variance between actual values and estimated values does not pinpoint causes of the variance and leads to hunch-based analysis.
- The law of averages works out only with a large number of projects; it is not reliable for any single project.
- The technique is reliable when considered over a large number of projects, but not for a single project, as it does not take into account the specific and unique aspects of the current project.

TASK-BASED ESTIMATION

The method for estimating software development effort directly without estimating the software size is task-based estimation. This method is also sometimes referred to as activity-based estimation. It is an improvement over the ballpark method of estimation, in the sense that it brings some structure to such methods of estimation. This is the de facto method for effort estimation in engineering projects in the manufacturing industry. Task-based estimation enumerates each of the tasks expected to be performed in the execution of a project in a systematic manner.

Initially, a software development project is divided into various phases. The common phases used in software development projects are described in table 9.4.

Normally, the design and construction phases are to be iterated for each module. However, in large projects, where each module itself is significantly large and in all likelihood would be assigned to an independent team, it is

Table 9.4. Task-based estimation phases for development projects

Ref. no.	Phase	Explanation
1	Project initiation	All activities necessary to start up the project, including identification and allocation of the team, setup of the development environment, kickoff meeting, etc.
2	Project planning	All activities related to preparing the project plans, such as estimation, project management, configuration management, quality management, training, schedule, etc.
3	Requirements analysis	All activities related to conducting requirements analysis and generating a user requirements specification document, such as conducting interviews with selected users, consolidating requirements, preparing requirements specifications, reviewing, obtaining approval, etc.
4	Software requirements specification	All activities related to converting user requirements specifications to software requirements specifications, such as process modeling, data modeling, architecture design, screen and report layout design, etc.

Table 9.4. Task-based estimation phases for development projects (continued)

Ref. no.	Phase	Explanation
5	Design (module-specific)	All activities related to software detailed design, including program design, table design, interface design, etc.
6	Construction (module-specific)	All activities related to coding, code review, and unit testing
7	Integration	All activities related to integration and integration testing
8	Test planning	All activities related to test planning and test case design
9	System testing	All activities related to final testing of the product, such as system testing, load testing, functional testing, etc.
10	Documentation	All activities related to preparation of necessary documentation, such as a user manual, operations manual, troubleshooting manual, etc.
11	User acceptance testing	All activities related to conducting user acceptance testing, such as preparing the test plan, reviewing, obtaining approval, setting up the environment for testing, conducting the test, rectifying defects, obtaining sign-off from the customer, etc.
12	User training	All activities related to conducting user training, including preparation of training materials and course materials, scheduling user training, conducting user training, etc.
13	Postdelivery	All activities that come after delivering the software, such as installation, pilot runs, rollout, warranty support, etc.
14	Project closure	All activities related to closing the project, such as documenting good and bad practices and lessons learned, handover of project records, release of resources, sharing experiences, etc.

suggested that each module be treated as a separate project for the purpose of estimation.

These phases can be tailored to suit any type of project, adding more phases or removing some depending on the project. The phases are different for different types of projects. Suggested phases for software testing projects are shown in table 9.5. Suggested phases for an enterprise resource planning rollout project are provided in table 9.6.

Table 9.5. Task-based estimation phases for testing projects

Ref. no.	Phase	Explanation
1	Project initiation	All activities necessary to start up the project, including identification and allocation of the team, setup of the development environment, kickoff meeting, etc.
2	Project planning	All activities related to preparing the project plans, such as estimation, project management, configuration management, quality management, training, schedule, etc.
3	Testing requirements analysis	All activities related to understanding the objectives of testing, including pass/fail criteria, the testing environment, types of testing needed, etc.
4	Test planning and design	All activities related to designing test plans and test cases, including test strategy, developing testing scripts for testing tools, etc.
5	Testing	All activities related to conducting planned tests, including documentation of the results, reviewing the test results, reporting the results, etc.
6	Regression testing	All activities related to conducting regression testing where necessary, including reviewing test results, reporting results, etc.
7	Postdelivery	All activities that come after delivering the software, such as certification, warranty support, etc.
8	Project closure	All activities related to closing the project, such as documenting good and bad practices and lessons learned, handover of project records, release of resources, sharing experiences, etc.

Table 9.6. Task-based estimation phases for enterprise resource planning implementation projects

Ref. no.	Phase	Explanation
1	Project initiation	All activities necessary to start up the project, including identification and allocation of the team, setup of the development environment, kickoff meeting, etc.
2	Project planning	All activities related to preparing the project plans, such as estimation, project management, configuration management, quality management, training, schedule, etc.
3	Gap analysis	All activities related to conducting gap analysis and generating a gap analysis document, such as conducting interviews with selected users, consolidating gaps, preparing a gap analysis document, reviewing, obtaining approval, etc.
4	Design	All activities related to generating a statement of work document based on the gap analysis, such as additional screen and report layout design, strategy for customization and implementation, etc.
5	Customization	All activities related to coding, such as code review, unit testing for the required customization, etc.
6	Testing	All activities related to testing, including planning and test case design, testing the final product, etc.
7	Documentation	All activities related to preparation of necessary documentation, such as a user manual, operations manual, troubleshooting manual, etc.
8	Product rollout	All activities related to implementing the software, including creating masters, pilot runs, etc.
9	User training	All activities related to conducting user training, including preparation of training materials and course materials, scheduling user training, conducting user training, etc.
10	Postimplementation	All activities that come after implementation, such as handholding support, defect fixing, warranty support, etc.
11	Project closure	All activities related to closing the project, such as documenting good and bad practices and lessons learned, handover of project records, release of resources, sharing experiences, etc.

Arriving at Software Development Effort Using Task-Based Estimation

The methodology for task-based estimation is as follows:

1. Begin by breaking down the software product into its constituent modules. A module is a significant part of a product, denoting a major functional grouping. It may consist of multiple screens and reports and associated scripts. Using material management software as an example, the major modules could be
   a. Warehouse module
   b. Purchasing module
   c. Inventory control module
   d. Payables module
2. For each module:
   a. List all applicable phases.
   b. List all applicable tasks for each phase.
   c. For each task, estimate the effort needed using three estimates— optimistic (best case), pessimistic (worst case), and most likely (normal case)—and arrive at the expected effort using the equation

$$\text{Expected effort} = \frac{(\text{optimistic effort} + \text{pessimistic effort}) + (4 \times \text{most likely effort})}{6}$$

   d. Use a consistent measure for estimating effort, either person-hours or person-days.
   e. It is suggested that each task be designed in such a way that the effort would be less than a person-week.
   f. It is suggested that more tasks be used per phase to increase granularity and to arrive at a more accurate estimate.
3. Estimate the effort required for the overall project phases (project initiation, project closure, project planning, etc.) by breaking each of them into its component tasks and estimating the effort required for each task. Next, sum the effort to arrive at the effort required for each phase. Then sum the phase effort to arrive at the effort for the module or project.
4. Document all assumptions. All estimates necessitate making some assumptions regarding technology, completeness of requirements, approvals, clarifications, environment, etc. that would impact the actual

effort. It would be advantageous if all assumptions made during estimation were recorded, as this would facilitate proper understanding of the estimate by decision makers for pricing (budgeting) the project.

An example of effort estimation for a software development project is given in table 9.7. Effort is shown in person-days. For the sake of brevity, only two modules are used. The effort required to develop the software for this project would be 255 person-days, with a minimum of 198.75 (or about 200) person-days and a pessimistic estimate of 335 person-days. Effort for other projects can be estimated in this manner.

The main advantage of task-based estimation is that it can be used in the case of full life cycle projects or partial life cycle projects, including software maintenance projects, testing projects, infrastructure projects, etc. While using a spreadsheet such as Microsoft Excel facilitates task-based estimation, a software estimation tool would make the task much easier.

Table 9.7. Task-based estimation example

Ref. no.	Phase	Task	Opti-mistic effort	Pessi-mistic effort	Most likely effort	Expected effort
Module: Overall project						
1	Project initiation	Review purchase order	1.00	2.00	1.00	1.16
2	Project initiation	Identify project manager	0.50	1.00	0.75	0.75
3	Project initiation	Prepare project initiation note	1.50	2.50	2.00	2.00
4	Project initiation	Project initiation meeting	0.25	0.50	0.25	0.30
5	Project planning	Effort estimation	3.00	5.00	4.00	4.00
6	Project planning	Prepare project management, configuration, and quality plans	4.00	6.00	5.00	5.00
7	Project planning	Prepare project schedule	1.00	2.00	1.50	1.50
8	Project planning	Prepare induction training plan	1.00	1.50	1.25	1.25
9	Project planning	Review project plans and schedule	2.00	2.50	2.25	2.08

Table 9.7. Task-based estimation example (continued)

Ref. no.	Phase	Task	Opti- mistic effort	Pessi- mistic effort	Most likely effort	Expected effort
10	Project planning	Project kickoff meeting	0.50	1.00	0.75	0.75
11	Project closure	Document best practices	2.00	4.00	3.00	3.00
12	Project closure	Document bad experiences	1.00	2.00	1.50	1.50
13	Project closure	Archive project records	3.00	5.00	4.00	4.00
14	Project closure	Release resources	1.00	1.50	1.25	1.25
15	Project closure	Conduct project postmortem	1.00	1.50	1.25	1.25
16	Requirements analysis	Plan interviews	2.00	4.00	3.00	3.00
17	Requirements analysis	Conduct interviews with subject matter experts	5.00	9.00	6.00	6.33
18	Requirements analysis	Consolidate interview findings	3.00	4.00	3.50	3.50
19	Requirements analysis	Document requirements	4.00	6.00	5.00	5.00
20	Requirements analysis	Review requirements document	1.00	1.50	1.00	1.08
21	Requirements analysis	Customer approval	2.00	4.00	3.00	3.00
22	Software requirements specification (SRS)	Design architecture	3.00	6.00	4.00	3.50
23	SRS	Design screen layouts	10.00	15.00	12.00	12.17
24	SRS	Design report layouts	12.00	16.00	14.00	14.00
25	SRS	Data modeling	8.00	15.00	10.00	10.50
26	SRS	Prepare SRS document	3.00	5.00	4.00	4.00
27	SRS	Review of SRS document	2.00	4.00	2.50	2.67
28	SRS	Coordinate and obtain customer approval	5.00	8.00	6.00	6.16

Table 9.7. Task-based estimation example (continued)

Ref. no.	Phase	Task	Opti- mistic effort	Pessi- mistic effort	Most likely effort	Expected effort
Module: Patient registration						
29	Design	Design screens	2.00	3.00	2.50	2.50
30	Design	Design reports	2.00	3.00	2.50	2.50
31	Design	Design tables	1.00	2.00	1.50	1.50
32	Construction	Code screens	4.00	6.00	5.00	5.00
33	Construction	Code reports	4.00	6.00	5.00	5.00
34	Construction	Deploy tables	2.00	4.00	2.50	2.67
35	Construction	Unit testing	3.00	5.00	4.00	4.00
36	Construction	Defect fixing	1.00	1.50	1.25	1.25
37	Construction	Defect closure	1.00	1.50	1.25	1.25
Module: Patient treatment						
38	Design	Design screens	3.00	4.00	3.50	3.50
39	Design	Design reports	4.00	6.00	5.00	5.00
40	Design	Design tables	1.00	2.00	1.50	1.50
41	Construction	Code screens	5.00	8.00	6.00	6.16
42	Construction	Code reports	6.00	9.00	7.00	7.16
43	Construction	Deploy tables	2.00	4.00	2.50	2.67
44	Construction	Unit testing	3.00	5.00	4.00	4.00
45	Construction	Defect fixing	1.00	1.50	1.25	1.25
46	Construction	Defect closure	1.00	1.50	1.25	1.25
Module: Overall project						
47	Integration	Design interfaces	3.00	5.00	4.00	4.00
48	Integration	Code interfaces	4.00	6.00	5.00	5.00
49	Integration	Prepare integration test plan	1.00	2.00	1.50	1.50
50	Integration	Conduct integration testing	3.00	5.00	4.00	4.00
51	Integration	Defect fixing	1.00	2.00	1.50	1.50
52	Integration	Regression testing	1.00	2.00	1.50	1.50
53	Test planning	Test strategy	1.00	2.00	1.50	1.50
54	Test planning	Develop test plans	4.00	8.00	5.00	5.33
55	Test planning	Review test plans	2.00	4.00	3.00	2.66
56	System testing	Set up test environment	4.00	8.00	6.00	6.00
57	System testing	Conduct system testing	3.00	6.00	4.00	4.16
58	System testing	Fix defects	1.00	1.50	1.25	1.25
59	System testing	Conduct load testing	3.00	5.00	4.00	4.00

Table 9.7. Task-based estimation example (continued)

Ref. no.	Phase	Task	Opti-mistic effort	Pessi-mistic effort	Most likely effort	Expected effort
60	System testing	Fix defects unearthed in load testing	3.00	6.00	5.00	4.83
61	System testing	Conduct functional testing	2.00	3.00	2.50	2.50
62	System testing	Fix defects found in functional testing	0.50	1.00	0.50	0.58
63	System testing	Review test results	2.00	3.00	2.50	2.50
64	User acceptance testing	Prepare test plan	3.00	5.00	4.00	4.00
65	User acceptance testing	Review test plan	1.00	2.00	1.50	1.50
66	User acceptance testing	Customer approval	5.00	8.00	6.00	6.16
67	User acceptance testing	Set up testing environment	1.00	2.00	1.50	1.50
68	User acceptance testing	Conduct user acceptance testing	4.00	6.00	5.00	5.00
69	User acceptance testing	Obtain sign-off	1.00	2.00	1.50	1.50
70	Documentation	Prepare user guide	2.00	3.00	2.50	2.50
71	Documentation	Prepare operations manual	1.00	2.00	1.50	1.50
72	Documentation	Review documentation	1.00	2.00	1.50	1.50
73	User training	Prepare training material	4.00	8.00	5.00	5.33
74	User training	Prepare course material	6.00	10.00	7.00	7.33
75	User training	Conduct user training	3.00	4.00	3.00	3.16
76	Postdelivery	Install	0.50	1.00	0.75	0.75
77	Postdelivery	On-site support	2.00	3.00	2.00	2.16
	Total effort		198.75	335.00		255.28

Merits and Demerits of Task-Based Estimation

Merits of task-based estimation include the following:

- It closely reflects the way work is normally carried out in software development organizations and therefore provides accurate estimates.
- It considers the uncertainty inherent in estimation and provides a mechanism to correct it.
- It is easy to learn and to implement.
- It does not depend on productivity to arrive at effort.
- It is most suitable for use with such software tools as Microsoft Project, PMPal, and Primavera.

These are the demerits of task-based estimation:

- It does not provide size estimation. Therefore, derivation of productivity and benchmarking is not possible.

SUMMARY

This chapter discusses the estimation of effort. Three methods—deriving effort from a software size estimate using a productivity figure, COCOMO, and task-based estimation—are explained. The use of multiple productivity figures when converting software size estimate into effort is suggested, in order to achieve greater accuracy in effort estimation. Appendix E gives a list of suggested phases and tasks that can be used for task-based estimation.

PRODUCTIVITY FOR SOFTWARE ESTIMATORS

Software estimation—that is, estimation of software size, effort, cost, and schedule (duration)—often causes animated discussions among software estimators, who are usually project leaders and project managers who normally carry out software estimation activity. Software development consists of a few disparate activities in which specialized knowledge is needed, namely:

- Requirements gathering, analysis, and management
- Software design
- Coding and unit testing
- Independent verification and validation
- Rollout, deployment, installation, and commissioning

Carrying out each of these activities requires persons with different skill sets, using different methods and tools.

PRODUCTIVITY

Productivity is a term that is used in the context of human beings. There are various ways to define productivity. One definition is *the rate of output per unit of input.* Another can be expressed as *number of units of output per person-day* or *number of units of output per person-hour*. Yet another way to define productivity is *the ratio of output to input*. Perhaps the simplest definition of productivity is *the rate of achieving or accomplishing something*.

In this chapter, **productivity** is defined as *the rate of producing some output, using a set of inputs in a defined unit of time and in a defined environment, by a qualified person who is acclimatized to the working environment and who is using a defined set of methods, at a pace that can be maintained day after day, without any harmful physical effects*.

CONCERNS WITH PRODUCTIVITY

At the outset, we need to understand the terms "productivity," "efficiency," and "capacity." These are words with similar meanings, but with marked distinctions:

- **Productivity**—In addition to the previous definitions, productivity can also be defined and expressed as *amount of output per unit of input*. The term is normally used in the context of human beings performing work. Productivity is used in reference to one type of homogeneous activity. A person's productivity depends on the activity itself and the working conditions. Productivity lends itself to improvement using better methods, tools, and techniques without adding more workstations.
- **Efficiency**—*Output divided by input, expressed as a percentage.* It is normally used in the context of a process or in the context of machines (for example, the efficiency of fuel in generating heat, the efficiency of a machine, etc.).
- **Capacity**—*The throughput of a system.* For example, a car factory produces 5,000 cars per day. The term capacity assumes that several disparate activities with varying rates of achievement are performed inside the system. Capacity is comprised of the final output of multiple heterogeneous activities. Capacity is used in reference to a facility such as an automobile manufacturing plant. Capacity for a facility or plant is designed before actually setting up the facility or plant. Once a specific capacity is designed and built, it is not possible to increase it without adding new workstations.

The software development industry is obsessed with giving a single, empirical, all-activities-encompassing figure for productivity. My observation is that the present models (techniques) of software effort estimation confuse the terms "productivity" and "capacity"—"productivity" is being used where "capacity" should be used.

Attempts have been made to express productivity in such figures as, for example, 10 person-hours per function point, but with a rider that this figure could vary from 2 to 135 depending on the product size and other factors. Sometimes ranges are given, such as 15 to 30 hours per use case point. Sometimes empirical formulas that depend on a set of factors are worked out, such as in the COCOMO method of software estimation.

These productivity figures lump all activities—requirements analysis, design, coding, review, testing, and so on—into a single measure. In reality, however, the skill requirements for each of these activities are different, the tools used are different, the inputs are different, and the outputs are different. Combining them under the heading "software development" and giving a single figure of productivity at best can only offer a rough estimate, never an accurate one.

The present focus in software estimation is on macro-productivity (but is this really capacity?), using one figure to represent the productivity of all activities in software development. This approach needs to change; we need to shift our focus from macro- to micro-productivity, using a figure for each activity involved in developing software. The way to achieve this is to either modify the timesheets if using empirical methods to determine productivity or have industrial engineers arrive at the productivity for each activity.

The benefits of productivity at a micro level include the following:

- Better predictability of software development, as effort for each specialized activity is estimated separately
- More accurate estimates for pricing assistance during the project acquisition and budget sanction stages
- More precise target setting when assigning work
- More accurate cost estimation
- Better prediction of skill requirements
- More precise variance analysis, which can lead to process improvement and the establishment of productivity norms

STANDARD TIME

The American Institute of Industrial Engineers (AIIE) defines standard time thus:

Standard time is the amount of time taken to accomplish a unit of work performed using a given method under defined working conditions by a qualified worker after adjustment at a pace that can be maintained day after day without any physical harmful effects.

Needless to say, standard time is the unit of measure for productivity. The key terms and phrases in the AIIE's definition are

- **Unit of work**—The amount of work in its smallest possible size. This implies that there must be an accepted unit of measure for the work for which productivity is being defined.
- **Given method**—The method of performing the work must be defined and the person performing it must adhere to that definition in letter and in spirit.
- **Qualified worker**—The person performing the work has the knowledge and skills (either by certification or by training) to do the work.
- **After adjustment**—The person is not doing the work for the first time; he or she has put in some time in the organization and is adjusted to the work environment and the methods of working.
- **At a pace that can be maintained day after day**—The pace must be one that can be achieved every day. Here is an analogy to illustrate: The Olympic record for the 100-meter dash is between 9 and 10 seconds, but the Olympic record for the marathon (26 miles or 42 kilometers) is disproportionately longer than what is obtained mathematically by calculating it using the record for the 100-meter dash. The average person is not an Olympian, so in the present context the pace is that of a normal (average) person running a marathon and not that of an Olympian running the 100-meter dash.

Having defined productivity (standard time), we still have to consider the aspect of an organization's personnel having a mix of skill levels. *The Handbook of Industrial Engineering*, edited by John Maynard, defines five skill levels:

1. **Super skill**—A person who has extensive experience and who knows all there is to know about the work, including all the best practices and all the shortcuts. This person is an authority and guides others in the subject.
2. **Very good skill**—A person who has much experience and who has learned all there is to learn about the work, but who perhaps has not personally applied all of this knowledge. This person knows all the

best practices and most of the shortcuts and can guide others in the subject.

3. **Good skill**—A person who has adequate experience and is capable of delivering results, but who perhaps needs reference to a document or clarification from a colleague or supervisor in advanced aspects of the work. This person does the work, but may not be able to guide others.

4. **Fair skill**—A person who is not a trainee and who has some experience, but who needs reference to documents or experts to complete the work. This person needs occasional guidance.

5. **Poor skill**—A person who is a new entrant and who has not completed a formal training period in the organization. This person needs guidance from someone with greater experience.

Another aspect we must consider is the level of effort one puts into performing the task. *The Handbook of Industrial Engineering* defines five levels of effort:

1. **Super effort**—Not a second is lost, all available time is used; does not take any allowed breaks; no trial and error; all effort is focused on the task.

2. **Very good effort**—Very high use of time; does not take all allowed breaks; no trial and error; all effort is focused on the task.

3. **Good effort**—Uses time fully; takes only the allowed breaks; very little trial and error; all effort is focused on the task.

4. **Fair effort**—Uses most of the available time; takes all allowed breaks; some trial and error; most of the effort is focused on the task.

5. **Poor effort**—Uses as much of the available time as possible; takes all the allowed breaks and more; keen to experiment; all effort is not focused on the task.

As you perhaps can infer, the output of a person with *super skills* but who is putting in *poor effort* may be equal to that of a person with *poor skills* but who is putting in *super effort*.

Productivity has to be defined based on a person of *good skill* and who is putting in *good effort*—that is, an average person. That an organization has a mix of workers with different skill levels raises three questions:

1. As advocated, if productivity is defined based on an average person, how do we reconcile the output of a super-skilled person and a poor-skilled person?

Obviously the super-skilled person comes at a much higher cost than a poor-skilled person does. That is, the costs are different for people of different skills. While we use the average person as a basis for estimating, target setting during execution is commensurate with the skill level of the person to whom the task is entrusted.

2. A mix of skill levels results in the actual time varying from the estimated time, right?

Absolutely. Yet in large projects, the combination of mixed skill levels and mixed effort levels averages out, and the actual time to complete the tasks required for the project comes very close to the estimated time.

3. If the resource estimation is performed using average skill and average effort, how does resource allocation ensure that all average resources are allocated to the project when the organization has a mix of resources?

Resource allocation is not just making available the requested number of resources. If a project manager requests for, let us say, ten software engineers, that means ten resources of average skill. If all super-skilled resources are allocated to the project, ten of them are not needed. Similarly, if all poor-skilled resources are allocated to the project, more than ten are needed. The people in charge of allocating resources to projects need to ensure that the project has the equivalent of the requested number of average-skilled persons. To accomplish this effectively, the organization ought to maintain conversion rates for converting one level of skill to another, such as one super-skilled person is equal to three poor-skilled persons. Table 10.1 is an example of a conversion rates table.

Suppose a project manager requests ten resources. The person allocating resources should use the organization's conversion rates, shown in table 10.1 for this example, to ensure that the equivalent of

Table 10.1. Conversion rates for skill levels

Skill level	Conversion rate
Super skill	2
Very good skill	1.5
Good (average) skill	1
Fair skill	0.60
Poor skill	0.50

Table 10.2. Resource allocation example

Skill level	No. of resources actually allocated	Equivalent number of average-skilled resources
Super skill	2	4
Very good skill	2	3
Good (average) skill	1	1
Poor skill	4	2
Total allocated	**9**	**10**

ten average resources are allocated to the project. The total number of resources can be any combination, and one is shown in table 10.2. Even though the actual number of resources allocated is nine, the requirements of the project manager have been met.

When it comes to the effort put in, everyone is expected to put in at least average effort, and the onus is on the project manager to ensure that everyone puts in a minimum of average effort. If the project manager ensures that everyone puts in more than average effort, then the project would be completed before the scheduled date. If the project manager fails to ensure that everyone puts in average effort, then the project would be completed later than the scheduled date.

THE PRODUCTIVITY PATH

Software development involves (but is not limited to) the following activities:

1. Preproject activities
   a. Feasibility study (proposal in the case of external projects)
   b. Financial budgeting and approvals for the project (negotiations in the case of external projects)
   c. Approvals, both financial and technical (receipt of purchase order in the case of external projects)
   d. Project go-ahead decision (project initiation in the case of external projects)
2. Project start-up activities
   a. Identification of the project manager
   b. Allocation of the project team
   c. Setting up the development environment

  d. Project planning
  e. Setting up various protocols
  f. Service level agreements and progress-reporting formalities
  g. Project-related training
 3. Software engineering activities
  a. User requirements analysis
  b. Software requirements analysis
  c. Software design
  d. Coding and unit testing
  e. Testing (integration, functional, negative, system, and acceptance)
  f. Preparation of the build and documentation
 4. Rollout activities
  a. Installation of the hardware and system software
  b. Setting up the database
  c. Installation of the application software
  d. Pilot runs
  e. User training
  f. Parallel runs
  g. Rollover
 5. Project cleanup activities
  a. Documentation of good practices and bad practices
  b. Project postmortem
  c. Archiving of records
  d. Release of resources
  e. Release of the project manager to enable him or her to take up another project
  f. Initiation of software maintenance

Industry rules of thumb for productivity are not clear as to how many of these activities are included in the productivity figure. Interestingly, no one would stake his or her life on the productivity figure, which is an industry rule of thumb!

If we draw a parallel to the manufacturing industry, the following are the tasks (in order) involved in punching a hole in a steel sheet:

1. Set up machine
2. Set up tool
3. Load job
4. Punch hole

5. De-burr hole
6. Clean up
7. Deliver workpiece for next operation

If multiple holes are punched, the time to complete activity #4 would be the number of holes to be punched multiplied by the time per hole, with times for the other activities remaining unaltered, as they are one-time activities.

If we look at the task of coding a unit, activities could involve:

1. Receiving instructions
2. Studying the design document
3. Coding the unit
4. Testing and debugging the unit for functionality
5. Testing and debugging the unit for unintended usage
6. Deleting trash code from the unit
7. Regression testing the unit
8. Releasing the unit for the next step

Similarly, we can come up with micro-activities for each software development phase.

CLASSIFICATION OF SOFTWARE DEVELOPMENT ACTIVITIES

The following are the major classes of software development work:

- **Requirements analysis**—This involves understanding what the user needs, wants, and expects and documenting this information so that the software designers understand the requirements and can design a system in strict conformance with them. Requirements analysis greatly depends on external factors.
- **Software design**—This involves considering the alternatives available for hardware, system software, and development platforms; arriving at the optimal configuration; designing an architecture that will meet the stated requirements and fulfill expectations, yet be feasible with the current technologies; and documenting the design in such a way that the programmers understand and can deliver a product that conforms to the original user specifications. Because

there are quite a few possible alternatives, this is a strategic activity, and errors made during this stage have strategic consequences.

- **Construction**—This involves developing software code that conforms to the design and that is as failure-free as possible (it is so easy to leave bugs inside!).

- **Review of requirements, design, and code**—This involves walking through the requirements and the design and code developed by another person, deciphering the functionality, and unearthing any possible errors.

- **Testing**—This involves trying to unearth all the defects that could be left in the software. It is an accepted fact that 100 percent testing—that is, testing for every possibility—is not practical.

- **Build preparation**—This involves linking all the components into one software product and preparing the product for rollout. With the onset of multi-tier software architectures, this stage is becoming a major specialist activity in itself.

- **Documentation**—Writing documentation for user guides, operation manuals, user training materials, and troubleshooting manuals can be a major activity in large projects, and many organizations employ technical writers for this task.

With such variety in the nature of these activities, it is obvious that their productivity cannot be uniform. The pace of working differs for each of these activities. They depend on the amount of software code produced as well as on other factors:

- Requirements analysis depends on the efficiency and clarity of the source of requirements, be it users or documentation.

- Software design depends on the complexity of processing, alternatives available, and constraints within which the functionality is to be realized.

- Code review depends on the style of coding.

- Testing depends on how well the code is written. The more errors, the more time it takes to test and retest.

- Coding itself depends on the quality of the software design.

- Build preparation depends on the number of tiers and components in the software architecture.

- Documentation depends on the size of functionality achieved by the software product.

Therefore, it is only logical that we need to have separate productivity figures for each of these activities.

HOW DO WE ARRIVE AT PRODUCTIVITY?

There are two distinct routes to determining productivity (standard time): empirical methods and work measurement.

Empirical Methods

Empirical methods involve collecting actual data from a large number of projects and computing an average (statistical mean, mode, or median) productivity and a standard deviation. The software industry, to a large extent, is following this methodology. My observation is that the software development industry perceives the term "average" to mean *arithmetic mean*. The drawback to the arithmetic mean is that it is influenced by extreme values (extreme values result from extreme circumstances). The *statistical mode* is the right measure to use to arrive at average productivity, as it is the most frequently occurring value in a population universe and therefore is not influenced by extreme values. The software industry often uses the arithmetic mean, which produces skewed results. It is a matter of concern that after nearly three decades of intense software development activity, there are no universally accepted norms for arriving at productivity in the software development field. The result is that software development is poorly managed and is costing more money for the end users.

One reliable and easily obtained source of data is historical data from timesheets. Most timesheet software available and being used in the industry is oriented toward payroll and billing rather than capturing data at the micro level so that it can be used to arrive at productivity data. Most timesheets capture data at two or three levels (the project level is always the first, and the second and third are either the module and component levels, component and activity levels, or a similar combination) in addition to date and time. Timesheets need to capture data from *five* levels—project, module, component, development phase, and the task accomplished, in addition to date and time for each employee. If timesheets supplied such information, the right data would be available to establish productivity data empirically in a realistic manner. Appendix D offers a suggested methodology for deriving productivity from past records of the organization.

One recommendation: if empirical methods are selected to arrive at productivity, use the statistical mode, and not the arithmetic mean, to arrive at an average. *The nature of the statistical mode, which is not influenced by extreme values, allows for more accuracy within the software development environment.*

Work Measurement

In the early 1980s, the International Labor Organization (ILO) released the *Compendium for Professional Workers*, which added a third category to the organizational workforce: *professional workers* (the original two categories were *workers* and *management*). This compendium treated software developers as professional workers. While the compendium separated programmers from management, providing them with certain benefits and facilities enjoyed by other workers, it did not suggest any methods for measuring their work, as it did for other workers. The premise was that programmers' work is creative and therefore cannot be measured. This is true in cases where programmers work not with the assistance of a document but with their own domain knowledge and experience in writing source code. However, this is not true in the case of software developers working in contract development, who work with defined user requirements and a design document; the work cannot be described as creative by any stretch of the imagination.

Work measurement involves defining the unit of measure for the work and setting the standard time required to perform it. The ILO approved a few methods for this activity, some of which are

- Time study
- Motion study
- Therbligs
- Synthesis
- Analytical estimation
- Work sampling

The method most often associated with work measurement is the time and motion study, and while this technique is commonly used in the manufacturing industry, it is not all that feasible in the software industry. Factory workers are not sitting in cubicles; a supervisor can scan each workstation from his or her seat to be sure that work is being carried out. In the software industry, however, such supervision is not possible. All the supervisor can see is that the programmers are in their cubicles, staring intently at their screens while their fingers are flying across their keyboards. Most programmers do productive work, but some may be

- Sending personal e-mails
- Surfing the Internet
- Chatting with an on-line friend
- Preparing their resume for submission to a recruiter
- Doing some similar nonwork-related activity

Initially, white-collar productivity was not thought to be measurable, but it is now, and norms for office work have been established. It is now possible to use work measurement techniques in the software industry.

If so, should we set productivity norms for every programming language that is being used by the software development industry? A common belief within the software industry is that programming languages differ vastly from one another. It is a myth that the productivity of programming in different languages varies vastly. Look at the facts:

- All programming languages have facilities for input functions, output functions, data manipulation functions, and other miscellaneous functions. While the syntax and semantics vary, the philosophy remains same—that is, to achieve the given functionality with defined quality in the minimum amount of time. Before you protest, let me state that I have programmed in many languages myself, and I am making this statement from my own personal experience.
- The software is written by programmers proficient in the language being used, with the help of a design document.
- Since programmers write programs with the help of a design document (just as factory workers use a drawing to perform their work), very little creativity is involved, although the work is not purely mechanical and repetitive. The same is true in the case of job-order manufacturing (shipbuilding, aircraft manufacture, construction, etc.) as well.

Another myth is that some programming languages are more complex than others. In my time, I have heard COBOL programmers called the top of the line. Then, by the turn of the century, the same COBOL programming was considered to be at the bottom of the line. I have seen Pascal, C, dBase III Plus, Oracle, and Visual Basic go through similar journeys. When any new programming language emerges on the scene, there are few teachers of that language, and programmers have to educate themselves in order to master and write code in the new language. As time passes, more and more teachers become available, so more programmers learn the language and master it. Any programming language is complex when it is new, but it becomes manageable and easy to master as time elapses. For Java programmers, DotNet is complex and vice versa perhaps, but no programming language is complex by nature.

From where, then, does the belief spring that some languages are more difficult than others? Perhaps it comes from those programmers who have spent a considerable amount of time learning a language on their own, believing they deserve a premium.

Thus the difficulty associated with a programming language is more in learning and mastering it than in using it. The problem organizations face is the lack of availability of programmers skilled in a particular new language. Programmers may say that it takes, for example, more time to produce 100 lines of code in Java than in DotNet, but why should it? Is it because Java requires more characters per line to achieve a given functionality than DotNet does? Or is it because programmers are not as well versed in Java as they are in DotNet? If a programmer says that DotNet may take more lines than Java would to achieve a given functionality, perhaps this is acceptable. But surely the same amount of time would be needed to produce the same number of lines of code, irrespective of the programming language. The reasoning here is

- Both DotNet and Java programmers have similar skill (proficiency) in their respective languages.
- Both are assisted by a (similar) design document.
- Both type at a similar speed.

Then the limiting factor is their typing speed!

A speed of 10,000 keystrokes per hour is the accepted norm for data entry operators. This works out to a typing speed of approximately 35 words per minute (with each word assumed to be five characters on average), which is considered low in typewriting and stenography circles. Perhaps not many programmers practice typing (it is not part of the software engineering curriculum, although in my opinion it should be, as software engineers spend their lives punching keys), so their speed is approximately 15 words per minute.

In using the work measurement technique for factory workers as well, two activities precede and follow the actual work when measuring work, namely:

1. **Setup time (prework)**—The time it takes to receive instructions, collect information, and study the information to understand it
2. **Cleanup time (postwork)**—The time it takes to deliver the output, clarify any issues, and hand over the artifacts

Thus it is both feasible and possible to carry out time studies to set standard times (productivity) for software development activities.

How to Conduct a Time Study in a Software Development Organization

In a software development organization, the work-sampling technique can be employed. Work sampling involves loosely observing employees at work and noting how they spend time on various activities—both productive and non-productive. It is normal to classify nonproductive activities into various categories for analysis purposes. Productive time is then separated from nonproductive activities and is set as the *basic time*. The basic time is corrected with the "rate (pace) of working," which is a percentage of normal working. Consider the following examples of established benchmarks, where the rate of working would be considered 100 percent if:

- In a game of bridge, the hand movement compares well with the motion of dealing cards when the 52 cards are dealt in a minute
- When walking, the rate is 3 miles per hour

Thus it is possible that the rate of working could be more than 100 percent.

The basic time corrected using the rate of working is called the *normal time*. Add to that the *relaxation allowance* based on factors defined by the ILO, and we obtain the *standard time*.

Whereas stopwatches are used for time studies in factories (the operations take only minutes), ordinary watches are adequate for carrying out work sampling for software development activities. Work measurement can be carried out for all seven types of software development activities described earlier in this chapter and productivity set for each of them.

CAPACITY VIS-À-VIS PRODUCTIVITY

As stated at the beginning of this chapter, I am of the opinion that the software development industry confuses "capacity" and "productivity." When dealing with the overall throughput for a facility, we use the term "capacity." For example, we say that an automotive plant has a capacity of 5,000 cars per day or that a shipyard has a capacity of 10 ships per year.

Capacity implies that various activities are performed at different workstations, that each activity may need different skill sets from the staff, and that each worker may have a different productivity (rate of achievement). The term can also refer to the overall output of a facility, such as number of units per a defined time period. In an automotive plant or a shipyard, the workflow is routed through different workstations. Some work takes more time to complete than other work does, and in such cases, these workstations are considered fully utilized. The remaining workstations are considered underutilized and have spare capacity. The capacity of the plant is limited by the fully utilized workstations. Thus, to increase capacity (produce more cars), the plant needs to add to only those workstations that are fully utilized.

Therefore, if an automotive plant has 500 persons working (500 person-days of effort) to produce 5,000 cars per day, and if production has to be increased to 10,000 cars per day, the required manpower and workstations would not double. This is an exercise called *line balancing* and *capacity planning*. It would take less than 1,000 person-days of effort to produce 10,000 cars. It is also not appropriate to say that since it takes 500 person-days to produce 5,000 cars per day, 1 person-day produces 10 cars! The productivity at each workstation differs. The capacity of each workstation needs to be worked out to ensure the desired production rate.

Capacity is finite at each workstation, irrespective of its utilization (for example, a car has five seats regardless of whether just one seat is occupied while it is being driven or all five seats are occupied). A plant is designed for a certain capacity. It is well understood and accepted that some "waste" is built into the system. Producing less would increase the cost per unit, but capacity planning is a different subject altogether. The same is true in software; we need to design a facility for a specified capacity. We need architects, designers, business analysts, programmers, testers, and so on.

To develop (produce) software, the skill sets previously mentioned in this chapter are needed. In practice, a person can be allocated for a minimum period of, say, a day, but a designer cannot be allocated, for example, for eight different activities in a day. Therefore, converting software size using a single figure does not seem to be right.

What needs to be done is this:

1. Determine the software size.
2. Estimate the effort required by each skill set to perform the necessary activities for the software size estimated. Round the effort up to the next person-day.
3. Determine the number of persons needed, and divide the effort among them. Round each effort up to the next person-day. The effort cannot

be rounded down to the next person-day, because the remaining time is lost due to fragmentation and the work still needs to be performed.

4. Sum the efforts of each skill set.
5. Arrive at the total effort needed.

MY RECOMMENDATION FOR HOW TO DETERMINE PRODUCTIVITY

My vote goes to setting up productivity norms using work-sampling techniques. Why? Because the method offers a fair result, arrived at through scientific study by unbiased, independent experts. Setting norms from past project records means accepting data without really knowing the causes for the pace of working (be it slow, average, or fast) and could result in skewed norms, which is not fair to either management or the programmers.

Conducting time studies to set a standard time is fair to both management and staff, as they set the "right" expectations and bring predictability to human endeavor and work results.

SUMMARY

This chapter discusses the software development industry's mistaken perception of the term "productivity," which in reality is "capacity." Productivity should be used in reference to an activity of human endeavor, while capacity should be used in reference to a facility or a plant. Software development consists of a few disparate activities that require persons of different skill sets. This chapter also challenges the myth that one programming language is more complex than another.

There are two means of arriving at productivity for software development activities. One is to derive productivity from past project records, and the second is to conduct productivity studies. This chapter discusses the method for conducting productivity studies to arrive at productivity of software development activities. Appendix D gives a methodology for arriving at productivity using past project records.

This book has free materials available for download from the Web Added Value™ Resource Center at www.jrosspub.com.

SCHEDULE ESTIMATION FOR SOFTWARE DEVELOPMENT PROJECTS

Scheduling is the setting of calendar dates to planned activities. Scheduling is an activity that calls for creativity and human ingenuity. When scheduling a project, we have to understand the following:

- The project consists of a number of activities (tasks), the performance of which results in the execution of the project.
- The project has a number of "milestones," the reaching of which signifies completion of a certain group of activities.
- The project has a start point, which is the project's first milestone, or "start" milestone.
- The project has an end point, which is the project's last milestone, or "end" milestone.
- All other activities in the project have to be performed between the start and end milestones.
- Some of these activities can be performed concurrent (in parallel) to each other.
- Some of these activities need to be performed in sequence (one after the other).

- Some activities can use multiple resources and some cannot.
- There is always a limit to the number of resources that can be deployed for any given activity.

A list of all activities (tasks) and milestones needed to execute and complete the project is commonly known as the work breakdown structure. The first item in this document is the start milestone and the last is the end milestone.

INITIAL WORK BREAKDOWN STRUCTURE

The first step in scheduling a project is the preparation of the work breakdown structure (WBS). Table 11.1 depicts a brief initial WBS for a material management software development project. Of course, a real-life project would have many more activities.

Having prepared the initial WBS, the next step is to determine the sequence of execution of the tasks listed in it. This is achieved by adding another column—the "predecessor" column—to table 11.1, as shown in table 11.2. Note

Table 11.1. WBS example

Task ID	Task description	Effort in person-days
1	Start	0
2	Project initiation	2
3	Project planning	5
4	Requirements analysis	10
5	Software requirements specification	4
6	Design	12
7	Construction of warehouse module	15
8	Construction of purchasing module	12
9	Construction of inventory control module	10
10	Construction of payables module	6
11	Integration	5
12	Integration testing and fixing defects	3
13	System testing	3
14	User acceptance testing	2
15	User documentation	5
16	User training	3
17	Software installation and master data creation	10
18	Pilot run	2
19	Handover and customer sign-off	1
20	End	0

Table 11.2. WBS example with predecessors

Task ID	Task description	Effort in person-days	Predecessor
1	Start	0	
2	Project initiation	2	1
3	Project planning	5	2
4	Requirements analysis	10	3
5	Software requirements specification	4	4
6	Design	12	5
7	Construction of warehouse module	15	6
8	Construction of purchasing module	12	6
9	Construction of inventory control module	10	6
10	Construction of payables module	6	6
11	Integration	5	6, 7, 8, 9, 10
12	Integration testing and fixing defects	3	11
13	System testing	3	12
14	User acceptance testing	2	13
15	User documentation	5	12
16	User training	3	14, 15
17	Software installation and master data creation	10	14
18	Pilot run	2	17
19	Handover and customer sign-off	1	18
20	End	0	19

that "start" would not have any predecessor, as it is the first milestone. The rest of the activities should have one or more predecessors.

WORK BREAKDOWN STRUCTURE WITH PREDECESSORS DEFINED

Looking at table 11.2, we can see not only the predecessor but also the successor for each task. For task 2, the predecessor is task 1 and the successor is task 3. For task 5, the predecessor is task 4 and the successor is task 6. Notice that task 6 is a predecessor for five tasks; that is, five tasks start upon completion of task 6. Task 11 has five predecessors; that is, task 11 cannot start until five tasks that converge on it are completed. Therefore, a task can have multiple predecessors or multiple successors.

Predecessors and successors can be mapped for each task. To create a proper schedule, every task must have one or more predecessors and one or more successors. The exceptions are the start milestone, which would not have any predecessor, and the end milestone, which would not have any successor. Additional milestones can be included in the WBS if they would enhance the team's clarity and understanding.

Notice that task 16 does not have a successor. This is an anomaly which has to be rectified in order to have a proper schedule. If there is no successor to an activity, its successor would be the end milestone; that is, the end milestone can have multiple predecessors.

Now the question of predecessor relationships arises. Look at tasks 2 and 3. Task 3 (project planning) cannot be started unless task 2 (project initiation) is completed. This relationship is called a *finish-to-start relationship*. That is, task 2 has to be finished before task 3 can be started.

Task 11 (integration) can start once task 6 (design) is completed, and other modules can be integrated as and when they are completed. Therefore, there is a finish-to-start relationship between task 6 and task 11. That is, task 11 can start when task 6 is finished, but it cannot be completed until tasks 7, 8, 9, and 10 are completed. This relationship is called a *finish-to-finish relationship*.

Now look at tasks 11 (integration) and 12 (integration testing and fixing defects). Should task 12 wait until all four modules are integrated? It can, but it is not necessary. As and when a module is integrated, its integration can be tested. This is a called a *start-to-start relationship*. That is, task 12 can be started after starting task 11, but with a time lag.

To account for all possible relationships, there is one more I would like to mention, and that is the *start-to-finish* relationship. In this type of relationship, task b must be started in order to finish task a. While there is application for this sort of relationship in other fields, I have not seen its applicability in software development.

Thus, to summarize, there are four types of predecessor relationships:

1. **Finish (predecessor)-to-start (successor)**—Denoted as FS-n, where n is the number of days the successor has to wait after finishing the predecessor. If n is not specified, that means $n = 0$.
2. **Start (predecessor)-to-start (successor)**—Denoted as SS-n, where n is the number of days the successor has to wait after starting the predecessor. If n is not specified, that means $n = 0$.
3. **Finish (predecessor)-to-finish (successor)**—Denoted as FF-n, where n is the number of days the successor has to wait after finishing the predecessor. If n is not specified, that means $n = 0$.
4. **Start (successor)-to-finish (predecessor)**—Denoted as SF-n, where n is the number of days the successor has to wait after starting the

predecessor in order to finish the successor. If n is not specified, that means $n = 0$.

For each of these relationships, a lag (waiting time) before the successor is started can be specified. Here are some examples:

- Task 3 can be started one day after finishing task 2. This means that the relationship of task 3 to predecessor task 2 is finish-to-start with a lag of one day.
- Task 12 can be started two days after starting task 11. This means that the relationship of task 12 to task 11 is start-to-start with a lag of two days.

WORK BREAKDOWN STRUCTURE WITH INITIAL DATES

Once we are done defining the WBS, defining the predecessors and the predecessor relationships, and ensuring that all tasks have predecessors and successors, we are ready to start assigning dates to the tasks. This is depicted in table 11.3. Note the following from the schedule:

- The start date for the start milestone is the project starting date.
- The end date for the end milestone is the project completion date.
- Weekends (Saturday and Sunday) are not counted as working days. Holidays are also excluded. For example, July 4 (American Independence Day) is excluded in task 18.
- Notice that task 3 starts on April 3, while task 2 is completed on April 2—the day before. Why? Because when somebody says that a task will be completed on April 2, it means that it will be completed by the end of the working day on April 2, and therefore the successor can only start on the next day.
- Notice that task 11 (which has five predecessors) starts on May 16, the day after completion of task 6. Task 11 has a finish-to-start relationship with task 6. Task 11 has a finish-to-finish with a two-day lag relationship with the rest of its predecessors. Therefore, task 11 is completed on June 9, two working days after completion of task 7. It is the predecessor that finishes last (on June 5) in all the predecessors of task 11. Because the lag is defined as two days, task 11 is completed on June 9, which is two working days after completion of its last predecessor.

Table 11.3. WBS with initial dates set

Task ID	Task description	Effort in person-days	Predecessor	Start date	Finish date
1	Start	0		1-Apr-08	1-Apr-08
2	Project initiation	2	1	1-Apr-08	2-Apr-08
3	Project planning	5	2	3-Apr-08	9-Apr-08
4	Requirements analysis	10	3	10-Apr-08	23-Apr-08
5	Software requirements specification	4	4	24-Apr-08	29-Apr-08
6	Design	12	5	30-Apr-08	15-May-08
7	Construction of warehouse module	15	6	16-May-08	5-Jun-08
8	Construction of purchasing module	12	6	16-May-08	2-Jun-08
9	Construction of inventory control module	10	6	16-May-08	29-May-08
10	Construction of payables module	6	6	16-May-08	23-May-08
11	Integration	5	6 (FS) 7 (FF-2) 8 (FF-2) 9 (FF-2) 10 (FF-2)	16-May-08	9-Jun-08
12	Integration testing and fixing defects	3	11	10-Jun-08	12-Jun-08
13	System testing	3	12	13-Jun-08	17-Jun-08
14	User acceptance testing	2	13	18-Jun-08	19-Jun-08
15	User documentation	5	12	20-Jun-08	26-Jun-08
16	User training	3	14, 15	27-Jun-08	1-Jul-08
17	Software installation and master data creation	10	14	19-Jun-08	2-Jul-08
18	Pilot run	2	17	3-Jul-08	7-Jul-08
19	Handover and customer sign-off	1	18	8-Jul-08	8-Jul-08l
20	End		16, 19	8-Jul-08	8-Jul-08

■ Notice that no relationship is mentioned for task 16. When no relationship is explicitly mentioned, there is a finish-to-start relationship with no lag. Task 16 has two predecessors—task 14 (completed on June 19) and task 15 (completed on June 26). Therefore, task 16 can start one day after task 15, which is the last of its predecessors to be completed.

■ The end milestone has two predecessors, both of which have to be completed for this milestone to be reached. Therefore, its start (as well as end) date is July 7, the day on which task 19 (which finished last) is completed.

From these explanations, we can draw the following inferences for future use:

■ The start date of an activity depends on its relationship with its predecessors:
   □ In a finish-to-start relationship, the start date depends on the predecessor that finishes last.
   □ In a start-to-start relationship, the start date depends on the predecessor that starts first.
   □ Other relationships have no impact.
■ The end date of an activity depends on, in addition to its duration, the relationship with its predecessors:
   □ In a finish-to-finish relationship, the end date depends on the predecessor that finishes last.
   □ Other relationships have no impact.

WORK BREAKDOWN STRUCTURE WITH RESOURCE ALLOCATION

Notice in table 11.3 that the effort is the same as the duration. This is so if we assume that only one resource is allocated to the project. In real-life projects, multiple resources are allocated to a project, and these resources have different skill sets. Naturally, these differences among the resources result in differences between effort and duration. For example, let's say that coding takes 100 person-days to complete. If one programmer is allocated to the task, the duration would be 100 days. If two are allocated, the duration would be 50 person-days. If four programmers are allocated, the duration would be 25 person-days.

Therefore, a resource column needs to be added to table 11.3 and the duration adjusted to create a realistic schedule. Look at table 11.4. Notice that the duration (effort/number of resources) is allocated for each task. Dates are set based on the duration. Duration depends on the effort in person-days and the number of resources allocated for the activity.

Table 11.4. WBS with resources allocated

Task ID	Task description	Effort in person-days	Resources allocated	Duration	Prede-cessor	Start Date	Finish Date
1	Start	0	0	0		1-Apr-08	1-Apr-08
2	Project initiation	2	1	2	1	1-Apr-08	2-Apr-08
3	Project planning	5	1	5	2	3-Apr-08	9-Apr-08
4	Requirements analysis	10	2	5	3	10-Apr-08	16-Apr-08
5	Software requirements specification	4	1	4	4	17-Apr-08	22-Apr-08
6	Design	12	4	3	5	23-Apr-08	25-Apr-08
7	Construction of warehouse module	15	3	5	6	28-Apr-08	2-May-08
8	Construction of purchasing module	12	4	3	6	28-Apr-08	30-Apr-08
9	Construction of inventory control module	10	2	5	6	28-Apr-08	2-May-08
10	Construction of payables module	6	3	2	6	28-Apr-08	29-Apr-08
11	Integration	5	1	5	6 (FS) 7 (FF-2) 8 (FF-2) 9 (FF-2) 10 (FF-2)	28-Apr-08	6-May-08
12	Integration testing and fixing defects	3	1	3	11	7-May-08	9-May-08
13	System testing	3	1	3	12	12-May-08	14-May-08
14	User acceptance testing	2	1	2	13	15-May-08	16-May-08
15	User documentation	5	1	5	12	12-May-08	16-May-08
16	User training	3	1	3	14, 15	19-May-08	21-May-08
17	Software installation and master data creation	10	2	5	14	19-May-08	23-May-08
18	Pilot run	2	1	2	17	26-May-08	27-May-08

Table 11.4. WBS with resources allocated (continued)

Task ID	Task description	Effort in person-days	Resources allocated	Duration	Prede-cessor	Start Date	Finish Date
19	Handover and customer sign-off	1	1	1	18	28-May-08	28-May-08
20	End		0	0	16, 19	28-May-08	28-May-08

SCHEDULING IN PRACTICE

In practice, we do not have to iterate so many times. We can take advantage of tools such as spreadsheets (Microsoft Excel, for example) and fill information in column by column. We can take advantage of Excel's date arithmetic capability. Specialized software tools such as Primavera, Microsoft Project, and PMPal can assist in scheduling.

Using an automated spreadsheet or specialized scheduling software makes recalculating subsequent schedules easier when the project start date is shifted or any of the tasks change.

GRAPHIC REPRESENTATION OF SCHEDULES

Two types of graphic representation are popularly used:

1. Bar charts (Gantt charts)
2. Network diagrams

A bar chart is shown in figure 11.1. Bar charts can be produced using Microsoft Excel spreadsheets or scheduling packages like Primavera and Microsoft Project.

Figure 11.2 depicts a network diagram. For the sake of brevity, only the task numbers are given in the network diagram.

There are various forms of network diagrams. In figure 11.2, each task is depicted in a circle. In more traditional network diagrams, a task is depicted on an arrow of a network and a circle depicts a milestone. In the form of network diagram currently being used in the software development industry, an arrow represents only a precedence relationship.

The most frequently used depiction of an activity is shown in figure 11.3. It is rectangular in shape and is divided into seven sections. Variations of this

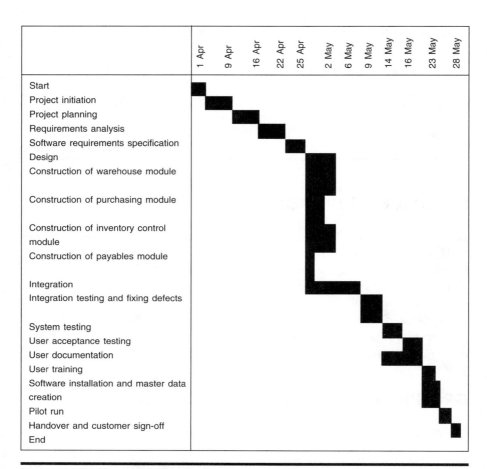

Figure 11.1. Bar chart (Gantt chart)

type of graphic task representation are found in different scheduling software tools. Scheduling can be carried out effectively using such software packages as Microsoft Project, Primavera, PMPal, EstimatorPal, etc.

SUMMARY

This chapter discusses the scheduling of software projects and offers a detailed example of a schedule. Also discussed is how to build an initial WBS, define predecessors, assign dates, and allocate resources to build a full schedule. Graphic representations are also shown.

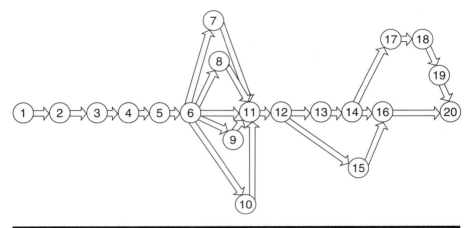

Figure 11.2. Example of a traditional network diagram

Early Start	Duration	Early Finish
Task Name		
Late Start	Slack	Late Finish

Figure 11.3. Popular graphic representation of an activity

12

SOFTWARE DEVELOPMENT COST ESTIMATION

Before embarking on cost estimation and its methods, it is necessary to understand pricing models. Why is this necessary? I have observed that most software estimators confuse cost estimation with pricing, so it is important to understand the difference between the two in order to be able to separate cost estimation decisions from pricing decisions.

Cost estimation is performed to understand how much money the organization has to spend to execute a project. Pricing is performed to understand how much the organization can profit from the project, or in other words, to determine how much the customer is willing to pay for the project.

PRICING MODELS

The following are some of the popular pricing models available to free-to-price organizations (that is, organizations not constrained by a government regulation in the matter of pricing or by market forces setting the price):

- **Cost-plus pricing**—In project pricing, this is considered fair pricing. The organization accounts for all the costs and adds a reasonable profit to the final cost. This method is commonly adopted between partners that have a strong, long-standing bond. The costs of the vendor are transparent to the purchaser.

- **Opportunity pricing**—Under this model, pricing depends on the opportunity presented by the purchaser. If the customer has no other choice than to buy from one organization, that organization charges top dollar. If there is too much competition, the organization may charge a lower price. If there is a prestigious project that would bring a lot of publicity to the organization, it may even price the project at a loss. Within this pricing model are two variants:

  - □ **Penetration pricing**—This model is adopted by a new entrant to a market already overflowing with existing providers. In order to gain a foothold in such a market, the new organization charges a lower price as an incentive to motivate purchasers to buy from it. Sometimes this model is also known as *introductory pricing.*

  - □ **Skimming pricing**—This model is used by an organization that has the advantage of being an early bird in an emerging market. It charges a higher price before competition enters the market and then lowers the price once competition is firmly established.

- **Going rate pricing**—This method is adopted by organizations in fields where there is plenty of competition and the price for a product is well known to purchasers. The model entails pricing the product or service at whatever price the organization envisages other suppliers in the market are offering.

- **Monopolistic pricing**—This model is a variant of going rate pricing. The seller plays up some unique feature of its product, and thus prices the product either higher or lower than the going rate. This model is frequently used when the two-bid system (technical bid and financial bid) is adopted by the purchaser.

- **Oligopolistic pricing**—This model is used when only a limited number of suppliers are present in the market. They collaborate (sometimes forming an association) to establish a fixed price for a product and enforce that price. No matter who the supplier is, the price is the same.

- **Transfer pricing**—This model is adopted by two departments within the same organization. In this scenario, only the actual cost is transferred from one department to another.

- **Loss leader pricing**—This model is adopted by an organization trying to lure clients away from their current vendors. The organization provides a product or service at a loss, speculating that future business will offset this loss and result in more business. Alternatively, the organization offers free publicity or prestige to new buyers, which can be converted into business from other potential buyers.

A request for proposal represents an opportunity for an organization. Either management or marketing considers the opportunity and decides how best to utilize it. The organization may take the opportunity at any cost or, in rare cases, reject it irrespective of the price offered. Therefore, the project-pricing model is always considered an opportunity-pricing model.

The following factors are considered when making a pricing decision:

- **Order book position**—If the organization's plate is empty (that is, it has no ongoing projects at the moment), it could price low so that the project would at least pay its variable costs. If the organization's plate is full and it does not wish to expand its capacity, it may price the project high.
- **Necessity to obtain the order**—Sometimes it is critical to win a particular order, and the organization may price the project low to win the bid. There are several reasons why this scenario may occur:
  - ☐ The project will open up a number of avenues for the organization.
  - ☐ The project will provide a lot of visibility for the organization.
  - ☐ The project will afford the organization a lot of free publicity.
  - ☐ The project will provide an opportunity to train a number of the organization's resources (personnel) in a cutting-edge technology, based on which it can win future orders.
  - ☐ The project will gain a foothold for the organization in a new and lucrative market.
- **Desirability of winning the order**—Sometimes the organization may not want the order and may price the project so high that it is certain not to win the bid. Reasons for this scenario include the following:
  - ☐ The organization does not have the technology to execute the order.
  - ☐ The organization does not wish to associate with the client, as the client may be slow to pay or otherwise have a bad reputation.
  - ☐ The project may involve obsolete technology or technology that is becoming obsolete, and therefore the organization's resources may be uninterested and unwilling to work on it.
- **Stiff competition in the field**—The organization may price the project with a bare minimum profit margin.

- **Monopoly situation**—Sometimes the organization is in the unique position of being the only supplier of a product or service. In such a case, it skims the opportunity and gets as much out of the order as possible.
- **Oligopoly situation**—Sometimes the organization collaborates with other vendors in the market to establish one price for a product or service that is profitable for all vendors involved.
- **Repeat orders**—The organization offers a service to an existing customer at a price that is fair to both the organization and the customer.
- **New market opportunity**—If an order facilitates entry into a new market, either geographical or domain based, the organization will price low.

Thus, pricing is a complex interaction between the above scenarios and the software estimate.

Normally, the steps in project pricing are as follows:

1. The technical team prepares the software estimates (software size, software development effort, and software development schedule) and presents them to the marketing team.
2. The marketing team prepares the cost estimation and presents it to the finance team.
3. The finance team suggests a floor price to the marketing team, below which the project will not be attractive financially.
4. Marketing coordinates pricing with senior management (in some cases, there might be a pricing committee) and determines:
   a. The price to be offered to the potential client
   b. The negotiation margin, if negotiations are foreseen

Therefore, software estimators should not link software estimation to pricing. Pricing is a commercial decision made by marketing in consultation with top management, based on the market opportunity at hand. However, the pricing decision would not go below the estimated cost, as no organization would want to work at a loss unless there are intangible benefits to be gained.

Cost estimation enables the business acquisition team to negotiate the best price possible for the organization. Once the cost to the company is known, the marketers make a decision such that the order will be won with as much profit margin as possible built into the price.

COST OF EFFORT

It is common practice to be asked for and to offer a per-person-hour cost (price) in the software outsourcing industry. How is this cost arrived at? Normally, it is the cost accountant's job to determine the per-person-hour cost. Table 12.1 gives an approximate method for computing per-person-hour cost.

Rounding-off rules are as follows:

- Round off to the nearest whole number
- Round up to the next whole number
- Round off to the nearest multiple of 5 or 10

While it is common to include overhead cost when quoting per-person-hour, this suffers from some drawbacks:

- Projects use staff with varying skills.
- The cost of resources most often varies depending on the skill levels of the staff.
- Some of the direct staff (who are allocated to one project at a time and work on revenue-earning work) are lower cost first-level programmers, while some are in the supervisory, higher cost cadre.

Therefore, it is advisable to estimate staff hours in various categories and add overhead to arrive at staff costs. Table 12.2 shows an example of this process. Other costs also have to be estimated, including the following:

- **Travel**—This includes travel to the client site to collect requirements, coordinate approvals, conduct review meetings, perform installation and rollout of the software developed, etc. Added here are the incidental costs of lodging, meals, local transportation, daily allowance to be paid to the staff on such visits, etc.
- **Special software tools needed for the project**—Sometimes software tools, either specified by the client or dictated by the project's technical requirements, need to be purchased. Included in this cost is any training that is needed to use these tools.
- **Special hardware**—It may be necessary to purchase additional hardware to execute the project. This may include communication equipment to be able to access the client's network, a test bed, etc. The cost of all such tools is included in the cost estimate.

Table 12.1. Sample method for determining per-person-hour cost

Ref. no.	Item description	Amount
1	Yearly cost of direct staff in terms of cost to the company, including salary, benefits, perks, contribution to long-term savings, vacation, etc. (Direct staff excludes all the staff members who do not work on revenue-earning work. Senior management is also excluded from this category. Those in middle management who are allocated to multiple projects concurrently are also excluded.)	X
2	Cost per person-hour (The number of person-hours per year, excluding weekends, holidays, and vacation. Normally, it is 2,000 hours per year for a year with 52 weekends and 2 weeks of vacation, but hours per year could be more or less depending on the number of weekends, holidays, and vacation days.)	$\dfrac{X}{\text{no. of direct staff hours}}$
3	Yearly cost of indirect staff (indirect staff includes senior management and staff that does not work on revenue-earning work, such as human resources, finance, etc.) in terms of cost to the company	A
4	Yearly cost of fixed costs such as rent, depreciation cost of capital equipment, annual maintenance costs, annual cost of debt servicing, etc.	B
5	Yearly cost of expenses such as power, communications, cleaning, supplies, employee goodwill, etc.	C
6	Any yearly miscellaneous costs	D
7	Overhead cost per person-hour	$\dfrac{A + B + C + D}{\text{no. of direct staff hours}}$
8	Per-person-hour cost	Results of #2 + results of #7 rounded off
9	Overhead percentage	$\left(\dfrac{A + B + C + D}{X}\right) 100$

Table 12.2. Cost estimation

Ref. no.	Staff category	Estimated hours Best case	Estimated hours Worst case	Rate per hour	Amount Best case	Amount Worst case
1	Programmers	100	125	15	1,500	1,875
2	Database administrators	25	30	20	500	600
3	Module leaders	30	40	30	900	1,200
4	Graphic designers	10	15	40	400	600
5	Business analysts	30	45	50	1,500	2,250
6	Application experts	15	20	60	900	1,200
7	Total direct effort cost	210	275		5,700	7,725
8	Overhead @ 25 percent				1,425	1,931
9	**Total effort cost**				7,125	9,656

- **Special training**—The cost of any special training needed to execute the project.
- **Other costs**— Any other necessary costs specific to the project are included in the cost estimate.

For each category, enumerate the items in a table and arrive at the costs. Always estimate the best-case and worst-case scenarios. Table 12.3 gives an example of a cost estimation summary.

Provide these two figures to the decision makers. Once they know the cost range, they will be able to manage the profit. If you happen to be that decision maker, the following guidelines will help you to make the cost decision:

- Use your organization's history as a source of information. If your organization has a history of tending toward any of the scenarios

Table 12.3. Cost estimation summary

Ref. no.	Item	Best-case scenario	Worst-case scenario
1	Effort cost	7,125	9,656
2	Travel cost	1,500	1,700
3	Special software tools cost	600	750
4	Special hardware cost	400	500
5	Miscellaneous expenses	100	150
6	**Total cost**	9,725	12,756

listed, then use the most commonly occurring scenario. If you have a large amount of data, the statistical mode is the best measure of central tendency. To avoid the influence of projects executed long ago, it is advisable to consider the projects completed only in the last six months.

■ Research the client's characteristics. Find out if the client has a tendency to overshoot schedules and request many changes, for example, or if the client tends to stick to the original requirements, is prompt to respond, etc. The information you discover can help you decide whether to use the best-case or the worst-case scenario estimate.

■ If you find no evidence to support either the best-case or worst-case possibility, use the average cost of both scenarios.

■ You can also use a cost that lies on either side of the average cost of both scenarios based on your assessment of your delivery team's competence and the client's tendencies.

Then use this estimated cost of the project to price the project based on the pricing model used by your organization.

SUMMARY

This chapter discusses the process of cost estimation for software projects. Pricing models are outlined in detail in order to understand that pricing is a commercial decision based on the opportunity presented by the project. Cost estimation is performed to assist decision makers in setting a winning price and managing the profit. An example of cost estimation is provided to illustrate all the steps, for a better understanding of the process.

13

TEST SIZE AND EFFORT ESTIMATION

Testing is carried out primarily to unearth any and all defects present in the system and to prevent a defective product from reaching the customer. Testing is also carried out to assure the customer that the product conforms to the specifications and functionality initially agreed upon.

Software testing is recognized as an essential activity in software development. Lately, the importance of *independent testing* (testing by persons not involved in the development of software) has been gaining wider acceptance, so much so that software companies specializing only in software testing have been established and are doing well. The increasing complexity and size of software has resulted in more complex testing, as well as more types of testing. As a result, there has been a paradigm shift from estimating testing effort as a percentage of development effort to independent size estimation and effort estimation.

Since testing is so varied and diverse, it is not possible to discuss test effort estimation without a brief introduction to testing itself first.

TESTING BASICS

There are two techniques used in testing: white box testing and black box testing. *White box testing* involves stepping through every line of code and every branch in the code. To use this technique, the tester should be knowledgeable in the software's programming language and should understand the structure of the program. In *black box testing,* a set of inputs is fed to the software, and the outputs delivered by the software are compared with the expected outputs. To use this technique, the tester should be familiar with the functionality of the system and should be able to administer the test.

TESTING SCENARIOS

Independent software testing is carried out in two scenarios:

1. **Project testing/embedded testing**—This is carried out as part of a software development project to ensure that the development work is defect free.
2. **Product testing**—This is carried out on a commercial off-the-shelf software product to ensure that the product works without any defects in a variety of customer scenarios.

Project Testing/Embedded Testing

When software is developed as a product either to be delivered to a single client or intended to be used at a single location, the following testing takes place in addition to software inspections (peer reviews):

- **Unit testing**—This is always carried out by both the person who wrote the code and by an independent peer, using the white box testing technique.
- **Integration testing**—This is carried out either as a one-off (when all integration is completed) or incrementally (whenever one unit of software is integrated, continually until all units are integrated). Black box testing is used for one-off integration testing, and white box testing is used for incremental integration testing.
- **System testing**—This type of testing is carried out to ensure that the software works in all intended target systems.
- **User acceptance testing**—This type of testing is carried out to obtain customer sign-off so that the software can be delivered and payment received.

Optionally, many other tests can be conducted at the request of the customer.

Product Testing

A product is developed as a project first and undergoes all the tests that a project normally undergoes (i.e., unit, integration, and system testing). System testing is carried out more rigorously than unit testing and integration testing and usually on multiple systems. In product testing, other more rigorous tests are carried out in addition to system testing:

- **Load testing**—In Web and multi-user applications, large numbers of users are logged in and using the software in a random manner. The objective of load testing is to see if the software is managing multiple requests and if it is either serving up accurate results or mixing up results. Load testing unearths issues connected with the bandwidth, database, sufficiency of RAM, hard disk, etc.
- **Volume testing**—This test subjects the software to a high volume of data to see if performance degrades as the amount of data increases.
- **Functional testing**—This tests the software to ensure that all its functions are working correctly.
- **End-to-end testing**—In this test, one entity is tracked from birth to death in the application. For example, in a payroll application, an employee joins the system and may be promoted or demoted; salary increases and decreases are effected, kept in abeyance, or transferred; and the employee then either retires, quits, or is terminated. End-to-end testing ensures that the state transitions designed in the application happen as desired.
- **Parallel testing**—This test is conducted on software where a number of users access the same function and are either inputting or requesting the same data. Parallel testing assesses the system's ability to handle requests made at the same time and to preserve the data integrity.
- **Concurrent testing**—Normally with the use of a testing tool, this test is carried out to unearth any issues that occur when two or more users access the same functionality and update or modify the same data with different values at the same time.

  Take, for example, a ticket reservation operation where there is only one seat left on a flight and it is shown to two people as available. When both confirm purchase of the seat at the same time, the system should accept only one request and reject the other one. The system should not collect money from both parties and reserve only one seat, because the credit card transaction of the rejected party would need to be reversed. Scenarios like this are tested with concurrent testing.

■ **Stress testing**—This test stresses the software by making expected resources unavailable, causing deadlock scenarios, not releasing resources, etc., to ensure that the software has built-in routines to handle such stress. Stress testing assesses the software's response to events like machine-reset, Internet disconnection, server timeouts, etc.

■ **Positive testing**—This tests the software as specified and does not try any actions that are not expected from a sincere user, to ensure that all defined functions are performing as expected. Positive testing is performed mostly during customer and end-user acceptance testing.

■ **Negative testing**—This test involves using the software in a manner in which it is not expected to be used, thereby revealing all other hidden defects not related directly to the defined functionality of the software. This is to ensure that even malicious usage will not affect the software or data integrity.

■ **User manual testing**—This test involves using the software in conformance with the user manual to ensure that the manual and the software are in sync with each other.

■ **Deployment testing**—This test simulates the target environment and deploys the software to ensure that the deployment specified is appropriate.

■ **Sanity testing**—This cursory testing ensures that the components of the software package are complete and the appropriate versions. Sanity testing is carried out before delivery to the customer or before making a software build.

■ **Regression testing**—This test is carried out after unearthed defects have been fixed.

■ **Security testing**—This test is carried out to gauge vulnerability against the threat of viruses and spyware.

■ **Performance testing**—This test is carried out to ensure that response times are in an acceptable range.

■ **Usability testing**—This involves testing the software for different types of usage to ensure that it satisfactorily fulfills the requirements of specified functional areas. Usability testing is performed in particular if the software is expected to be used by persons with certain disabilities.

- **Install/uninstall testing**—This tests the software on all target platforms to ensure that install and uninstall operations are satisfactorily performed.
- **Comparison testing**—This involves testing the product against competing products to compare the differences and determine the relative position of the product.
- **Intuitive testing**—This tests the software to see if the product can be used with little or no reference to user guides.

It is rare for all these tests to be carried out on every project executed in an organization, but it is common for product testing to include many of these tests. Every organization carries out some combination of the test types described here, but all organizations conduct at least the following four types of testing:

1. **Functional testing**—To ensure that all functionalities allocated to the software are working and that, when used properly, there are no inaccuracies
2. **Integration testing**—To ensure that the coupling between various software modules is in order
3. **Positive testing/acceptance testing**—To confirm that the customer accepts the software
4. **Load testing**—To ensure that the system does not crash when heavy loads are placed on it

Sometimes organizations carry out the other types of testing, but only if time and budget are available or if mandated.

THE "HOW" OF TESTING

When it comes to the methodology of testing, there are two approaches that can be taken:

1. **Test-cases-based-testing**—This testing is performed when there is a set of test cases, and testing is carried out only against these test cases.
2. **Intuitive testing**—There may be a general description of the functionality and suggestions or guidelines for intuitive testing that ex-

plain how to go about unearthing defects. Testing is carried out using the experience and intuition of the tester. A certain amount of creativity or common sense is expected from the tester.

Every software project has a high-level test plan. For every intended test, there ought to be a set of test cases against which testing is carried out. However, consider the following implications:

- For every numeric data input (including date type data), there needs to be five test cases, using the partitioning and boundary value analysis techniques:
  - □ One value in the acceptable range, which will be accepted by the system
  - □ One value in the above acceptable range, which will be rejected by the system
  - □ One value in the below acceptable range, which will be rejected by the system
  - □ One value at the upper boundary of the acceptable range, which will be accepted by the system
  - □ One value at the lower boundary of the acceptable range, which will be accepted by the system
- Size checks need to be performed for all nonnumeric data, one per data item.
- Logical testing is needed to check for the presence of invalid data, such as two decimal points in numeric data, numeric and special characters in name data fields, etc.

Thus, the test case set for even a moderately complex unit is huge. Modern projects are large in size, and the effort required to prepare exhaustive test case sets is significant. Therefore, it is common to prepare test cases when it is expected that the tester cannot intuitively figure out the test cases on his or her own. The following tests usually come with guidelines:

- Graphical user interface testing
- Navigation testing
- Negative testing
- Load testing
- Stress testing

- Parallel and concurrent testing
- Unit testing

Organizations make use of these guidelines to avoid preparing exhaustive test cases, and it is not uncommon for unit testing to be carried out without any test cases. Integration testing, system testing, and acceptance testing are normally carried out against test cases.

TEST STRATEGY

Before we can start our discussion on test effort estimation, an understanding of test strategy is necessary:

> *Test strategy* is concerned with unearthing as many defects as possible within the allocated budget of time and cost and with maximizing the impact of such testing.

The first step in finalizing the test strategy is to set testing objectives, such as the following:

- **Quality objectives**—These are concerned with the level of unearthing of defects, including:
  - □ All defects, irrespective of time or cost
  - □ Almost all possible defects within the time available, with cost and time being the main criteria
  - □ All possible defects within the time available, with time being the main criterion
- **Customer acceptance objectives**—These relate to the main objective of testing, which is to obtain customer sign-off and be paid by the customer for the product.
- **Product certification objectives**—The tests are carried out as specified by the customer, and the product is certified as requested by the customer. The product can be certified in any of the following areas:
  - □ Free of viruses and spyware
  - □ Functionality
  - □ Usability
  - □ Comparison and relative position
  - □ Product rating

In addition to objectives, the following are also part of test strategy:

- **Types of tests to be included in testing**—Determining which tests need to be conducted to achieve the project objectives
- **How to test**—Determining the methodology of testing, such as:
  - ☐ Test-plan-based and test-case-based testing or intuitive testing
  - ☐ White box or black box testing
  - ☐ Manual testing or tool-based testing
- **Regression testing**—Determining the number of iterations for regression testing (only once or iterated until all defects are fixed)
- **Criteria for successful completion of testing**—Determining whether the criteria are time based and cost based and what the criteria include (discovery of all defects, repair of all defects, etc.)
- **Mechanisms for defect closure and escalation, when necessary**— Such as who will close defects, how to close defects, who can escalate, when and to whom to escalate, how to escalate, etc.
- **Progress reporting**—To be performed during project execution
- **Defect analysis**—Determining whether such analysis as ABC analysis, category analysis, etc. is required

Now we are ready to discuss test effort estimation.

TEST ESTIMATION

> *Test estimation* is the estimation of the testing size, testing effort, testing cost, and testing schedule for a specified software testing project in a specified environment, using defined methods, tools, and techniques.

The key terms and phrases in this definition are

- **Estimation**—Defined in earlier chapters
- **Testing size**—The amount (quantity) of testing that needs to be carried out, although sometimes this may not be estimated, especially in cases of embedded testing (testing is embedded in the software development activity itself) and in cases where it is not necessary
- **Testing effort**—The amount of effort, in either person-days or person-hours, necessary for conducting the tests
- **Testing cost**—The expenses necessary for conducting testing, including person-days of testing effort

■ **Testing schedule**—The duration, in calendar days or months, that is necessary for conducting the tests

With this definition of test estimation in mind, let us look at the approaches to test effort estimation.

APPROACHES TO TEST EFFORT ESTIMATION

The following approaches are available for carrying out test effort estimation:

■ Delphi technique
■ Analogy-based estimation
■ Software-size-based estimation
■ Test-case-enumeration-based estimation
■ Task (activity)-based estimation
■ Testing-size-based estimation

The Delphi technique and analogy-based estimation for estimating software development projects were explained in chapter 5. The techniques are the same for testing projects, so they will not be discussed again here. Let us look at each of the remaining techniques more closely.

Software-Size-Based Estimation

By the time a testing project is in its initiation phase, the software size is already known. This software size is adopted as the testing project size, and then a productivity figure (rate of achievement) needs to be assigned for the software size to arrive at the effort required to execute the testing project.

Let's say it takes 2 person-hours to test software 1 function point in size. Using this norm, we can arrive at the amount of effort required for the testing project based on the size of the software to be tested. Suppose the size of the software to be tested is 1,000 function points. Using the norm of 2 person-hours per function point, the effort for testing the software is 2,000 person-hours.

However, such norms for converting software size to effort are not available from any standards body. Therefore, an organization needs to develop and maintain its own norms using its historical data, adhering rigorously to an established process. Norms must be derived for all the software size measures used in the organization, and the norms must be maintained.

Merits and Demerits of Software-Size-Based Estimation

Merits of software-size-based estimation include the following:

■ It is very simple to learn and use.
■ It arrives at the effort estimate very quickly.
■ If an organization derives and maintains these norms using the right process, the results of effort estimation using this technique can be surprisingly accurate.

These are the demerits of software-size-based estimation:

■ It is too simplistic, and it is not auditable.
■ As a testing size is not available, productivity cannot be derived. However, testing productivity can be derived against the software size.
■ The amount of testing differs depending on the application type, even though the size may be same. For example, a stand-alone software application and a Web-based software application need different amounts of testing even though their sizes may be same. Therefore, the per-software-size norm may not be applicable in all cases.
■ Organizations have to keep meticulous records and employ full-time specialists to derive norms and to maintain them. Timesheets need to be tailored to capture suitable data for deriving these norms accurately. Data collection has to be rigorous.

To use this technique, an organization needs to maintain a table of conversion factors similar to table 13.1.

Table 13.1. Conversion factors

	Person-hours per unit size					
Type of application	Function points	Use case points	Object points	Mark II function point analysis	Feature points	Software size units
Stand-alone	0.25	0.50	0.25	0.50	0.25	0.50
Client-server	0.30	0.65	0.30	0.65	0.30	0.65
3-tier application	0.50	0.90	0.50	0.90	0.50	0.90
4-tier application	0.75	1.10	0.75	1.10	0.75	1.10

Test-Case-Enumeration-Based Estimation

This technique is comprised of the following steps:

1. Enumerate all the test cases.
2. Estimate the testing effort required for each test case, using either person-hours or person-days consistently.
3. Use best-case, normal-case, and worst-case scenarios for estimating effort needed for each test case.
4. Compute the expected effort for each test case using beta distribution:

$$\frac{\text{best case} + \text{worst case} + (4 \times \text{normal case})}{6}$$

5. Sum the following:
   a. Expected times to obtain expected effort estimate for the project
   b. Best-case times to obtain best-case effort estimate
   c. Worst-case times to obtain worst-case effort estimate
   d. Normal-case times to obtain normal-case effort estimate

Table 13.2 is an example of test effort estimation using test case enumeration.

Table 13.2. Test effort estimation example

| Test case ID | Test case description | Effort in person-hours | | | |
		Best case	Worst case	Normal case	Expected
US1	**Set up test environment**				
US1.1	Check test environment	1.00	2.00	1.50	1.500
US1.2	Install screen recorder	0.75	1.50	1.00	1.042
US1.3	Ensure defect-reporting mechanism	1.25	3.00	2.00	2.042
UI1	**Login screen on Internet Explorer**				
UI1.1	Correct login	0.05	0.20	0.10	0.108
UI1.2	Wrong ID and correct password	0.07	0.20	0.10	0.112
UI1.3	Correct ID and wrong password	0.07	0.20	0.10	0.112
UI1.4	Forgot password functionality	0.15	0.30	0.20	0.208
UF2	**Login screen on Firefox**				
UF2.1	Correct login	0.05	0.20	0.10	0.108
UF2.2	Wrong ID and correct password	0.07	0.20	0.10	0.112
UF2.3	Correct ID and wrong password	0.07	0.20	0.10	0.112
UF2.4	Forgot password functionality	0.15	0.30	0.20	0.208
	Total effort estimate	3.68	8.30	5.50	5.663

Merits and Demerits of Test-Case-Enumeration-Based Estimation

Merits of test-case-enumeration-based estimation include the following:

- It is an auditable estimate, as it has an adequate amount of detail so that a peer can review it and ensure that the estimate is comprehensive and as accurate as possible.
- It is fairly accurate due to all test cases being enumerated and three values being used to arrive at the expected effort.
- It facilitates monitoring progress because it marks the test cases completed, and a completion percentage can be computed easily.
- It facilitates giving a range of values for the estimates. For example: *The project can be executed with a minimum effort of X person-hours and a maximum of X person-hours, with an expected effort of X person-hours.* This allows the decision makers to set negotiation margins in their quotes.

These are the demerits of test-case-enumeration-based estimation:

- It has no testing size. Therefore, productivity cannot be derived.
- All test cases and attendant overhead need to be enumerated, which increases the time to complete the estimation.

Task (Activity)-Based Estimation

This method looks at the project from the standpoint of tasks to be performed. Projects are executed in phases, and phases in a testing project are

1. Project initiation
2. Project planning
3. Test planning
4. Test case design
5. Test environment setup
6. Conduct testing, including:
   a. Integration testing
   b. System testing
   c. Load testing
7. Test result logging and reporting
8. Regression testing

9. Test report preparation
10. Project closure

Of course, the phases may differ from project to project and organization to organization.

Each of these phases can be further broken down into tasks. Here is an example:

Phase: Project initiation
1. Study the scope of testing and get any necessary clarification.
2. Identify the (testing) project manager.
3. Retrieve data from similar past projects and make it part of the project dossier.
4. Prepare the project initiation note and obtain approval.
5. Conduct the project kickoff meeting and hand over the project dossier to the project manager.

Phase: Project planning
1. Prepare the effort estimates.
2. Determine the resource requirements.
3. Initiate resource request forms.
4. Prepare the project management plan.
5. Prepare the configuration management plan.
6. Prepare the quality assurance plan.
7. Arrange for peer review of the project plans.
8. Obtain approval of the project plans.
9. Baseline the project plans.

Each phase can be broken down into its constituent tasks, and using these tasks, test effort estimation can be carried out. The following are the steps in task-based effort estimation:

1. Assign durations for each of the tasks, in either person-hours or person-days consistently.
2. Use three time estimates (best-case, worst-case, and normal-case scenarios) for each task.
3. Compute the expected time using the formula

$$\frac{\text{best case} + \text{worst case} + (4 \times \text{normal case})}{6}$$

4. Make adjustments for project complexity, familiarity with the platform, skill of the developers, tools usage, etc.
5. Sum the total effort estimate for the project:
   a. Expected times to obtain expected effort estimate for the project
   b. Best-case times to obtain best-case effort estimate
   c. Worst-case times to obtain worst-case effort estimate
   d. Normal-case times to obtain normal-case effort estimate
6. If in doubt about the result, use the Delphi technique to validate the estimate.

Table 13.3 shows an example of task-based effort estimation for testing projects.

Merits and Demerits of Task-Based Estimation

Merits of task-based estimation include the following:

- It most closely reflects the way projects are currently executed.
- It takes into consideration all the activities that are performed and gives effort estimates as accurately as practicable.
- It offers an adequate amount of detail, making it amenable to review, audit, and postmortem analysis, by comparing the actual values with estimated values.
- It is simple to use and makes preparing an estimate easy.
- It makes monitoring project progress easy because it marks completed tasks.
- It is suitable to use with analogy-based test effort estimation.

These are the demerits of task-based estimation:

- Testing size is not computed. Therefore, testing productivity cannot be derived.

ISSUES IN SIZING TESTING PROJECTS

When we attempt to specify a unit of measure, there must be a clear definition of what is included in it. There must also be a means to measure the size for which we are specifying a unit of measure. Then there must be some uniformity

Table 13.3. Task-based estimation example

Task ID	Phase	Task	Effort in person-hours			
			Best case	Worst case	Normal case	Expected
1	Test planning	Study specifications	2.00	5.00	3.00	3.167
2	Test planning	Determine types of tests to be executed	0.50	1.00	0.65	0.683
3	Test planning	Determine test environment	0.50	1.00	0.65	0.683
4	Test planning	Estimate testing project size, effort, cost, and schedule	2.00	4.00	3.00	3.000
5	Test planning	Determine team size	0.50	1.25	0.75	0.792
6	Test planning	Review of estimation	1.00	2.00	1.50	1.500
7	Test planning	Approval of estimation	0.50	2.00	0.75	0.917
8	Design test cases	Design test cases for module 1	5.00	8.00	6.00	6.167
9	Design test cases	Design test cases for module 2	6.00	9.00	7.00	7.167
10	Design test cases	Design test cases for module 3	4.00	6.00	5.00	5.000
11	Conduct tests	Conduct tests for module 1	15.00	18.00	16.00	16.167
12	Conduct tests	Conduct tests for module 2	16.00	19.00	17.00	17.167
13	Conduct tests	Conduct tests for module 3	14.00	16.00	15.00	15.000
14	Defect report	Defect report for module 1	1.00	2.00	1.50	1.500
	Total effort estimate		68.00	94.25	77.80	78.908

in the testing practices, specifically in the preparation of test plans, comprehensiveness of test cases, the types of testing carried out, and the availability of empirical data, to normalize various situations to a common measure. The following aspects need consideration:

- **Type of application**—Stand-alone, client-server, or Web based
- **Type of testing**—White box or black box
- **Stage of testing**—Unit, integration, system

- **Purpose of testing**—Reliability, client acceptance, to ensure functionality
- **Test case coverage**—How much is covered by test cases and how much is left to the intuition of the tester
- **Definition of test case granularity**—Whether one input field tested with five input values is one test case or five test cases
- **Size of the test cases**—Because size varies at the unit, integration, and system levels, a normalization factor is needed to bring them all to a common size
- **Usage of tools**—Impact of tools and the effort needed to program them
- **Environmental factors**—Tester experience and knowledge, complexity of the application, resources (time and budget) allowed for testing, existence of a clean testing environment, etc. and the impact of these factors on testing
- **Code walk-through**—Whether done before testing software in the organization

The literature and practices I have seen so far do not suggest that all these aspects are well considered or covered when defining the size measure for testing effort. Is size measure necessary to estimate testing effort? No, testing effort can be estimated using the estimation techniques mentioned, but the size measure is essential for being able to make comparisons between two projects, as it is important to assess the reasonableness of the effort estimates. Size measure also facilitates computation of testing productivity, or rate of achievement.

Who Needs Test Size Estimation?

1. **Testing organizations**—Their main line of business is to test software created by others and to certify the product. Their objective is to ensure that the product meets the customer specifications and expectations. This test case set carries out the following:
   a. Black box testing (mainly)
   b. Functional testing
   c. System testing
   d. Negative testing
   e. Regression testing
2. **Customers**—They have entrusted their software development to a vendor, and their objective is to ensure that they get what they pay for.

SIZING A TESTING PROJECT

"Test point" is a catchy term for the unit of measure for testing size and effort estimation, and it is popular among software developers and testers for sizing software-testing projects. I prefer software test unit (STU) over test point (the argument for using "unit" over "point" for size measures was presented in chapter 2). STU can be extracted from a software size estimate.

> *STU is a size measure for measuring the size of a software testing project. It is equivalent to a normalized test case that has one input and one corresponding output.*

It is common knowledge that test cases differ widely in terms of complexity and the activities necessary to execute them. Therefore, test cases need to be normalized, just as function points are normalized to one common measure, using weighting factors. There are currently no agreed-upon measures for normalizing test cases to a common size. The question also remains as to what their relationship is to other software size measures, such as function points or use case points. Would it be fair to say that 1 adjusted function point results in 1 normalized STU? Perhaps we could say that 1 adjusted function point results in 1 (or 1.2, 1.3, etc.) STU.

Many types of testing are carried out on software. Is there a standard for which tests should be used for a testing project? I am afraid there is no agreement on this matter either. Generally, though not always, a testing project includes integration testing, system testing, and acceptance testing—all using the black box testing technique.

But the reality could be different. The variety in applications on which testing depends is significantly large. There is no standard, agreed-upon method for normalization between various application types. Testing types vary from project to project, and there is no standard to refer to regarding the type of testing that should be carried out on any given project. There is barely enough research and empirical data available from which accurate guidelines can be drawn, as the profession of independent testing itself is still in its nascent stages. However, we can estimate STU by converting the software size estimate, using a set of conversion factors and adjusting the STU size using various weights.

Weights

The following weights (all project specific) could be considered when converting the software size estimate:

1. Application weight
2. Programming language weight
3. Weights for each type of testing, namely:
   a. Unit testing
   b. Integration testing
   c. System testing
   d. Acceptance testing (positive testing)
   e. Load testing
   f. Parallel testing
   g. Stress testing
   h. End-to-end testing
   i. Functional testing (negative testing)

STU has a weight equal to 1 when the combined weight of integration, system, and acceptance testing is equal to 1. That is, the sum of the weights of these three tests cannot be more than 1 or less than 1. When other tests are added to the project, their weights may be assigned and added to the STU weight. Organizations need to compile weight data for all these tests and maintain them in-house by comparing the estimated values with actual values at the end of every testing project, once a rigorous causal analysis for each case has been conducted.

Use of testing tools is expected to reduce the effort, even though some are of the opinion that tools do not reduce the effort for the first iteration of testing. Perhaps this is true, but it really depends on the tool itself. Therefore, the weight for tools usage should also be assigned based on the tool itself and the project in question. A weight of 1 for tools usage indicates that the tool will not have any impact on the effort required for testing. A weight of more than 1 indicates that the tool would increase the testing effort, and a weight of less than 1 indicates that the tool would reduce the testing effort.

If unit testing is included in the proposed tests for the project, another weight needs to be assigned for the programming language used to develop the code. This means independent unit testing carried out by a person who did not write the code. These are the reasons for this additional weight:

1. Unit testing is white box testing—that is, from within the code.
2. The development environment for different languages differs from one to another and differs in the amount of effort required for the testing project.

Table 13.4. Software test unit estimation example

Ref. no.	Aspect	Test points
1	Product size in function points	2,500
2	Conversion factor (STU per function point)	4.5
3	Unadjusted software test units	11,250
4	Application weight for client-server application	1.1
5	Composite weight factor	1.375
6	Adjusted software test units	15,468.75
7	Productivity factor in person-hours per STU	0.2
	Test effort in person-hours	3,093.75

The methodology for computing the testing project size in STU follows. The software size is being used as the basic input for this model:

1. Use an existing software development size.
2. Convert the software size to unadjusted STU using a conversion factor based on the application type.
3. Compute the composite weight factor:
   a. Sum all individual weights of the selected tests.
   b. Multiply the sum of weights by the application weight.
   c. Multiply the sum of weights by the language weight if unit testing is selected.
   d. Multiply the sum of weights by the tools weight if tools usage is selected.
4. Multiply the unadjusted STU by the composite weight factor to obtain the testing size in STU.
5. Compute the testing effort in person-hours by multiplying the STU size by the productivity factor. The productivity factor indicates the amount of time for a test engineer to complete the testing of one STU.

Table 13.4 illustrates STU estimation. Table 13.5 gives the various test weights used in computing the composite weight factor in table 13.4.

Merits and Demerits of Software Test Unit Estimation

Merits of STU estimation include the following:

Table 13.5. Test weights

Ref. no.	Aspect	Test weights
1	Functional test	0.35
2	System test	0.30
3	Acceptance test	0.20
4	Virus-free test	0.20
5	Spyware-free test	0.20
	Total weight	**1.25**

■ It facilitates computation of productivity, comparison, and benchmarking because size is estimated.
■ It is useful in analogy-based estimation.

These are the demerits of STU estimation:

■ It is not as simple as other test effort estimation methods.
■ There is no universally accepted or benchmarked data available on various weights used in the method. This data has to be developed and maintained in-house, adhering to rigorous methodology and record-keeping, which can result in more overhead for the organization.
■ Timesheets have to be oriented toward deriving the required data.

Well, nothing good ever comes free or easy, as they say. Such is the case with STU estimation for sizing testing projects. One needs to spend effort and time to set the norms, as one would have to do in any other case. (A software tool for estimating software testing project size, effort, cost, and schedule is available from the Web Added Value™ Download Resource Center at www.jrosspub.com.)

FINAL WORDS ABOUT TEST EFFORT ESTIMATION

Here is an area where it is obvious that further work is necessary. However, there are methods that make it possible to estimate the effort required to execute testing projects. STU estimation is emerging as a valid method for sizing software-testing projects.

It is suggested that a testing project be scheduled in the same way that software development projects are scheduled, with resources allocated and the schedule reworked with resource constraints. Only then should a commitment to schedule and effort be given to decision makers for further use. It is also suggested that the presentation of test effort estimate be subjected to the format suggested for software development project estimates, to ensure that all aspects of estimation are communicated to the decision makers.

SUMMARY

This chapter looks at estimation of effort for testing projects. Methods of arriving at testing effort from software size, enumeration of all test cases, Delphi estimation, analogy-based estimation, and task-based estimation are discussed. The use of the STU is recommended for estimating testing size, and a methodology is presented for estimating STU for a software-testing project.

PITFALLS AND BEST PRACTICES IN SOFTWARE ESTIMATION

In the software development industry, we often hear that software estimates vary from 25 to 200 percent! Is such a huge range unavoidable? Well, 30 years back, what one often heard was, "Estimate, add a safety factor of 100 percent, then multiply that by 2.5—and pray to God that the developers meet it."

In those days, lines of code was the predominantly used software size measure, and though other size measures have come about, software size estimation still continues to dodge the accuracy needed in estimation. In all these years, if there is one thing that has given credence to Parkinson's first law—*work expands to meet the time available for its completion*, it is software development and project execution.

We can minimize the problem and narrow down the variance between actual values and estimated values by following best practices, thus avoiding the pitfalls of software estimation. How to do this is discussed below.

There are two sides to the coin of software estimation success and failure:

1. Proper and methodical estimation coupled with well-developed and maintained norms
2. Tight project execution with proper controls, operated within the assumptions made during the estimation

The variances between estimated values and actual values can be the result of shortfalls either in the estimation process or in the norms (or both) or due to lax project management or project management process—or all the above. While I am not trying to exonerate project execution from being a possible culprit for variance between estimated and actual values, I am focusing on the organizational pitfalls in software estimation that can render estimated values erroneous.

PITFALLS IN SOFTWARE ESTIMATION

The following are the most frequent pitfalls into which I have seen software development organizations fall.

Inexperienced Estimators

Who is the estimator? The answer is simple: whoever is carrying out the activity of estimation. But are there any key attributes that make an estimator a *good* estimator? Yes, I say.

First and foremost, the estimator should be a software engineer who has risen to a project leader level. The estimator must be experienced in software development work in general and in the domain of the project in question in particular. The estimator should also be able to properly break a project down into its constituent components, be trained in the art and science of software estimation, and be thorough in all that he or she does.

I have seen many cases where a software engineer with a couple of years of experience tries to carry out software estimation. It is my opinion that no matter how bright that engineer may be and regardless of from which premier institution he or she may have graduated, that software engineer is not the right choice to carry out software estimation. He or she simply does not have the necessary real-life experience that can only come from being involved in multiple projects. A software estimator needs to be able to code programs, lead small teams as a module leader (senior programmer), and then grow to manage projects as a project leader. Once a software engineer has this experience, then he or she is qualified to carry out software estimation.

A person at a programmer level is competent to develop an efficient and effective program unit and achieve desired levels of productivity and defect injection in that program unit. The programmer's knowledge about productivity and quality is limited to his or her own personal capability—he or she does not know how others are performing. Therefore, a programmer is not the right person to carry out software estimation.

A senior programmer, through mentoring others in developing efficient and effective software, learns and comes to understand the differences in productivity levels and defect injection levels of different programmers. That knowledge, however, is limited to one or a few projects in which he or she has been involved. Therefore, even a senior programmer is not the right choice for entrusting software estimation activity. However, a senior programmer is a better choice than a programmer.

A project leader learns and comes to understand functional decomposition of projects into their constituent modules and software artifacts. Based on the projects he or she has executed, a project leader has learned the variances in the skill levels, effort levels, productivity, and quality of different persons in different projects. After executing a few projects, a project leader is ready to be an estimator, as he or she has converted user specifications into software artifacts and thereby has gained expertise in both sides of software development—requirements and software. Therefore, a project leader is the right choice for carrying out software estimation. Many organizations use the designations project manager and project leader interchangeably; therefore, when I refer to a project leader, it means that a project manager is also the right choice for carrying out software estimation.

Software estimation carried out by inexperienced estimators is one major cause of software estimation going awry.

Lack of Training

Software estimators need to be thoroughly trained in the following five areas before being able to competently take on an estimation project:

1. Concepts of estimation in general
2. Techniques of software size estimation in particular
3. Handling uncertainty
4. Functional decomposition
5. Productivity concepts

There are no certification agencies for software estimation other than the International Function Point Users Group (IFPUG), which offers certification in function point usage only. Though function point is a commonly used unit of measure for software size, it is not the only one; use case points, object points, Mark II function point analysis, and software size units are others, and they have been outlined and discussed in previous chapters of this book. Also, function point analysis is not software estimation—it is only a part of software estimation. Anyone who knows the IFPUG's *Counting Practices Manual* by heart can become certified in function point usage, and while such a person may be an expert in function point analysis, that certainly does not mean he or she is an expert in software estimation.

Therefore, training in software estimation is a prerequisite even for Certified Function Point Specialists. Preferably, the trainer should be a software engineer who has done software estimation within the organization, but the cardinal rule is that the trainer be an *experienced estimator*. To my knowledge, such training is the exception rather than the rule in many organizations.

Lack of Historical Data

For estimation to be accurate, an organization must initiate and maintain a knowledge repository, which should contain, among other artifacts, estimation-related data such as:

- Project estimates
- Actual values of software size, effort, cost, and schedule, derived from projects, after adjustment for assignable causes of variance
- Causal analysis of variances between estimated and actual values
- Adjustment of actual values based on causal analysis for use in future projects
- Productivity norms for various:
  - □ Application domains
  - □ Software development platforms
  - □ Software size measures, such as function points, use case points, object points, Mark II function point analysis, and software size units

For this data to assist estimators in arriving at more accurate software estimates, the knowledge repository should be organized in such a way that it is easily accessible, and the data it contains should have been validated previously. Many organizations claim to have such an initiative set up, but in reality, this resource of information is not very comprehensive.

Inadequate Duration for Estimation

It may sound improbable, but the normal time allowed for software estimation is about one to two calendar days. A week is a luxury—rarely would such time be allowed for software estimation. When the time allowed is short, shortcuts are usually resorted to in order to meet the deadline. Peer review may have to be abandoned, or just a cursory review may be performed. Managerial review itself may become hasty. In addition, the estimator may not have adequate time to think through the project scope, to ask for clarification to bridge any gaps in specifications, to understand the project, or to locate and refer to data from past projects. As the adage goes, "haste makes waste," and it is not conducive to producing high-quality estimates upon which project execution can rely.

Preparing a software estimate remains in the creative domain. By making available a comprehensive knowledge repository, estimation process, training in estimating, and estimation tools, estimate variances can be brought down to predictable levels. Still, adequate time must be allowed for estimation as well as for reviews.

What is a reasonable amount of time to make an estimate? This is a very difficult question to answer without saying "it depends . . ." It depends on the size of the project. I would say that a reasonable amount of time is at least three business days for a small software project and more for medium-size and bigger software projects. This is one of the norms that should find its place in an organization's knowledge repository.

Nonconformance to Reviews

As with any other software development activity, reviews are essential for software estimation. I advocate two types of reviews:

1. **Peer review**—This review should be conducted by an estimator on a similar level, who has similar experience and, more importantly, who has knowledge in the application domain. This is a closer review, focused on details at the micro level.
2. **Managerial review**—This review should be conducted by a person senior to the estimator. This reviewer will focus on macro details, such as productivity and software size, effort, cost, and schedule, at an overall level, using his or her past experience and highly developed hunches.

Both types of review add value and reveal errors that are not so obvious. Errors not obvious in a peer review are obvious in a managerial review and vice versa. Oftentimes, one of these reviews—usually the peer review—is skipped. I strongly advocate not skipping either of these reviews.

Not Measuring the Software Size of the Software Product Delivered

While it is common to size software during project acquisition, it is not common to collect the actual values for software estimation, especially the software size. Effort comes from the timesheets, cost comes from the finance department, and schedule is monitored by the client and escalated in cases of slippage. What seems to escape the attention of everyone is the software size. To obtain the actual software size, a member of the project team has to size the product delivered at the end of the project.

In my experience, determining the size of the software product actually built and delivered is the exception. In the absence of this vital piece of information, it is not possible to derive productivity. If productivity is derived based on the estimated software size, as is the normal practice, the productivity figures can never be right. When erroneously derived productivity figures are used, obviously the estimates cannot be right as well. This is one pitfall I have observed in most organizations.

Lack of Causal Analysis of Variances

Conducting a true project postmortem has yet to become a universal custom within software development organizations. It is usually left to the project manager to document the best practices, lessons learned, and causal analysis of variations between estimated and actual values of the software product, which include not just software estimation but many other aspects, such as requirements.

Final causal analysis ought to be carried out by independent entities that are trained in analysis techniques such as critical examination and statistical analyses (such as correlation, goodness of fit, interpolation, extrapolation, etc.). Causal analysis also needs to be carried out at the organizational level for all projects so that trends and patterns, if any, can be detected. The trend analysis technique can expose organizational-level shortfalls and shed light upon opportunities for improvement in organizational processes.

It is my observation that conducting professional and thorough causal analysis with respect to variances between actual values and estimated values is the exception rather than the rule in many organizations.

Usage of a Single Productivity Figure

Normal practice is to apply one productivity figure to convert software size to software development effort. For example, use 10 person-hours per function point and multiply the software size by this norm to obtain the software development effort. Software development has moved away from one software engineer being a jack-of-all-trades and performing all activities related to software development. Software development now requires four distinct skill sets—if not more, namely:

1. **Requirements analysis**—Normally conducted by business analysts
2. **Software design**—Normally carried out by software architects
3. **Construction**—Normally carried out by programmers
4. **Software testing**—Normally carried out by testers

Each of these skill sets is highly specialized, has different costs associated with it, and takes different amounts of time to perform for different projects.

Some projects are construction intensive, while some or design intensive. Some may consume more effort in requirements elicitation, and others may take much more time in testing. I therefore advocate the application of four productivity figures to convert the software size into software development effort.

Again, it is rare in most organizations with which I am familiar that this method is applied to derive software development effort from estimated software size.

Absence of Software Estimation Tools

More often than not, software estimates are done using spreadsheets such as Microsoft Excel. There is no question that a spreadsheet is an excellent tool, but each estimate is saved in a separate file. Storing files is easy, but locating and retrieving the right file when needed is not. Retrieving a file that you created may be simple, but when multiple people create files for estimates using different naming conventions, retrieving the required estimate becomes exceedingly difficult and time consuming.

Another potential problem with using spreadsheets arises when an estimator needs to find the methodology (i.e., the formulas, complexity rules, size adjustment factors, etc.) used to arrive at a past estimate in order to apply it to arrive at a new estimate. Certain methods (function points for example) use seven worksheets. Even if an existing estimate is used and saved as a new estimate, the modifications to the existing estimate, if not done carefully, can introduce errors in the new estimate. Collaboration between software size and effort estimation with cost estimation and schedule estimation is also difficult to achieve with spreadsheets.

Software estimation tools resolve these issues. A software estimation tool stores all estimates within the tool itself, and retrieval of estimates becomes easier. It also alleviates the issue of finding the formulas and the estimation methodology, as such information is built into the tool itself.

Tools improve the productivity and quality of preparing software estimates. They provide for collaboration among all four aspects of estimation: software size, effort, cost, and schedule.

Over- or Underestimation

This is another common pitfall in the practice of estimation. Marketing wants a lower estimate to gain a competitive edge. The project team wants a higher estimate so as to have enough time to deliver a perfect product. This conflict, if not well managed, leads to erroneous estimates.

The first factor that can lead to overestimation is when the estimate is influenced by commercial decisions. It should be propagated throughout the organization that price and delivery schedule commitments are commercial decisions and that estimates should not be influenced by them. If the estimated schedule is longer than the delivery date committed to, ways to improve upon the delivery schedule need to be found. In most cases, this can be achieved by an infusion of more resources, temporary expansion of capacity by working overtime, or by subcontracting a portion of the work. The project teams and estimators must be assured that the estimate is not linked to commercial decisions, thus promoting their confidence and discouraging any chance of overestimation.

The second factor that leads to overestimation is when management expects no variance between the estimated and actual values or at least when the project team *thinks* that is management's expectation. Management needs to dispel this misconception and make its expectations clear to the project team.

The third factor that causes overestimation is marketing's or management's use of ballpark estimates as real estimates. Ballpark estimates are needed sometimes (for example, temporarily at the beginning of a project acquisition), but if a project is realized based on a ballpark estimate, it must be reestimated immediately before work on the project starts. This new estimate must be the one used in all matters relating to project monitoring. Only in extreme circumstances, such as when there is a lack of time to prepare a comprehensive estimate (one that includes all aspects of estimation), should a ballpark estimate be used. Even in such circumstances, however, it should be understood by all parties involved that if the project is acquired, a comprehensive estimate will be prepared, and the project will be monitored based on this new, comprehensive estimate. Otherwise, ballpark estimates should not be used at all.

One factor that leads to underestimation is marketing's or management's belief that the estimate includes a buffer. Marketing and management often remove this buffer when considering price and delivery schedules. It is sometimes true that an estimate includes a buffer, but even so, the question remains as to how much of the buffer should be removed when price and schedule are being determined. Some of the buffer has to remain to absorb unforeseen issues that arise during project execution.

Another factor that results in underestimation is when the project scope is misunderstood by the estimator. This could also result in overestimation. It is essential that the estimator obtain clarification to understand the project scope clearly before starting to estimate. A peer review will go a long way toward filling in gaps for a thorough understanding of the project scope.

Management ought to encourage right-sizing estimates by creating an environment conducive to doing so in the organization.

BEST PRACTICES IN SOFTWARE ESTIMATION

The following best practices were discussed in the previous section on common pitfalls in software estimation, but they are reiterated here for quick reference:

1. Only experienced persons at the level of project leader and above carry out software estimation work.
2. All estimators are trained in the art and science of software estimation by experienced estimators, preferably from within the organization.
3. Historical data, validated through rigorous causal analysis at both the project level and the organizational level, is maintained in conformance with a well-defined knowledge repository process and is made available to estimators in an easy-to-retrieve manner.
4. Adequate time is allowed for making software estimates.
5. Both peer reviews and managerial reviews are mandatory.
6. The software size of the software product delivered is always measured after project execution is completed, and productivity is derived from this size.

7. Causal analysis of the variance between estimated values and actual values is always carried out before adjusting the organizational norms.

8. To convert software size into software development effort, more than one productivity figure is applied.

9. Software estimation tools, which are evaluated in conformance with a well-defined tool evaluation process, are made available to software estimators. Chapter 15 of this book discusses the criteria for selecting a software estimation tool. All estimators are trained in the usage of such tools to derive maximum effectiveness in estimation.

10. An environment conducive to building the confidence of estimators is maintained by the organization, where estimators do not feel the need to build unnecessary buffers into their estimates. The estimates subjected to both peer reviews and managerial reviews are treated as sacrosanct for the purposes of project execution. Pricing is recognized as a commercial decision within the organization, thereby discouraging any possibility of under- or overestimation.

11. The practice of using ballpark estimates to monitor projects needs to be discouraged.

In addition to these best practices, there are others that should be discussed.

Organizational Support for Software Estimation

The organization plays a significant role in fostering best practices in software estimation. Many of the practices essential to the success of software estimation can only be performed at the organizational level. These are outlined below.

Having a Defined Process for Software Estimation

Definition of a good process for software estimation is essential for arriving at accurate and reliable software estimates. A process provides guidance for the new estimator, a set of reference documentation for the experienced estimator, and a checklist for the reviewers. A well-defined software estimation process ought to include procedures, guidelines, formats, templates, and checklists. These aspects are discussed in greater detail later in this chapter.

Knowledge Repository

An organization's knowledge repository should include an estimates repository, which should include every estimate ever prepared in the organization, along with their actual values and causal analysis of variance between actual and estimated values. Validated values are recorded in the repository for all cases where a project was awarded to the organization based on the estimate. In cases where a project was not awarded based on the estimate, an analysis should have been performed and the results recorded in the repository. Such causal analysis helps to determine what a winning estimate would have been. All the data in an estimates repository helps an organization to benchmark against other organizations.

Setting Productivity Norms

Most of the practices I have seen in organizations and most of the literature I have studied indicate the use of historical records to arrive at productivity norms. Appendix D outlines a methodology for using empirical methods to derive norms from past records.

Empirical data—collected and sifted diligently, analyzed scrupulously, and with norms determined to conform to a well-defined process—is also used for setting productivity norms. However, this method has the following drawbacks:

- Past data tells us what was achieved, not what should have been achieved.
- There is no way to infer whether the achievement was the "right" achievement. That is, the productivity figure could represent either underachievement or overachievement.
- The law of averages can help to arrive at a more accurate productivity figure, but only if there is a very large quantity of data. To illustrate, if you toss a coin 25 times, the results may not necessarily be 50 percent heads and 50 percent tails, but if you toss a coin a million times, the ratio of heads to tails would certainly hover close to 50 percent.

  Normally, software development organizations infer and set norms based on small amounts of data. When the volume of data is not large, skewness creeps in and extreme values influence the average. Norms cannot be determined until, say, a thousand projects have been executed in order for the law of averages to work its magic.
- Although using empirical data is not the right method to set productivity norms, past records should be used to validate existing norms and to adjust them.

What is the solution, then? The solution that industries have adopted (except the software development industry) is industrial engineering studies. That's right—those studies that have been setting productivity norms for the manufacturing and construction industries, in fact all other industries—for over 50 years!

Some portions of software development, such as development of system software or software design, are still considered part of the creative domain, but the rest of the work is now largely regarded as white-collar work. Most white-collar work has been studied and productivity norms have been set. Therefore, I am of the opinion that most software development work can also be studied and that productivity norms can also be set by using industrial engineering techniques.

The industrial engineering techniques that readily come to mind for setting productivity norms in the software development industry are

- Work sampling
- Synthesis
- Analytical estimation

I advocate that productivity norms be set based on industrial engineering studies, at least initially. I also advocate that these norms be validated through analysis of historical records. I consider this a best practice.

Unit of Measure for Measuring Software Size

Because a software development organization executes different projects, it sometimes becomes necessary for estimates for different projects to be prepared in different units of measure. By all means, I accept this. What I suggest is that an organization standardize and use one unit of software size measure. By this I mean:

- Whenever possible, the organization should use a standard unit of measure.
- When it becomes essential to use a unit of measure other than the established standard, by all means use it, but convert the software size into the organization's standard unit of measure using a conversion factor for internal records. Many software estimation tools allow for such conversion, and the organization can develop and maintain these conversion factors.

A standard unit of measure allows for the benchmarking of projects in terms of productivity and quality. Productivity can be computed at the organizational level (e.g., 6 hours per function point). A standard unit of measure also facilitates computation of quality metrics for the organization in terms of defect density per unit of measure (e.g., 0.1 defect per function point). With this measurement of software size and quality, it becomes possible to determine if the organization is improving in real terms, meaning free from factors such as inflation, currency conversion rate, etc.

Single Estimate or a Range of Estimates

The normal practice is to present only one set of figures. This is fine if the situation is deterministic, which means we know with certainty the size and effort required. This certainty can only come about through maturity of the process, as can be found in the construction field. Construction is an ancient activity; plenty of studies have been carried out and productivity levels validated. The units of measure used in construction are also well defined and universally accepted. The same can be said of some areas of manufacturing. A large body of knowledge in these two industries has been collected through the scientific method and has been validated through research. Therefore, these fields and others similar to them can afford to be deterministic.

When it comes to software development, however, there is no universal agreement on any units of measure for software size or for productivity figures. True, much research has been carried out and there is a body of knowledge available, but whether it will stand the scrutiny of the scientific method is doubtful. Therefore, using deterministic methods and giving only one figure each for software size, effort, cost, and schedule is stretching it a bit.

Even when cost estimates are prepared in the construction industry, which is considered deterministic in the matter of estimation, the estimates need to present costs in the three figures specified by the Construction Specifications Institute, the de facto standard for cost estimation of construction projects in the United States. These three figures are

1. Normal estimate
2. Pessimistic estimate—10 percent above the normal estimate
3. Optimistic estimate—10 percent lower than the normal estimate

If the construction industry—a field supported by a large body of validated knowledge and with a central body that provides validated data—needs three estimates, how is it that the software industry views using a single deterministic estimate as acceptable? It is more appropriate to present estimates (of software size, software development effort, project cost, and project schedule) in three figures, namely:

1. Normal-case scenario estimates
2. Best-case scenario estimates
3. Worst-case scenario estimates

I strongly advocate this presentation—a range of three values—as a best practice.

SOFTWARE ESTIMATION PROCESS

The software estimation process is an organization-level activity. This book discusses software estimation as it is carried out in an organization. When individuals carry out work and they answer only to themselves, their output is what is evaluated; the method they use to do the work likely is not questioned. In organizations, whether small or big, the methods used for working are very important, as the results depend upon those methods. In addition, multiple persons working on a single project need to collaborate and cooperate with each other, and the quality of their collective output depends on how well the team functions as a unit and on each team member's efforts to work shoulder to shoulder with the others. The moment the word *cooperation* comes into play, coordination and methods of working follow.

Methods of working are usually documented and referred to as a "process." Since 1994, when the International Organization for Standardization (ISO) released its ISO 9000 series of standards, a process-driven way of working has taken its place in many organizations. The concept of process-driven working was strengthened when the Software Engineering Institute of Carnegie Mellon University introduced its Capability Maturity Model. Today, process-driven working is normal practice in an overwhelming majority of software development organizations.

Process

> A **process** is the normally documented methods of working in an organization, consisting of procedures, standards, guidelines, checklists, formats, and templates.

The key terms in this definition are

- **Documented methods of working**—The methods of working are documented and available for reference to all concerned persons in the organization. Documentation facilitates identical understanding and bringing everyone onto the same page. It acts as a point of reference when in doubt or when a tricky situation needs clarification. Documentation also facilitates critical examination of all facets of working, which makes improvements possible. Documenting implies well-structured documentation. That is, it follows specific formats, templates, and language to ensure comprehensiveness and uniformity in all documents, irrespective of who prepared them.

- **Procedures**—Step-by-step instructions for how to carry out an organizational activity, including the what, how, who, and when. Some examples are
  - ☐ Estimation request procedure
  - ☐ Estimation presentation procedure

- **Standards and guidelines**—These two terms are now used interchangeably. Previously, "standards" meant implementation as is, in toto, without any modification whatsoever, and without any exceptions in the content of the standard; "guidelines" meant there was room for interpretation and change in certain situations. Examples include:
  - ☐ Productivity standards for conversion of function points to effort
  - ☐ Guidelines for selection of the appropriate estimation methodology for a given software project

- **Checklists**—A checklist is a list of items to be checked off that assists a person in ensuring completeness when carrying out an activity. Some examples are:
  - ☐ Code review checklist
  - ☐ Delivery inspection checklist

- **Formats and templates**—These assist the organization in achieving uniformity in the output of different persons and assist the individual in producing comprehensive output. The estimation process has:
  - ☐ Templates for software size estimation
  - ☐ Templates for software development effort estimation
  - ☐ Formats for presentation of software estimates

Based on the above, an organization ought to have the following as part of its software estimation process:

1. **One software estimation process** as the top-level document
2. **Procedures** for:
   a. Estimation request
   b. Estimation revision/reestimation
   c. Estimation presentation
   d. Variance analysis (between actual values and estimated values)
   e. Setting estimation norms
   f. Estimate review
3. **Standards** for:
   a. Productivity norms for conversion of software size to software development effort, for each approved software size measure
   b. Approved software size measures in the organization
4. **Guidelines** for:
   a. Software size estimation for each approved size measure
   b. Using Delphi estimation
   c. Using analogy-based estimation
   d. Using task-based estimation
   e. Estimation for software maintenance projects
   f. Test effort estimation, if applicable to the organization
   g. Selecting the appropriate software estimation methodology for a given project
   h. Each analysis technique to be used in variance analysis between actual values and estimated values
   i. Tailoring the process/procedure to suit the project at hand
   j. Estimation tool usage, if used in the organization
5. **Checklists** for:
   a. Review of each software size estimation, one for each approved size measure
   b. Peer review of software estimate
   c. Review of cost estimate
   d. Review of schedule estimate
6. **Formats and templates** for:
   a. Presentation of software estimates
   b. Estimation of software size for each approved software size measure
   c. Estimation of software estimate using Delphi estimation
   d. Estimation of software estimate using analogy-based estimation
   e. Estimation request

Now let us discuss what each of these documents should contain.

Process Document

A process document is the top-level document for software estimation in the organization. All other documents are subordinate to this document. The process document must contain the following:

- **Preliminaries**—The purpose and scope of the process document and entry and exit criteria
- **Process description**—A detailed description of how estimation is to be carried out, including:
  - ☐ Estimation during the project acquisition stage
  - ☐ Reestimation during the project execution stage
  - ☐ Estimation for internal projects
  - ☐ Tailoring guidelines to make the process suitable for the current project
- **Estimate preparation and review**—A list of persons who can prepare the estimation and who can review it
- **Software size measures**—A list of approved software size measures for the organization or reference to a document that contains the measures
- **Variance analysis procedure**—The procedure or reference to such a procedure for reconciling actual values with estimated values

A sample software estimation process is provided in Appendix F.

Procedure Documents

A procedure document should list the step-by-step instructions for carrying out work. It generally contains the following:

- **Preliminaries**—The purpose and scope of the document and entry and exit criteria
- **Procedure description**—Either a description of or a diagram depicting the procedure, including the steps to be followed, roles and responsibilities of concerned persons, etc.
- **Quality assurance mechanism**—Should describe the vehicles for ensuring quality of the work, such as reviews and the people who can perform these reviews

Standards and Guidelines

These documents describe the suggested method(s) for carrying out work in the organization. Examples are guidelines for estimating software size using function points, guidelines for estimating software size using object points, etc. These documents generally contain:

- Preliminaries, including the purpose and scope of the document and entry and exit criteria
- A description of the standard
- Precautions that need to be taken, if any
- Applicability and nonapplicability guidelines
- References to templates or formats
- Reference to further information, where necessary

Checklists

Checklists are normally used for a specific activity, such as review of an estimate. A checklist is normally in tabular form, with two main columns:

1. One column describes a state or condition, normally in question form.
2. The second column allows the person completing the checklist to indicate "yes," "no," or "not applicable."

"No" in the second column indicates a shortfall in the state or condition, which needs to be improved. When an activity passes on to its next stage, all entries in the checklist should be either "yes" or "not applicable." A checklist can be used by the person carrying out the activity to ensure that the activity is completed comprehensively or by the reviewer to ensure that the output is exhaustive.

Formats and Templates

A template is similar to a format, except that a template has guidelines for every entry in the format and may even contain possible options and examples. These documents do not have any standard or suggested entries, as they are specific to a situation. Both facilitate filling in information in a uniform manner across the organization.

Final Words on the Software Estimation Process

It is essential to define processes in order to carry out software estimation efficiently. The estimation process outlined here can be adapted to suit the unique needs of any organization.

PRESENTATION OF SOFTWARE ESTIMATES

It is one thing to prepare a software estimate, which in itself is an onerous task that requires experience in software development, knowledge of software estimation, and a well-honed forecasting instinct for the execution of a project in the future. It is quite another to present the software estimate in a form that is comprehensive and that conveys it accurately. If not properly presented to the requester, a software estimate, prepared as the result of your knowledge acquired through diligent effort, could be subject to misuse and misinterpretation, with the final blame for a poor estimate placed squarely on your shoulders.

My opinion, based on my observations, is that it is not poor estimates that have given software estimation a bad name, but rather poor presentation of estimates. I have witnessed estimates conveyed over the telephone or in a two-line e-mail. The receiver is happy with such a presentation. That person's job is easy—no need to exercise the brain and no need to make a decision. That person receives a single figure and can build a proposal around it. If the project is lost due to overestimation, the perception is that it is the fault of the estimator and a poor estimation process. If the project is awarded and results in a monetary loss because of underestimation, again the estimator and the process are blamed.

We must keep in mind that as estimators, our job is to estimate. Pricing is the job of management, the marketing department, the finance department, or whoever in the organization is entrusted with the job of making the pricing decision. If you happen to be the person who is deciding the price, separate the two activities; consider software estimation apart from the pricing decision. The topic of pricing is discussed in greater detail in chapter 12.

I suggest that estimation never be communicated in an informal manner. The software estimate should be presented properly—in a documented form. Figures for software size and development effort, cost, and schedule are vital parts of a software estimate—but they are not the entire estimate. The following information needs to be presented as well:

- The scope of work that is covered by the estimate
- Underlying assumptions made in defining the scope of work
- All aspects explicitly included in the estimate
- All aspects explicitly excluded from the estimate
- Project-related information, such as the project name, a brief description, technology used, etc.

These details offer the person requesting the estimate all the information he or she needs to know to make appropriate decisions based on the objectives of the situation.

Further, I suggest the estimate be presented using a format or template the organization has created specially for this purpose. I recommend the following entries be included in the presentation of the estimate:

- **Estimation request note**—An estimation request note is raised by the person requesting a software estimate, and reference to it should be included along with any other details of the estimation request. An example of an estimation request note can be found in Appendix H.
- **Project details**—The project name, project ID, customer information, a brief project description, project type, application domain, and technology domain. These details set the background for the estimate.
- **Estimate preliminaries**—Such as the initial gut feeling about the prospective client's budget, effort needed to execute the project, etc. This information may be used to indicate the allocable funds for internal projects and the client's budget.
- **Time available for preparing the estimate**—The amount of time allowed by the requester to prepare the software estimate. It allows for assessment of the amount of focus the estimate received.
- **Estimator information**—The name of the estimator and any other relevant details.
- **Reviewer information**—The name of the person who conducted the peer review of the estimate.
- **Estimation methodology**—A brief explanation of why a certain methodology was chosen and the reasons other methodologies were not chosen.
- **Risks**—Every project has risks associated with its execution, and these risks may be foreseen during estimation. Enumerate and ex-

plain all the risks foreseen as potential stumbling blocks to a successful estimate.

■ **Assumptions**—Assumptions are always made while preparing an estimate, especially one made at the project acquisition stage. Enumerate all the assumptions, with a brief explanation of each one. Include the reasons behind each assumption, as this puts the estimate accuracy in proper perspective. This is a vital part of the estimate that should not be neglected.

■ **Estimation details**—The figures for software size, effort, cost, and schedule. It is best to include the three scenarios: the best-case scenario, worst-case scenario, and normal-case scenario. Calculate an average of these three scenarios, which is the expected scenario, using the formula

$$\frac{\text{best case } + \text{ worst case } + \ (4 \times \text{ normal case})}{6}$$

■ **Reference documents**—All the documents referred to while preparing the estimate. Examples of such reference documents include:

☐ The organizational software estimation process documentation, including procedures, standards and guidelines, formats and templates, and checklists

☐ Estimation request note

☐ All client-supplied documents, including the request for proposal

☐ Minutes of meetings relevant to the estimate, if any

☐ Past estimates

☐ Any documents that were used as reference material during the estimation, such as publications, journals, seminar proceedings, etc.

☐ Estimation methodology guides

■ **Inclusions**—Identify all the components specifically included in the estimate. Clearly define the scope of the work for which the estimate is prepared. Enumerate all software engineering activities, including quality assurance activities expected to be performed during project execution. Enumerate all deliverables for the project.

■ **Exclusions**—Identify all components that are not included in the estimate. Enumerate all software engineering activities that are not specifically excluded in the scope of work, which could be the creation of master data files, warranty support and limitations, and such other aspects that might mistakenly be understood as included.

- **Remarks or comments**—Include any other relevant information that was not included in any of the above sections.
- **Appendices**—Enumerate all documents that are included as appendices, which can include:
  - ☐ Estimation worksheets for size, effort, cost, and schedule
  - ☐ Document extracts that support the assumptions made in the estimate or information used in the estimate

I suggest that a managerial review of this document be conducted and approval obtained before transmitting it to the requester of the estimation. A template for presenting software estimation is suggested in Appendix G. You can use it as is or modify it to suit the unique requirements of your organization, or you can develop your own template. The point is, whatever you do, use a template.

SUMMARY

It is very easy for organizations to fall prey to pitfalls in software estimation. This chapter discusses in detail the common pitfalls in software estimation and suggests best practices that will help organizations avoid them. An organizational process, including procedures, standards, formats, and templates, is an important best practice. Another is diligently setting productivity norms, either through industrial engineering studies or through a careful study of the organization's historical records. Another best practice is to give three figures—normal-case, best-case, and worst-case scenarios—for each of the four aspects of estimates (software size, software development effort, project cost, and project schedule). Finally, the importance of proper presentation of an estimate is also emphasized.

CRITERIA FOR SELECTING A SOFTWARE ESTIMATION TOOL

Software estimation includes the following four elements:

1. Software size
2. Software cost
3. Software effort
4. Software delivery schedule

A plethora of tools are available in the market, and it is often difficult to arrive at an educated decision on which tool to purchase. Each vendor claims that its tool is better than the others, the most scientific, and suitable for any type of software project and for any organization. This chapter attempts to help the professional make an educated choice when selecting a software estimation tool.

UNITS OF MEASURE FOR SOFTWARE SIZE

Throughout this book, I have reiterated the fact that there is no universal agreement on the unit of measure for software. Here are a few reasons why this is so:

- Programming platforms differ widely.
- Graphical user interface (GUI) programming has added one more dimension to the variety of software development platforms, and there is confusion on how to measure the size of a GUI.
- Several project types are not full life cycle projects. These include software maintenance projects, testing projects, implementation projects, etc., and there is confusion on how to measure the size of such projects.

Therefore, criterion #1 for selecting a software estimation tool is

1. **The tool must allow the use of multiple units of measure for software size.**

In other words, the tool must have provisions for using the different popular techniques for software size measurement.

A COMMON UNIT OF MEASURE FOR SOFTWARE SIZE

If the size measurement is carried out using different measures, how does the organization measure its overall productivity? Measurement of an organization's software development productivity is possible only when the software size is measured using one unit of measure.

Therefore, criterion #2 for selecting a software estimation tool is

2. **The tool must enable conversion of multiple units of measure into one unit of measure for software size to achieve standardization for the organization.**

SOFTWARE COST ESTIMATION

There are no differences of opinion among estimators when it comes to the estimation of software cost. All agree that the estimation of software cost must be in the currency of the organization's home country, meaning the price can be in dollars, euros, rupees, etc. While development effort (in person-days or person-hours) is the major cost source in software cost estimation, other cost items come into play when estimating the cost of the software to be developed.

It is likely that these additional cost items vary from organization to organization in terms of variety and unit cost. It is also likely that person-day costs vary from project to project. Therefore, a software estimation tool must allow for the maintenance of cost items, meaning it must be able to add, modify, and delete cost item data, not just keep static cost item data that cannot be modified by the user organization.

Therefore, criteria #3, #4, and #5 for selecting a software estimation tool are

3. **The tool must allow for software cost estimation.**
4. **The tool must provide for parameterization of person-day cost.**
5. **The tool must provide for maintenance of cost items.**

SCHEDULING THE SOFTWARE PROJECT

Effort is estimated essentially for three reasons:

1. To commit to the delivery schedule of the client, management, or users
2. To estimate the resources required to execute the project
3. To estimate the cost of the project in order to allocate funds or price the project, with the objectives of cost and profit optimization.

That the tool should cater to the first and second reasons is of little debate. The first reason a schedule is developed is to commit to stakeholders, which is by no means insignificant. Scheduling is a creative task and an activity that calls for human ingenuity, which cannot be fully automated. Equally important is the fact that there is no universally accepted or standard way of apportioning a percentage of project effort to a given phase or activity. The objectives of achieving a schedule from an estimate are as follows:

- Scheduling should be quick.
- The tool should cater to allocation of resources in the schedule.
- The tool should allow for allocating effort to the different phases of schedule creation.
- The tool should generate a schedule of sufficient detail that is exportable to an intermediate file, from which it can be imported into a full-fledged program evaluation and review technique or critical path method package such as Microsoft Project and Primavera.

Therefore, criteria #6 to #11 for selecting a software estimation tool are

6. **The tool must provide for scheduling the project.**
7. **The schedule must be derived from the estimated effort.**
8. **The tool must automate schedule generation to the extent that is practically possible.**
9. **The tool must allow for human intervention when creating the schedule.**
10. **The schedule generated must have adequate detail and must be exportable to a popular intermediate file such as Microsoft Excel or directly to Microsoft Project and Primavera.**
11. **When the effort in person-days is honestly estimated and then scheduled, the scheduled number of person-days can still overshoot the estimated number of person-days due to loss of time in personnel allocation, idle time, and finish-to-start relationships. Therefore, the tool must be able to estimate the number of person-days, but must also allow for the number of scheduled person-days to be different from the number of estimated person-days.**

ESTIMATION FOR PARTIAL LIFE CYCLE PROJECTS

There are several significantly large projects that are not considered full life cycle projects, such as software maintenance, enterprise resource planning implementation, and testing projects. The tool has to cater to such projects as well, using a technique such as task-based estimation, so that partial life cycle project types can be defined and used for estimation by the organization.

Therefore, criterion #12 for selecting a software estimation tool is

12. **The tool must cater to partial life cycle project estimation.**

USABILITY

Any software needs to be built with users in mind. An expert can work with any tool, but *the main distinguishing characteristic of a good tool is that it can produce an expert-quality output even when used by a person of average expertise.* Such a tool has an intuitive interface that makes learning how to use it easy. The availability of GUI tools makes this possible. Tools that have the wrong controls on their screens put a strain on the user rather than make usage easier. The tool must cater more to functionality than to jazziness. A simple user interface is always the better user interface.

Therefore, criterion #13 for selecting a software estimation tool is

13. **The tool must be built with usability in mind, with an intuitive interface that makes it easy for the average-skilled person to quickly master it.**

USAGE OF POPULAR TECHNIQUES

Software estimation is perhaps as old as software development itself. Some size estimation techniques have become popular and are used by many organizations. Especially popular are the lines of code, function point analysis, and use case points techniques. Other techniques commonly used are object points, Mark II function point analysis, and software size units.

Therefore, criterion #14 for selecting a software estimation tool is

14. **The tool must provide for as many popular software size estimation techniques as is feasible.**

AUDITABILITY

"Two heads are better than one" is a well-known dictum, and it forms the basis of software inspections, reviews, and walk-throughs. An estimate made by one person, however diligent and expert he or she may be, needs to be reviewed by one or more peers. The tool must be able to show the details of the estimate so that it can be reviewed and improved upon if necessary. This detail also assists in reconciling the actual values spent on the project so that lessons may be drawn from the experience and improvements made in the estimation process for subsequent projects.

Therefore, criterion #15 for selecting a software estimation tool is

15. **The tool must provide for making estimates that are auditable.**

REPORTING CAPABILITY

The purpose of estimation is to submit the results, in the form of a report, to the client, management, or user. This report should present essential details and hide those that are unnecessary. However, the tool must provide a detailed report for every estimate made.

Therefore, criterion #16 for selecting a software estimation tool is

16. **The tool should provide for generation of a detailed report for every estimate made, as well as a summary report of all estimates made using the tool.**

ESTIMATOR PRODUCTIVITY

It is extremely important to keep in mind the pressures placed on estimators, who are usually either project leaders or project managers and who already have a number of tasks to which they must attend. Usage of any tool necessitates data entry, but data entry is a manual process (typing) that takes time to perform. A tool that provides choices from which to select, to the extent possible, reduces this effort and increases the estimator's productivity when using the tool. Therefore, the tool must facilitate selection of choices and reduce as much as possible the amount of typing necessary to input data.

It is likely that most projects in an organization are similar in nature, although certainly not identical. Therefore, the tool must provide for copying an existing estimate and allowing it to be modified to generate a new estimate. Such a feature saves an immense amount of time for the estimators and therefore money for the organization.

Therefore, criteria #17 and #18 for selecting a software estimation tool are

17. **The tool must provide for selection from a list of choices as much as possible to make estimates.**
18. **The tool must provide a "copy-modify-generate" feature for making new estimates.**

SUMMARY

Software estimation is a critical activity for an organization engaged in software development. A software estimation tool helps an average-skilled person generate a professional, quality estimate. There are a plethora of tools available for software estimation. The criteria listed and explained in this chapter will help professionals make an educated choice of an appropriate tool for software estimation.

APPENDIX A: VARIANCE ANALYSIS BETWEEN ACTUAL AND ESTIMATED VALUES

Variances between actual and estimated values can stem from the following reasons:

- **Chance variation**—It is a well-acknowledged fact that even in a tightly controlled and stable process, slight variances can occur randomly due to chance. However, the variance in such cases is small, usually less than 5 percent.
- **Assignable variation**—Sometimes assignable reasons cause variations, such as:
  - ☐ Unforeseen events
  - ☐ Changes in the working environment
  - ☐ Changes in requirements, specifications, or design
  - ☐ Quantity of work to be performed either increases or decreases
  - ☐ The skill levels or the motivation levels of the human resources employed in the project may be different from the assumed levels
  - ☐ Erroneous productivity norms

The main purpose of analyzing variances between actual and estimated values is to validate norms used for estimation and to derive preventive actions for future projects so that repetition of the same variances does not occur. If the results of the analysis indicate that the variances are due purely to chance variation, the norms are retained and the variances are accepted as normal, random occurrences. However, if it is discovered that variance is still beyond chance variation in multiple projects even after adjusting the values for assignable variation, it can be determined that the estimation norms may need another look, but the estimation norms are not changed until the variation begins to show a trend.

Thus, three types of analyses need to be carried out at the close of every project:

1. **Project variance analysis**—Allows us to place the variance in its proper perspective and isolate assignable reasons
2. **Trend analysis**—Shows the trend of the variances between estimated values and actual values
3. **Correlation analysis**—Shows the relationship between two sets of values

PROJECT VARIANCE ANALYSIS

Let us use the project data in table A.1 and work out a sample analysis to gain better insight into the data. We can see some variations, but are they significant? That is, are the variations due to chance or not? This will become clearer by adding two more columns, as shown in table A.2.

Looking at table A.2, the absolute variance may not allow us to draw any firm conclusions, but the percentage variance allows us to draw two educated inferences:

1. There is a significant increase in software size.
2. The variances in development effort, cost, and schedule are not proportionate with the increase in size.

Table A.1. Project data

Aspect	Estimated value	Actual value
Software size (in function points)	100	120
Software development effort (in person-hours)	1,000	1,300
Software development cost (in dollars)	30,250	33,150
Software development schedule (in workdays)	125	136
Software productivity	10	10.8333

Table A.2. Project data with variance

Aspect	Estimated value	Actual value	Absolute variance	Variance as percent of estimate
Software size (in function points)	100	120	20	20.00
Software development effort (in person-hours)	1,000	1,300	300	30.00
Software development cost (in dollars)	30,250	33,150	2,900	9.59
Software development schedule (in workdays)	125	136	11	8.80
Software productivity	10	10.8333	0.833	8.33

The second point indicates that the increase in software size did not cause proportionate increases in other aspects. Surprising, isn't it? Other things being constant, an increase in size should result in a proportionate increase in effort, cost, and schedule—common sense tells us this is so. But the fact is, such "other things" are rarely constant in real life. The "other things" can be kept constant only in controlled experiments.

Notice that the effort is disproportionately higher. The following are possible reasons for this:

1. The team members took more time than expected. Perhaps they faced issues we are not aware of yet.
2. The project team was less motivated.
3. The project team was comprised of more novices than originally estimated.
4. All of the above.

Couple these possible reasons with the increases in cost and schedule, which are both disproportionately lower! These figures allow us to infer that the project team was comprised of more novices to cut costs, and the team worked extra hours to reduce the impact on schedule. We can also see that the team was expected to work 8 hours per day, but actually worked about 9 hours per day, which obviously helped to lessen the impact on the schedule.

This can be summarized in a critical examination table, as shown in table A.3. A critical examination table contains the following four columns:

1. The "what" column contains the event being analyzed.
2. The "why" column contains the possible reasons for the event in the "what" column.

Table A.3. Critical examination table

Aspect	What	Why	What else	What should
Size	20 percent increase	Two change requests	Nil	Nil
Effort	30 percent increase	Increased size	Could contain the 20 percent increase	Should have contained the 20 percent increase
Cost	9.59 percent increase	Increased size	Could have increased by 20 percent	9.59 percent is a good achievement
Schedule	8.8 percent increase	Increased size	Could have increased by 20 percent	This is a good achievement
Productivity	8.33 percent increase	Better motivation	Could be maintained at 10 function points per hour	This is a good achievement

3. The "what else" column contains possible alternatives for the event in the "what" column.
4. The "what should" contains the desirable alternative to what was described in the "what" column.

The project team can advise us on filling in the "why" column Similarly, the "what should" column can be filled in with the assistance of the technical head, delivery head, or whoever is responsible for delivery. Now we can draw inferences based on the explanation in the "what should" column; thus:

1. The size increase is due to change requests, for which there are no alternatives.
2. The increase in cost is lower than the possible 20 percent increase, so we can infer, or have the project team confirm, that less costly (and thereby less experienced) persons were used for the project. We can safely infer that the increase of more than 20 percent in effort is due to this fact.
3. We can also see that the project team worked more hours per day to reduce the impact on schedule.
4. The increase in productivity was due to better motivation.

Since we have assignable reasons for the variances, we retain the estimation norms.

The variances between actual values and estimated values need to be analyzed for all projects, as shown in this example, soon after a project is closed.

TREND ANALYSIS

Trend analysis needs to performed at the organizational level to find out if there is a perceptible trend in the variances of individual projects. Control charts can also be used for this purpose, but there needs to be a stable process and a large number of projects must be executed before using them.

Trend analysis involves plotting the values on a line graph to find out if the line shows a trend, and if so, whether it is an increasing or decreasing trend. Table A.4 shows some project productivity data.

From the data in this table, we can plot line graphs, as shown in figure A.1. We can also plot a trend line through the data so that the trend becomes

Table A.4. Project productivity data

Project	Schedule variance	Effort variance	Cost variance	Productivity in hours per function point
Project A	5%	8%	6%	10.00
Project B	7%	5%	5.50%	9.00
Project C	4%	3%	3%	11.00
Project D	−1.25%	−2%	−2.50%	14.00
Project E	−2%	−1.50%	−1%	12.50
Project F	2%	3%	4%	10.20

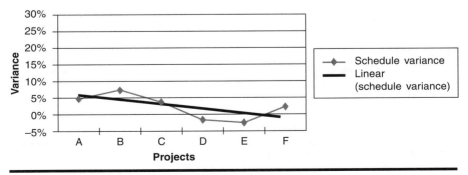

Figure A.1. Line graph for productivity data

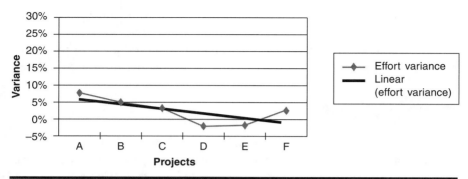

Figure A.2. Effort variance trend graph

obvious. Microsoft Excel can be used to plot these graphs, but with one caution: ensure that the projects are entered in chronological order, from top to bottom, to get an accurate picture of the trend. If the order of projects is altered, the graphs will depict a wrong trend.

The data line in figure A.1 indicates that the schedule variance has been decreasing, which is positive, but the last data point indicates an increase. The trend line (diagonal line) indicates that the trend for schedule variance is a decreasing trend.

In figure A.2, the data line indicates a negative trend that is increasing. Variance for the last project indicates that the effort variance is increasing. The trend line indicates that the trend for effort variance is a decreasing trend.

In figure A.3, the last two projects on the data line show an increasing trend, but the trend line still shows a decreasing trend for cost variance.

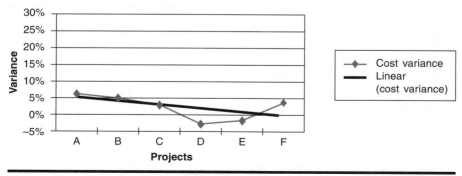

Figure A.3. Cost variance trend graph

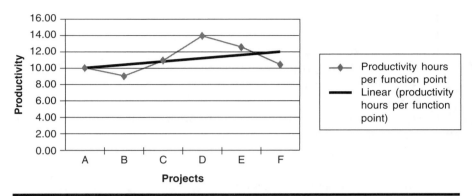

Figure A.4. Productivity variance trend graph

In figure A.4, while the overall trend shows an increasing trend for productivity, the data line indicates a decreasing trend for the last two projects. Given all this information, the following becomes obvious:

1. The overall trend is satisfactory.
2. The trend for project E is not satisfactory, as it is in the opposite direction of the overall trend in all aspects. This trend calls for closer examination to derive preventive actions for future projects.
3. The trend for project F is in the opposite direction of the overall trend for cost variance and productivity, but is close for schedule variance and effort variance. Therefore, a critical examination of this project needs to be conducted to derive preventive actions for future projects.

To summarize, a trend analysis needs to be carried out at the organizational level for every project once it is completed. Based on trend analysis, preventive actions can be formulated for future projects.

CORRELATION ANALYSIS

Often, we would like to know if the software size or the team size has an impact on productivity. To find out, we need to carry out correlation analysis. Correlation analysis allows us to establish the relationship, if any, that exists between two sets of data. This is especially helpful, in the context of software estimation, to establish if any of the following variables impact productivity:

- Software size
- Team size
- Average experience of the team
- Location of work (in-house or client site)
- Programming language

Once we establish that a relationship exists, we can use causal analysis to effect changes that will improve productivity.

Correlation has three aspects:

1. Positive and negative correlation:
   a. A positive correlation is a directly proportional correlation.
   b. A negative correlation is an inversely proportional correlation.
2. Simple, partial, and multiple correlation:
   a. A simple correlation refers to a relationship between two variables.
   b. A multiple correlation refers to a relationship between three or more variables, studied simultaneously.
   c. A partial correlation refers to a relationship between three or more variables, but studied between two variables and assuming that the other variables remain constant.
3. Linear and nonlinear correlation:
   a. A linear correlation is when the influence is based on a constant ratio.
   b. A nonlinear correlation is when the influence is not based on a constant ratio.

Pearson's coefficient of correlation is the popular method used to carry out correlation analysis between two variables and is explained below. The formula is

$$r = \frac{\sum (X - X_{bar}) \times (Y - Y_{bar})}{N(\sigma_x \sigma_y)}$$

where r is coefficient of correlation, X_{bar} is the arithmetic mean of variable X, Y_{bar} is the arithmetic mean of variable Y, σ_x is the standard deviation of variable X, σ_y is the standard deviation of variable Y, and N is the number of pairs of observations.

The correlation coefficient always lies between $+1$ and -1. A plus value indicates a positive correlation, and a minus value indicates a negative correlation.

Table A.5. Correlation between project size and productivity

Project	Project size in function points	Productivity in person-hours per function point
Project A	250.00	10.00
Project B	500.00	9.75
Project C	750.00	9.85
Project D	1,000.00	9.50
Project E	1,500.00	8.25
Project F	2,000.00	8.00

The value of the correlation coefficient is interpreted as follows:

- A value of 0 indicates no correlation at all.
- A value of 1 indicates a perfect correlation in the direction of the plus or minus sign.
- A value tending toward 0 indicates a weaker correlation.
- A value tending toward 1 indicates a stronger correlation.

Microsoft Excel is equipped with formulas for computing correlation.

Table A.5 is an example of a correlation between project size and productivity. The coefficient of correlation using Microsoft Excel for the data in this table is −0.96. That is, there is a very strong correlation between the project size and productivity in an inverse direction, which means that as the project size increases, productivity decreases.

Table A.6 depicts an example of productivity comparisons among projects using Java and Visual Basic as development platforms. Productivity is measured in person-hours per function point.

Using the line graph shown in figure A.5, we can see if there is a correlation in table A.6. In this graph, the productivities parallel each other but do not coincide with one another at any point. Therefore, we can safely infer two

Table A.6. Productivity comparison

Project	Java	Visual Basic
Projects A and B	9.50	10.00
Projects C and D	8.25	9.75
Projects E and F	8.00	9.85

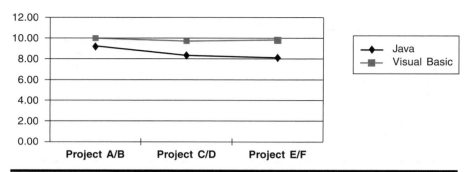

Figure A.5. Line graph for productivity comparison

things: productivity for these two development platforms is not the same and the development platform impacts productivity.

CONTROL CHARTS

Control charts assist us in assessing whether or not a specific value is within control. They are widely used in process flow production to control quality. The prerequisite for using control charts is a stable process, which means it is producing predictable results and variances are due only to pure chance and random variation.

In control charts, four values are plotted on a graph:

1. **Standard value**—Normally the arithmetic mean, but an organizational baseline can also be used.
2. **Upper control limit**—The maximum permissible value above the standard value. It is normally the arithmetic mean plus three times the standard deviation. In practice, however, the value of the upper bound is set as the maximum permissible higher value.
3. **Lower control limit**—The minimum permissible value below the standard value. It is normally the arithmetic mean minus three times the standard deviation. In practice, however, the value of the lower bound is set as the minimum permissible lower value.
4. **Actual data**—The actual data resulting from the process for which the control chart is produced.

Table A.7. Productivity data for control chart

Project	Standard	Upper control limit	Lower control limit	Productivity in hours per function point
Project A	11.00	12.00	9.00	10.00
Project B	11.00	12.00	9.00	9.00
Project C	11.00	12.00	9.00	11.00
Project D	11.00	12.00	9.00	14.00
Project E	11.00	12.00	9.00	12.50
Project F	11.00	12.00	9.00	10.20

Table A.7 provides sample productivity data. Using Microsoft Excel, a control chart can be produced for this data, as shown in figure A.6. From this chart, we can easily infer that projects E and F have crossed the upper boundary and are therefore out of control. Thus, we need to investigate the reasons for this through critical examination and derive preventive actions for future projects.

Control charts can also be used during the execution of a project so that all the aspects can be kept from going out of control.

More information on variance analysis, trend analysis, and control charts can be obtained from any good book on statistical inferencing or business statistics. More information on critical examination can be obtained from any book on work study.

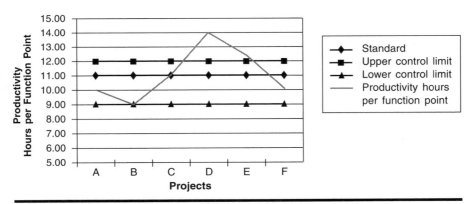

FIGURE A.6 Control chart for project productivity

APPENDIX B: PROJECT TYPES AND SUITABLE SOFTWARE ESTIMATION TECHNIQUES

Project type	Suitable estimation methods
Full life cycle	Software size estimation, task-based estimation, Delphi estimation, analogy-based estimation
Testing	Software test units, test-case-enumeration-based estimation, software-size-based estimation, task-based estimation, Delphi estimation, analogy-based estimation
Independent verification and validation	Task-based estimation, Delphi estimation, analogy-based estimation
Other partial life cycle projects	Task-based estimation, Delphi estimation, analogy-based estimation
Implementation of commercial off-the-shelf software	Task-based estimation, custom estimation methods, Delphi estimation, analogy-based estimation

Project type	Suitable estimation methods
Software porting	Task-based estimation, Delphi estimation, analogy-based estimation
Software migration	Task-based estimation, Delphi estimation, analogy-based estimation
Conversion	Task-based estimation, Delphi estimation, analogy-based estimation
Software maintenance: defect fixing	No estimation for short durations, task-based estimation for longer durations, Delphi estimation, analogy-based estimation
Software maintenance: operational support	No estimation for short durations, task-based estimation for longer durations, Delphi estimation, analogy-based estimation
Software maintenance: odd behavior	No estimation for short durations, task-based estimation for longer durations, Delphi estimation, analogy-based estimation
Software maintenance: software modification	Task-based estimation, Delphi estimation, analogy-based estimation
Software maintenance: functional expansion	Software size estimation, task-based estimation, Delphi estimation, analogy-based estimation

APPENDIX C: ESTIMATION SHEET FOR DELPHI TECHNIQUE

1. Originator information
Name (*the requester*):

Designation:

Department:

2. Client information
Client name:

Nature of business:

Address:

Phone:

Contact person:

3. Project details
Name of project:

Development platform (*programming language, database, number of tiers, etc.*):

Application domain (*describe the application in as much detail as possible*):

Date by which estimate is required (*to be filled in by the originator*):

Budget specified (*if available*):

Size measure specified (*if predetermined or desired*):

4. Project type
☐ Development
☐ Maintenance
☐ Reengineering
☐ Conversion
☐ Software implementation
☐ Other (*specify*)

5. Estimation inputs (*list of documents supplied along with this note*)
☐ Request for proposal
☐ Briefing by marketing
☐ Direct briefing from the client
☐ User requirements
☐ Statement of work
☐ Software requirements specification
☐ Design document
☐ E-mail from marketing
☐ Inputs provided by the bidding process (*applicable for projects initiated by marketing*)
☐ Other (*specify*)

6. Experts selected (see example below)

| Name of expert | Domain expertise | | Development platform expertise | |
	Expertise description	Number of years	Expertise description	Number of years
Expert 1				
Expert 2				
Expert 3				
Expert *n*				

7. Estimate convergence (see example below)
Use a separate table for each iteration of convergence.

Name of expert	Size	Effort
Expert 1	A	X
Expert 2	B	Y
Expert 3	C	Z
Expert n	K	L

8. Convergence average method
☐ Arithmetic average
☐ Statistical mode

9. Final convergence
Software size and size measure:

Software development effort in person-hours:

10. To be filled in by the project management office
Actual software size:

Actual software development effort:

Actual software development cost:

Actual scheduled delivery date:

APPENDIX D: DERIVING PRODUCTIVITY FROM PAST PROJECTS

This appendix is intended to provide assistance to an organization that is trying to derive a productivity figure for the first time. Such an organization would have completed at least one or a few projects. Of course, other organizations may also adopt this procedure. One attribute is used as an example, but the method shown here to derive productivity can be applied to other attributes as well.

Consider a project that is based on Java programming. To derive the productivity for programming in Java, we need the figures for lines of code (LOC) developed and the effort spent developing the LOC. The project data is shown in table D.1.

Before proceeding with this example, a discussion of averages is necessary. More specifically, we need to discuss *measures of central tendency,* of which *average* is one. I trust you are already knowledgeable in statistics, but in support of some of my suggestions below, I will provide a very brief discussion on the measures of central tendency. Refer to a textbook on statistics to learn more on the subject.

It is very difficult to consider a mass of data and make sense of it, but a single value gives us a fair idea of the population universe. Let us say, for example, that the average height of Indians is 5 feet 6 inches and the average height of Americans

Table D.1. Productivity data

Person	Size	Effort in person-hours	Productivity in LOC per person-hour
Programmer A	420	9.0	46.67
Programmer B	350	8.0	43.75
Programmer C	500	7.5	66.67
Programmer D	450	9.0	50.00
Programmer E	365	7.5	48.67
Programmer F	1,100	18.0	61.11
Programmer G	250	10.0	25.00
Programmer H	1,600	20.0	80.00
Programmer I	90	2.5	36.00
Programmer J	520	10.0	52.00
Programmer K	380	8.0	47.50
Programmer L	1,400	18.0	77.78

is 5 feet 11 inches. From this, we can infer that generally Americans are taller than Indians. However, if we are provided height values of a thousand Indians and a thousand Americans, it is very difficult to draw any meaningful inference about the heights of these two groups. A single value that gives representative information about a mass of values is called the *central value* or a *measure of central tendency*. That is, when we plot a graph of the values, most values gather around this value. The most commonly used measure of central tendency is what we refer to as the "average," which in statistics is called the *arithmetic mean* or simply the *mean*.

The measures of central tendency are

■   Arithmetic mean, which includes the *simple mean* and *weighted mean*
■   Mode
■   Median
■   Geometric mean
■   Harmonic mean

All these measures can be called the "average."

When the population universe is very large or symmetrical, the *mean* is the best measure of central tendency, but when the universe is small (that is, there are few values) or if the data is not symmetrical, the mean is affected by extreme values and gives an inaccurate picture.

The *median* is the middle value.

The *mode* is the most frequently occurring value. The advantage of the mode is that it is not influenced by extreme values. Therefore, for a smaller population of values, the mode is suggested for determining the average value.

Since most of the time we deal with small amounts of data, we should first determine if the data is symmetrical, which means whether it is uniformly distributed. The data is likely to be symmetrical if we have in the organization a mix of novices, experts, and persons with intermediate skill (that is, nonuniform skill sets) performing work and delivering results. While this may be true, determining if the data is symmetrical is recommended.

Statistics provides a measure with which to gauge symmetry of data—or rather lack of it. This measure is called the *skewness coefficient*. Although the skewness coefficient can be computed by a few formulas, I will use one here that is simple to calculate and accurate enough. It is Pearson's coefficient of skewness. The formula is

$$\text{Skewness coefficient} = \frac{\text{mean} - \text{mode}}{\text{standard deviation}}$$

Ideally, the skewness coefficient should be 0 or as close to 0 as possible. The skewness coefficient normally lies between +1 and −1. As the skewness coefficient moves away from 0, skewness of the data increases. If the skewness coefficient is positive, then the data is skewed on the higher side of the mean; if the coefficient is negative, the data is skewed on the lower side of mean.

What does this mean for us?

- When the data is skewed on the positive side:
  - If all team members are of homogeneous skill, then some members have put in more effort than others.
  - If the team members are of heterogeneous skill, then it is possible that the project team has more experts than novices or persons of average skill.
- When the data is skewed on the negative side:
  - If all team members are of homogeneous skill, then some members have put in less effort than others.
  - If the team members are of heterogeneous skill, then it is possible that the project team has more novices than experts or persons of average skill.

If the skewness coefficient is close to 0, then we can use the mean to determine the average, but if it moves closer to 1, then there are extreme values in the data that need to be eliminated. The best way to eliminate the impact of extreme values is to use the mode in place of the mean. Therefore, my first recommendation is this: until an organization builds up data from a large number of projects, it should use the statistical mode to derive the average value for each attribute and not the mean. The statistical mode removes extreme achievements from consideration while allowing the organization to establish standard norms.

Getting back to table D.1, we can infer the following:

- Productivity ranges from a minimum of 25 LOC per person-hour to a maximum of 80 LOC per person-hour.
- The simple mean productivity (the average of all productivities) is 53 LOC (rounded to the nearest whole number) per person-hour.
- The weighted mean productivity (the sum of LOC divided by the sum of effort in person-hours) is 59 LOC (rounded to the nearest whole number) per person-hour.
- The median productivity is 50 (rounded to the nearest whole number).
- The standard deviation of productivity achieved by programmers is 16.30.

To be able to compute the mode, the productivity values need to be rounded off to the nearest 5 or 10. Table D.2 depicts productivity rounded off to the nearest 5. In this table, we can observe that the productivity value 50 occurs six times, which is the maximum frequency. Therefore, productivity using the statistical mode is 50 LOC per person-hour.

Using the mode, we can now compute the skewness coefficient:

1. Skewness coefficient in terms of a simple mean is 0.18.
2. Skewness coefficient in terms of a weighted mean is 0.505.

Microsoft Excel offers the formulas to derive the mean (average), median, mode, and skewness coefficient, and we can use them to obtain the required values. These values are summarized in table D.3.

In this table, we can observe that the simple mean productivity, median productivity, and modal productivity are very close to one another, while the weighted mean productivity is off by a larger margin. The skewness coefficient is 0.272, indicating that the data is skewed toward higher values. Therefore, we can say that there are more experts on this project team. Any data with a skewness coefficient higher than 0.05 is considered skewed data.

Table D.2. Productivity data rounded off

Person	Size	Effort in person-hours	Productivity in LOC per person-hour	Productivity rounded to nearest 5
Programmer A	420	9.0	46.67	45.00
Programmer B	350	8.0	43.75	45.00
Programmer C	500	7.5	66.67	65.00
Programmer D	450	9.0	50.00	50.00
Programmer E	365	7.5	48.67	50.00
Programmer F	1,100	18.0	61.11	60.00
Programmer G	250	10.0	25.00	25.00
Programmer H	1,600	20.0	80.00	80.00
Programmer I	90	2.5	36.00	35.00
Programmer J	520	10.0	52.00	50.00
Programmer K	380	8.0	47.50	50.00
Programmer L	1,400	18.0	77.78	80.00

Since we have established that the data in this example is skewed, calculating the mean will likely give us a wrong value. With a large volume of data, the mean, median, and mode would all result in values very close to one another. Therefore, if you are deriving productivity from one or a few values, my recommendation is to use the statistical mode. How much constitutes "a few"? My answer to this question is to *use the mode until you have a thousand values with which to work.* The fact is, the statistical mode is the value used most frequently in the industry; it is used more often than the arithmetic mean. I will even go one step further and recommend using *only* the statistical mode for setting productivity standards in your organization.

Another aspect that needs attention is currency of data. Depending on your organization's preference, I recommend including data from the achievements of the last 6 to 12 months for deriving productivity through the mode. Data over a year old, in my opinion, is not likely to be relevant, as circumstances change, newer tools are used for development, and the development environ-

Table D.3. Summary of measures of central tendency

Simple mean productivity	52.93
Weighted mean productivity	58.24
Median productivity	49.33
Mode productivity	50.00
Standard deviation of productivity	16.30
Skewness coefficient using Excel formula	0.272

ment may have undergone significant change. This concept is known as the *moving average.*

Many software development organizations group all development activities, including effort and size of the software, to derive an all-encompassing productivity figure, which means:

- The effort is computed by totaling the effort spent on all software development activities, including:
  - Coding
  - Review
  - Testing
  - Requirements analysis
  - Software design
- The size of the software product for computing productivity is arrived at
- The formula used is size divided by effort (that is, software size per unit of effort)

This gives misleading figures for productivity. In fact, what it gives is *capacity.*

In summary, use the following best practice steps to derive productivity from past projects:

1. Compute productivity from the values of completed projects.
2. Compute the skewness coefficient of data to decide whether to use the mean or the mode. My suggestion is to use the statistical mode for arriving at average productivity.
3. Compute productivity only at the organizational level to set organizational standards.
4. Use the organizational productivity standard for monitoring project productivity during execution.
5. Calculate productivity as size per unit of effort.
6. Calculate effort in either person-hours or person-days, but consistently use the same measure for all attributes.
7. When using size, choose:
   a. A size that is specifically right for the attributes, such as
      - LOC or a size measure such as function point analysis or software size units for coding
      - LOC or a size measure such as function point analysis or software size units for code review

- □ Number of pages for documentation
- □ Software test units for software testing
  b. A software size that is standardized for the organization, such as
- □ Function points
- □ Use case points
- □ Object points
- □ Mark II function point analysis
- □ Software size units
8. Compute productivity separately for each attribute:
  a. Programming language for coding and code review
  b. Testing productivity for each type of test carried out in the organization
  c. Documentation for different types of documents produced in the organization

How often should productivity be computed and norms for the organization set? There is no point in changing the norms frequently. Consider the following guidelines:

1. Unless a running project is completed, do not change the norms.
2. It is common to set norms once every quarter, as doing so every month may be too short a time frame and half a year may be too long.
3. Conduct variance analysis and remove assignable causes from the data before considering the data for setting norms.

APPENDIX E: SUGGESTED PHASES AND TASKS FOR TASK-BASED ESTIMATION

Phase 1: Project initiation
1. Project start
2. Receive and review contract
3. Review commitments
4. Amend commitments
5. Identify project manager
6. Prepare project initiation note

Phase 2: Project planning
1. Estimate software size, effort, cost, and schedule
2. Arrange for review of software estimates
3. Implement review feedback in software estimates
4. Arrange for approval of software estimates
5. Baseline software estimates
6. Prepare project plans:
   a. Project management plan
   b. Configuration management plan
   c. Quality assurance plan

    d. Induction training plan

    e. Project schedule

    f. Risk management plan

    g. Defect prevention plan

7. Arrange for review of all plans
8. Implement review feedback in project plans
9. Arrange for approval of project plans
10. Baseline all project plans
11. Raise resource requests
12. Obtain required resources for the project
13. Obtain sign-off for service level agreements
14. Arrange project kickoff meeting
15. Arrange for phase-end audit
16. Close nonconformance reports of the audit, if any

Phase 3: Requirements analysis
1. Prepare list of executives to be interviewed
2. Prepare interview questionnaires and validate them
3. Conduct interviews
4. Compile interview findings
5. Prepare list of documents to be perused
6. Peruse the documents
7. Compile findings from perusal of documents
8. Prepare data model
9. Arrange for review of data model
10. Implement review feedback in data model
11. Prepare process model
12. Arrange for review of process model
13. Implement review feedback in process model
14. Establish scope of the project and determine project boundaries
15. Establish hardware requirements
16. Establish database requirements
17. Establish performance requirements
18. Establish input requirements
19. Establish output requirements
20. Establish functional requirements
21. Establish security requirements
22. Establish user interface requirements
23. Establish external interfaces
24. Prepare traceability matrix

25. Prepare requirements specification document
26. Arrange for review of requirements specification document
27. Implement review feedback in requirements specification document
28. Arrange for approval of requirements specification document
29. Baseline requirements specification document
30. Arrange for phase-end audit
31. Close nonconformance reports, if any

Phase 4: Software design
1. Conduct phase kickoff meeting
2. Identify database design standards
3. Identify user interface design standards
4. Identify report design standards
5. Design database schema
6. Design table structures
7. Design user interfaces
8. Design external interfaces
9. Design navigational model
10. Develop object model
11. Design class diagrams and classes
12. Develop collaboration and sequence diagrams
13. Develop implementation plans
14. Develop test plans
15. Develop program (unit) designs and specifications
16. Prepare software design description document
17. Arrange for review of software design description document
18. Implement review feedback in software design description document
19. Obtain internal approvals for software design description document
20. Transmit the software design description document for client approval
21. Implement client feedback, if any, in the software design description document
22. Obtain client approval for the software design description document
23. Baseline software design description document
24. Conduct phase-end audit
25. Close nonconformance reports, if any

Phase 5: Construction
1. Identify and set up development environment
2. Identify and train team in coding guidelines
3. Create development database

 4. Create table structures
 5. Review database and table structures
 6. Implement database review feedback, if any
 7. Create test data
 8. Conduct code and unit test of module 1—self testing
 9. Code review module 1
10. Prepare test cases for unit testing of module 1
11. Review test cases to be used in unit testing of module 1
12. Conduct independent unit testing of module 1
13. Fix defects uncovered in unit testing of module 1
14. Conduct code and unit test of module n—self testing
15. Code review module n
16. Prepare test cases for unit testing of module n
17. Review test cases to be used in unit testing of module n
18. Conduct independent unit testing of module n
19. Fix defects uncovered in unit testing of module n
20. Conduct phase-end audit
21. Close nonconformance reports, if any

Phase 6: Integration
 1. Determine integration approach and procedure
 2. Identify modules to be integrated
 3. Identify order of integration
 4. Develop integration testing plan and test cases
 5. Identify and set up integration environment
 6. Code interfaces
 7. Integrate modules in the order determined
 8. Arrange for review of integration, as needed
 9. Implement review feedback, if any
10. Conduct integration testing—self testing
11. Fix defects, if any
12. Conduct independent integration testing
13. Fix defects, if any
14. Obtain sign-off for integration testing
15. Conduct phase-end audit
16. Close nonconformance reports, if any

Phase 7: System testing
 1. Conduct phase kickoff meeting
 2. Prepare system testing test cases

3. Arrange for review of system testing test cases
4. Implement review feedback, if any
5. Determine and set up system test environment
6. Create test data
7. Conduct system test on target environment 1
8. Log and analyze defects in target environment 1
9. Fix defects in target environment 1
10. Conduct regression testing and defect closure for target environment 1
11. Conduct system test on target environment n
12. Log and analyze defects in target environment n
13. Fix defects in target environment n
14. Conduct regression testing and defect closure on target environment n
15. Obtain sign-off for system testing
16. Conduct phase-end audit
17. Close nonconformance reports, if any

Phase 8: Acceptance testing
1. Obtain dates from client and schedule user acceptance testing
2. Set up test environment for user acceptance testing
3. Set up test database
4. Arrange test data
5. Assist client in user acceptance testing
6. Fix defects unearthed in user acceptance testing, if any
7. Obtain sign-off from client representative for user acceptance testing
8. Conduct phase-end audit
9. Close nonconformance reports, if any

Phase 9: Documentation
1. Document installation and commissioning manuals
2. Arrange for review of installation and commissioning manuals
3. Implement review feedback, if any, on installation and commissioning manuals
4. Document user guides
5. Arrange for review of user guides
6. Implement review feedback, if any, on user guides
7. Document operations manual(s)
8. Arrange for review of operations manual(s)
9. Implement review feedback, if any, on operations manual(s)
10. Document troubleshooting manual(s)
11. Arrange for review of troubleshooting manual(s)

12. Implement review feedback, if any, on troubleshooting manual(s)
13. Obtain approval for all documentation
14. Conduct phase-end audit
15. Close nonconformance reports, if any

Phase 10: Delivery
1. Assemble all software artifacts for delivery
2. Assemble all documentation for delivery
3. Assemble all review logs for delivery
4. Assemble all test logs for delivery
5. Assemble all approvals and sign-offs for delivery
6. Package all the deliverables on specified media for delivery
7. Arrange for delivery inspection
8. Implement feedback, if any, on the deliverables
9. Deliver the software to the client
10. Obtain receipt acknowledgment from client
11. Conduct phase-end audit
12. Close nonconformance reports, if any

Phase 11: Data migration
1. Conduct database mapping at field level
2. Document data field mapping
3. Arrange for review of data field mapping
4. Implement review feedback, if any, for the data field mapping document
5. Develop software utilities for data migration
6. Test software utilities
7. Implement test feedback, if any, on data migration software utilities
8. Back up databases as required to preserve "before migration image" of the databases
9. Run data migration utilities
10. Inspect databases for accurate data migration
11. Improve data migration utilities, if necessary
12. Restore "before migration image" to the databases
13. Rerun the migration utilities
14. Inspect and ensure that the migration was accurately carried out
15. Arrange for data entry, if necessary, for new fields
16. Test the databases with the software
17. Implement testing feedback, if any
18. Migrate the database to production

19. Conduct phase-end audit
20. Close nonconformance reports, if any

Phase 12: Postdelivery (warranty phase)
1. Receive defect reports, if any, from client representatives
2. Analyze and fix defects
3. Deliver fixes back to client
4. Provide handholding assistance to end users as and when necessary
5. Continue support until end of the warranty period
6. Obtain sign-off for warranty period from client
7. Conduct phase-end audit
8. Close nonconformance reports, if any

Phase 13: Project closure
1. Document best practices implemented in the project
2. Document pitfalls faced in the project
3. Submit reusable components, if any, to the organization's configuration control board
4. Derive project metrics
5. Conduct causal analysis for variances between actual values and estimated values
6. Hand over project metrics and causal analysis to the organization's metrics council
7. Document opportunities for organizational process improvement, if any, and hand them over to the software engineering process group
8. Submit project records to the project management office
9. Release all remaining resources
10. Conduct project closure meeting
11. Conduct phase-end audit
12. Close nonconformance reports, if any

APPENDIX F: SAMPLE PROCESS DEFINITION FOR SOFTWARE ESTIMATION

1. Purpose

This document is used to describe the estimation process and software estimation techniques to be followed in the organization.

2. Scope

This document defines the process for carrying out software estimation in the organization.

3. Entry criteria

The estimation process can be triggered by the following events:

- An estimation request note (ERN) requesting software estimation for a project
- Phase completion of a software development project, necessitating reestimation

4. Exit criteria

The estimation is deemed complete upon delivery of estimate documents to the originator of the estimation request and approval of the estimate for reestimation during project execution.

5. Process description

5.1. Estimation during project acquisition stage

When an ERN triggers the estimation process, the following steps are carried out:

1. Marketing raises the ERN to the project management office (PMO).
2. The PMO identifies and assigns a suitable project leader or project manager to carry out the required estimation.
3. The estimator studies the ERN and obtains clarification, if necessary, from its originator.
4. The estimator selects the appropriate software size measure from the organization's approved list of software size measures if one is not specified in the ERN.
5. The estimator carries out estimation of the software size, software development effort, software development cost, and software development schedule, using the formats specified in the organizational process.
6. The estimator arranges for a peer review. To be effective and to conserve time, this review follows the guided walk-through method of review.
7. The estimator implements feedback and obtains sign-off from the reviewer.
8. The estimator arranges for a managerial review by his or her superior and obtains managerial approval after implementing feedback, if any.
9. The estimator submits the estimate to the originator and provides any necessary clarification.
10. The estimator completes the necessary entries in the ERN and submits it to the PMO to keep as a record.

5.2. Reestimation during project execution

Reestimation is necessary during project execution in the following circumstances:

- After the completion of requirements analysis or software design
- Whenever a change request is received

The project manager is responsible for reestimation of the project estimate. The following steps are carried out:

1. The project manager either performs the work of reestimation or assigns the work to an appropriate project leader.
2. The project manager or project leader carries out the reestimation and revises the project estimate.
3. The project manager or project leader also updates the revision history of the estimate documents.
4. The project manager carries out the managerial review and approves the estimate.
5. The documents are baselined for use in the project.
6. The configuration register is updated accordingly.

In the case of change requests, the following additional steps are required:

1. The change request is reviewed to make sure it conforms to the change request approval procedure in the project's configuration management plan.
2. Once the change request is approved, reestimation as described above is carried out.
3. The impact of the change request on cost and schedule is communicated to the originator of the change request, and approval is obtained from the originator.
4. Once the originator's approval of impacts on cost and schedule is received, the documents are updated, reviewed by the project manager, and baselined for use in the project.

5.3. Internal projects
In internal projects, the end software product is delivered to the system administration group for use within the organization. These software products can be

- Office automation, for the purpose of automating certain organizational processes
- Tools for general internal use or for project-specific use during software development in order to improve productivity and quality

The following steps are utilized to carry out estimation:

1. The software engineering process group (SEPG) raises the necessary project initiation note to the PMO to initiate project execution.

2. The PMO arranges for approval of the project initiation note by senior management.

3. The PMO identifies the estimation work and assigns a suitable project leader or project manager. However, it is not mandatory to assign a project leader or project manager, as internal projects may be used to mentor team members in software estimation.

4. Estimation of software size for internal projects is not mandatory. It needs to be carried out when the project is expected to consume more than 6 person-months. However, at the discretion of the project manager, software estimation may be carried out for any project.

5. The estimator carries out estimation of software development effort, software development cost, and software development schedule, using the formats specified in the organizational process.

6. The estimator arranges for a peer review. To be effective and to conserve time, this review follows the guided walk-through method of review. The reviewer is either a project leader or a project manager.

7. The estimator implements feedback, if any, and obtains sign-off from the reviewer.

8. The estimator arranges for a managerial review by his or her superior and obtains managerial approval after implementing feedback, if any.

9. The estimator submits the estimate to the originator and provides clarification, if necessary.

10. The estimator completes the necessary entries in the ERN and submits it to the PMO to keep as a record.

5.4. Tailoring guidelines

The process described above is adhered to except under the following circumstances:

- The effort required for the project is less than or equal to 3 person-months.
- The time available for estimation is less than 4 clock hours.

In such situations:

1. A peer review might be exempted from the estimation process described above. However, approval of the SEPG must be obtained for such exemption. When an estimate is not reviewed, it must be referred to as a ballpark estimate.

2. Only an experienced estimator is assigned the work in ballpark estimation.
3. The estimator must include the list of assumptions.

5.5. The estimator and the reviewer
The estimator for new projects is a project leader or a project manager, previously trained in software estimation. The reviewer of the estimate is a peer of the estimator, selected by the PMO.

5.6. Software size measure approved for use in estimation
The following are the approved software size measures:

- Function point analysis
- Object points
- Software size units
- Use case points
- Software test units
- Mark II function point analysis
- Lines of code

Guidelines for these size measures are documented in the organizational standards.
The following are the approved types of software development effort estimates:

- Task-based estimation
- Delphi technique
- Analogy-based estimation

5.7. Software size measure selection
The following guidelines may be used to determine the technique best suited for an estimation:

- A size measure preferred by the customer or the originator of the ERN
- Function points for a third-generation-language project
- Use case points for a UML-based project
- Object points for a client-server project
- Task-based estimation for conversion, porting, migration, and re-engineering projects
- Software test units for software-testing projects
- Lines of code for defect-fixing projects
- Software size units when other size measures are not suitable

If none of the above project types are applicable, the estimator may use his or her best judgment in selecting an appropriate software size measure.

5.8. Reconciliation with actual values

It is possible that some projects for which estimates were prepared may be lost to the competition. In such cases:

- Marketing tries to obtain the estimates prepared by the party that won the project.
- The metrics council (a part of the SEPG) conducts a causal analysis using the critical examination, trend analysis, and correlation analysis techniques to compare actual values with the estimated values of the following:
  - □ Software size
  - □ Software development effort
  - □ Software development cost
  - □ Software development schedule
- The metrics council then draws inferences about the competition's norms vis-à-vis the organizational norms and uses the data for benchmarking.

When projects are closed, the PMO arranges for the metrics council to perform a causal analysis of the variance between estimated values and actual values of the following:

- Software size
- Software development effort
- Software development cost
- Software development schedule

Based on the results of the causal analysis, the metrics council decides whether organizational norms need to be adjusted, and if so, proposes these adjustments to the SEPG.

6. Comments and feedback

Comments or feedback for improvement on this process may be raised to the SEPG using the formats defined in the software process improvement process.

APPENDIX G: ESTIMATION PRESENTATION TEMPLATE

1. Project name

2. Project details

Include the following information:
1. Brief description of the project
2. Time allowed for estimation
3. Initial information available for estimation (basic/obtained more information from client/detailed)
4. Domain experience of the organization (limited/moderate/extensive)
5. Initial gut feeling
6. Project type:
    a. Development
    b. Maintenance
    c. Reengineering
    d. Conversion
    e. Enterprise resource planning implementation

3. Software effort estimation method selected

Include the reason for the selection.

4. Estimator information (see example below)

Ref. no.	Estimator	Planned		Actual	
		Start date	End date	Start date	End date

5. Reviewer information (see example below)

Ref. no.	Reviewer	Planned		Actual	
		Start date	End date	Start date	End date

6. Risks (see example below)

Describe the risks that might have been identified. These will be addressed during the proposal process. Later, in the project execution phase, these risks will have to be addressed in the project plan. Classification of risks will be required.

Risk	Low	Medium	High	Critical
Requirement change			✓	
Response time to offshore queries			✓	
Change in offshore team			✓	

7. Assumptions

Describe various assumptions made by the estimator during the estimation.

8. Estimation details (see example at top of next page)

For example, software size measure (function points, object points, use case points, Mark II function point analysis, software size units, lines of code, software test units).

Aspect	Best case	Worst case	Normal case	Expected
Software size				
Software development effort				
Software development cost				
Software development schedule				

9. Reference documents

Mention the various reference documents that might have been used during the estimation. Examples of such documents include:

- Internal documents (estimation processes, standards, and guidelines)
- Client-supplied documents
- Marketing documents
- Minutes of meetings
- Published documents

10. Inclusions

Enumerate all activities or software components that are included as part of the estimation, such as master data creation, on-site support during warranty period, etc.

11. Exclusions, if any

Enumerate all software components or activities that may be mistakenly assumed to be included in the estimate by marketing or the client, such as master data creation, on-site support during warranty, etc.

12. Remarks

Include any other information relevant to the estimation.

13. Appendices

Enclose all the documents (estimation worksheet and other related documents).

APPENDIX H: ESTIMATION REQUEST NOTE TEMPLATE

1. Originator information
Name (*requester*):

Designation:

Department:

2. Client information
Client name:

Nature of business:

Address:

Phone:

Contact person:

3. Project details
Name of project:

Development platform (*programming language, database, number of tiers, etc.*):

Date by which the estimate is required (*to be filled in by the originator*):

Budget specified (*if available*):

Size measure specified (*if predetermined*):

Size of the project (*initial gut feeling*):

4. Project type
- ☐ Development
- ☐ Maintenance
- ☐ Reengineering
- ☐ Conversion
- ☐ Software implementation
- ☐ Other (*specify*)

5. Estimation inputs (*list of documents supplied along with this note*)
- ☐ Request for proposal
- ☐ Briefing by marketing
- ☐ Direct briefing from the client
- ☐ User requirements
- ☐ Statement of work
- ☐ Software requirements specification
- ☐ Design document
- ☐ E-mail from marketing
- ☐ Inputs provided by the bidding process (*applicable for projects initiated by marketing*)
- ☐ Other (*specify*)

6. To be filled in by the estimator
Name of estimator:

Estimation completion date:

Name of reviewer:

Review defects closed on (*date*):

Submitted to the originator on (*date*):

Software size measure used:

Estimated software size:

Estimated software development effort in person-hours:

Estimated software development cost:

Duration of software development:

7. To be filled in by the project management office
Actual software size:

Actual software development effort:

Actual software development cost:

Actual scheduled delivery date:

APPENDIX I:
QUICK REFERENCE

Capacity vis-à-vis productivity—"Capacity" refers to the overall throughput of a facility, whereas "productivity" refers to the rate of achievement for a specific type of work.

Cost estimation—Performed to understand how much money the organization has to spend to execute a project.

Estimation—The intelligent anticipation of the quantum of work that needs to be performed and the resources (human resources, monetary resources, equipment resources, and time resources) required to perform the work at a future date, in a defined environment, using specified methods.

- **Software estimation**—Estimation of the software size, software development effort, software development cost, and software development schedule for a specified software product in a specified environment, using defined methods, tools, and techniques.

Pricing—Performed to understand how much the organization can profit from the client, or in other words, to determine how much the customer would be willing to pay for the project.

Procedure—A step-by-step instruction for how to carry out an organizational activity, including the what, how, who, and when aspects of that organizational activity.

Process—Documented methods of working in an organization, which consist of procedures, standards, guidelines, checklists, formats, and templates.

Productivity (standard time)—The rate of producing some output using a set of inputs in a defined unit of time and in a defined environment, by a qualified person who is acclimatized to the working environment and who is using a defined set of methods, at a pace that can be maintained day after day, without any harmful physical effects. Productivity is determined through two distinct routes: empirical methods and work measurement.

Scheduling—The setting of calendar dates to planned activities, using the following steps:
1. Define the work breakdown structure
2. Define predecessors
3. Set initial dates
4. Allocate resources
5. Modify the dates based on resource availability
6. Ensure that the network diagram has no hanging nodes

Software test unit—A size measure for measuring the size of a software testing project. It is equivalent to a normalized test case, with one input and one corresponding output.

Standard time—The amount of time it takes to accomplish a unit of defined work carried out by a qualified worker after adjustment, using a given method, under specified working conditions, at a pace that can be maintained day after day, without any harmful physical effects.

Test effort estimation—The estimation of the testing size, testing effort, testing cost, and testing schedule for a specified software testing project in a specified environment, using defined methods, tools, and techniques. The following are six approaches:
- Delphi technique
- Analogy-based estimation
- Software-size-based estimation
- Test-case-enumeration-based estimation
- Task (activity)-based estimation
- Testing-size-based estimation

Units of measure for software estimation—Five commonly used units of measure for software estimation are as follows (in alphabetical order):
1. **Function point**—A rough equivalent of a unit of delivered functionality of a software project. This is the most popular size measure. A function point is derived from the following five function point transactions:

- **External input**—Each user input is an elementary process that provides distinct application-oriented data to the software.
- **External output**—Each user output is an elementary process that provides distinct application-oriented information to the user.
- **External inquiry**—An elementary process that accepts an on-line input, which results in the generation of an immediate software response in the form of an on-line output.
- **Internal logical file**—All logical data files ("create," "read," "update," and "delete"—CRUD) maintained by the system being developed.
- **External interface file**—Any machine-readable interfaces, including data files that are maintained by another system.

Tables I.1 to I.5 show the rules for determining complexity and the corresponding weights for various function point transactions.

The value adjustment factor is computed from 14 general system characteristics (GSC) using the following formula:

$$\text{Value adjustment factor} = 0.65 + \left(\frac{\text{sum of GSC ratings}}{100} \right)$$

Table I.1. Complexity rules for external inputs

File types referenced	Data element types		
	1 to 4	**5 to 15**	**More than 15**
Less than 2	Low (3)	Low (3)	Average (4)
2	Low (3)	Average (4)	High (6)
Greater than 2	Average (4)	High (6)	High (6)

Table I.2. Complexity rules for external outputs

File types referenced	Data element types		
	1 to 5	**6 to 19**	**More than 19**
Less than 2	Low (4)	Low (4)	Average (5)
2 or 3	Low (4)	Average (5)	High (7)
Greater than 3	Average (5)	High (7)	High (7)

Table I.3. Complexity rules for external inquiries

Record element types	Data element types		
	1 to 5	**6 to 19**	**More than 19**
Less than 2	Low (3)	Low (3)	Average (4)
2 or 3	Low (3)	Average (4)	High (6)
Greater than 3	Average (4)	High (6)	High (6)

Table I.4. Complexity rules for internal logical files

Record element types	Data element types		
	1 to 19	**20 to 50**	**More than 50**
1	Low (7)	Low (7)	Average (10)
2 to 5	Low (7)	Average (10)	High (15)
Greater than 5	Average (10)	High (15)	High (15)

Table I.5. Complexity rules for external interface files

Record element types	Data element types		
	1 to 19	**20 to 50**	**More than 50**
1	Low (5)	Low (5)	Average (7)
2 to 5	Low (5)	Average (7)	High (10)
Greater than 5	Average (7)	High (10)	High (10)

2. **Mark II function point analysis**—As defined by the U.K. Software Metrics Association, Mark II function point analysis is a method for the quantitative analysis and measurement of information-processing applications. It quantifies the information processing requirements specified by the user to provide a figure for the size of the resulting software product. Size is expressed as Mark II function points or Mark II function point index. Mark II function point analysis uses logical transactions to estimate software size.

Table I.6 depicts the weights of the input, processing, and output components for a functional size.

Mark II function point analysis indicates software size as function point index. It is computed using the following formula:

$$\text{Function point index} = (W_i \times \Sigma N_i) + (W_e \times \Sigma N_e) + (W_o \times \Sigma N_o)$$

Table I.6. Weights of the input, processing, and output components

Ref. no.	Element	Weight
1	Entity	1.66 (We)
2	Input data element type	0.58 (Wi)
3	Output data element type	0.26 (Wo)

where function point index is the functional size, Wi is the weight of the input data element types, We is the weight of the entities, Wo is the weight of the output data element types, ΣNi is the number of all input data element types, ΣNe is the number of all entities, and ΣNo is the number of all output data element types.

The technical complexity adjustment factor (TCAF) is used to adjust the size of software. It is computed using the following formula:

$$\text{TCAF} = 0.65 + (\text{sum of DI} \times 0.005)$$

where DI is the degree of influence for each of the 20 complexity factors.

3. **Object point**—Software artifacts (screens, reports, and third-generation-language components) are enumerated and rated on a complexity level (simple, medium, or difficult). Tables I.7, I.8, and I.9 give the complexity rules and corresponding weights for object point transactions.

4. **Software size unit**—An input process element that has five numeric data elements.

   ■ **Data elements**—The data that enters the system, is processed, and is either stored for future use or given out as output. Each element can be a constant (when used as a parameter for the

Table I.7. Complexity levels for screens

Number of views contained	Number and source of data tables		
	Total <4 (1 server, 1 or 2 clients)	Total between 4 and 8 (2 or 3 servers, 3 to 5 clients)	Total >8 (>3 servers, >5 clients)
2 or less	Simple	Simple	Medium
3 to 7	Simple	Medium	Difficult
8 or more	Medium	Difficult	Difficult

Table I.8. Complexity levels for reports

Number of sections contained	Number and source of data tables		
	Total <4 (1 server, 1 or 2 clients)	Total between 4 and 8 (2 or 3 servers, 3 to 5 clients)	Total >8 (>3 servers, >5 clients)
1	Simple	Simple	Medium
2 or 3	Simple	Medium	Difficult
4 or more	Medium	Difficult	Difficult

Table I.9. Weights for objects

Object	Weight based on complexity level		
	Simple	Medium	Difficult
Screen	1	2	3
Report	2	5	8
Third-generation-language component	NA	NA	10

software system) or a variable. Data elements are classified into three types:

- **Numeric data element**—Consists of the digits 0 to 9, one decimal point, and a positive or negative sign. A numeric data element transforms and is transformed in the system.

- **Alphanumeric data element**—Consists of all humanly readable characters, including the space character. An alphanumeric data element passes through the system.

- **Control data element**—Triggers some process within the system. Links on a Web site and command buttons on a screen are examples of control data elements.

■ **Process elements**—Act on data elements and transform input to desired outputs. Process elements are classified into three types:

- **Input process element**—Receives data elements into the system from the external environment.

- **Output process element**—Sends data elements from the system to the external environment.

- **Associate process element**—A process element that helps either input process elements or output process elements or assists in maintaining certain system functions, the results of which are sometimes not seen by users.

5. **Use case point**—Used in conjunction with UML and RUP for software size and effort estimation. Use cases of the proposed system are enumerated, and each is classified by complexity, with each complexity category classified by number of transactions or by number of classes. Each use case is comprised of actors. Each actor is classified into one of three levels based on complexity.

■ *Classification of use cases:*

  □ *Simple use case*—1 to 3 transactions or 5 or fewer classes in the software; carries a weight of 5.

  □ *Average use case*—4 to 7 transactions or 6 to 10 classes in the software; carries a weight of 10.

  □ *Complex use case*—8 or more transactions or 11 or more classes in the software; carries a weight of 15.

■ *Classification of use case actors:*

  □ *Simple actor*—A system interface; carries a weight of 1.

  □ *Average actor*—A protocol-driven interface; carries a weight of 2.

  □ *Complex actor*—A graphical user interface; carries a weight of 3.

Technical and environmental complexity factors adjust the software size. These are computed using the following formulas:

$$\text{Technical complexity factor} = 0.6 + \left(\frac{\text{technical factor}}{100} \right)$$

$$\text{Environmental complexity factor} = 0.4 + (-0.03 \times \text{environmental factor})$$

APPENDIX J: ABBREVIATIONS

ADE	Alphanumeric data element
AFPI	Adjusted function point index
AIIE	American Institute of Industrial Engineers
APE	Associate process element
AUCP	Adjusted use case point
CDE	Control data element
CFPS	Certified Function Point Specialist
CMM®	Capability Maturity Model
CMMI®	Capability Maturity Model Integration
COCOMO	Constructive Cost Model
COTS	Commercial off-the-shelf
CRM	Customer relationship management
CWF	Composite weight factor
DET	Data element type
DI	Degree of influence
EAF	Effort adjustment factor
ECF	Environmental complexity factor
EF	Environmental factor
EI	External input
EIF	External interface file
EO	External output
EQ	External inquiry
ERN	Estimation request note

ERP	Enterprise resource planning
FF	Finish-to-finish
FP	Function point
FPA	Function point analysis
FPI	Function point index in Mark II function point analysis
FS	Finish-to-start
FTR	File type referenced
GSC	General system characteristic
GUI	Graphical user interface
IFPUG	International Function Point Users Group
ILF	Internal logical file
ILO	International Labor Organization
IPE	Input process element
ISO	International Organization for Standardization
JAD	Joint Application Development
KLOC	Thousand lines of code
LOC	Lines of code
MK II FPA	Mark II function point analysis
MRP	Material requirements planning
NDE	Numeric data element
NOP	New object point
OP	Object point
OPE	Output process element
PC	Personal computer
PMO	Project management office
RAD	Rapid Application Development
RAM	Random access memory
RDBMS	Relational database management system
RET	Record element type
RFP	Request for proposal
RUP	Rational Unified Process
SCM	Supply chain management
SEPG	Software engineering process group
SF	Start-to-finish
SQL	Structured Query Language
SRS	Software requirements specification
SS	Start-to-start
SSU	Software size unit
STU	Software test unit
TCAF	Technical complexity adjustment factor

TCF	Technical complexity factor
TDE	Total data elements
TF	Technical factor
3GL	Third-generation language
UCP	Use case point
UKSMA	U.K. Software Metrics Association
UUCP	Unadjusted use case point
VAF	Value adjustment factor
WBS	Work breakdown structure

INDEX

A

ABC analysis, 180
Acceptance testing, 14, 27, 35, 37, 38, 39, 102, 118, 174, 177, 179, 189, 190, 192, 255
Access privileges, 41
Activity, 161, 163
Activity-based estimation, see Task-based estimation
Actors, 84–85, 87, 279
Actual values, estimated values versus, 15–17, see also Variance analysis; Variation
ADE, see Alphanumeric data element
Ad hoc approach, 49, 50
Ad hoc reports, 41
Adjusted function point count, 82
Adjusted function point index (AFPI), 94
Adjusted use case points (AUCP), 85, 87
AFPI, see Adjusted function point index
Agile Manifesto, 44
Agile methods, 119, 120
Agile software development project, 32, 44–45
AIIE, see American Institute of Industrial Engineers
Albrecht, Allan J., 73
Alphanumeric data element (ADE), 98, 100, 101, 278
American Institute of Industrial Engineers (AIIE), 12, 137, 138
American National Standards Institute, 53
Analogy-based estimation, 33, 34, 37, 39, 41, 42, 43, 44, 51, 53, 57–64, 70, 186, 210, 237, 238
    merits and demerits of, 64
    selection of similar past projects, 58–60

shortlisting of past projects, 60–64
in software maintenance, 64
test effort, 181
Analytical estimation, 16, 146, 206
APE, see Associate process element
Apple Computer, 1
Application domain, 21, 24, 51, 53, 54, 56, 58, 61, 63, 198, 199
    selection of projects and, 60, 61
Application server, 45, 46
Application software, 1, 2, 33
Application tiers, 59, 61, 62, 63, 99
Application weight, 189, 191
Architecture design, 102
Arithmetic average, 62
Arithmetic mean, 56, 145, 232, 234, 244, 247
Artifact measurement, 69–70
Artifacts, 88, 89, 90, 110, 197, 277, 278
Assignable cause, 249
Assignable variation, 225, 226, 229
Associate process element (APE), 99, 100, 104, 105, 278
Assumptions, 214, 215, 263
    documenting, 128–129
AUCP, see Adjusted use case points
Auditability, tool selection and, 221
Average, 18, 56, 62, 145, 243, 244, 246
Average performer, 70

B

BaaN, 51
Back end, 59, 61, 63
Back-end programs, 46
Backups, 41
Ballpark estimate, 124, 202–203, 204, 262–263

285

Bandwidth, 175
Bar chart, 161, 162
Basic time, 149
Batch processing, 83
Benchmarking, 13, 27, 53, 70, 83, 117, 133, 192, 264
Best-case scenario, 27–28, 29, 116, 117, 128, 129, 171, 183, 185, 186, 187, 207, 208
Best guess, 3, 51, 55
Beta distribution, 18, 183
Bidding process, 10
Black box testing, 173, 174, 180, 187, 188, 189
Boehm, Barry, 51, 120, 123
Boundary value analysis, 178
British Standards Institute, 53
Budget, 4, 5, 10, see also Cost estimation
Buffer, 203, 204
Build preparation, 144
Business processing logic, 43

C

Capability Maturity Model, 208
Capacity, 13, 69, 248
  defined, 136
  expansion of, 202
  productivity versus, 137, 149–151, 273
Capacity planning, 150
Category analysis, 180
Causal analysis, 29, 50, 123, 189, 198, 203, 205, 264
  lack of, 200, 204
CDE, see Control data element
Central tendency, 172, 243, 244, 247
Central value, 244
Certified Function Point Specialist (CFPS), 53, 198
CFPS, see Certified Function Point Specialist
Chance variation, 15, 29, 225, 226
Change request, 40, 43, 260, 261
Character user interface, 73
Check box, 76
Checklist, 204, 209, 210, 212
Cleanup time, 148
Clear case, 119
Client locations, 58
Client-server, 88, 182, 187, 263
CMMI® 3, 61, 63
CMMI® 5, 61, 63
COBOL, 83
COCOMO, 51, 88, 89, 117, 120–123, 137
Code walk-through, 13, 34, 188
Coding, 13, 16, 27, 102, 135, 144, 248
Coefficient of correlation, 232–233

Co-location of customer/end user with development team, 44, 119
Combo box, 76, 77, 104
Command button, 76
Commercial off-the-shelf (COTS) software, 1–2, 31, 32, 35–36, 174, 237
Commissioning, 135
Comparison, 192
Comparison testing, 177
Competition, 54, 55, 166, 167, 264
Complexity, 107, 275–276, 277, 278, 279
  of components, 22, 25–26
  density versus size, 112–113
  factors, 107
  function point and, 83
  limitations and, 109–110, 111–112
  object points and, 88, 89
  paradox of in relation to size, 108–112
  points and, 97
  programming language and, 147–148
  ratings for external inputs, 75–76
  ratings for external inquiries, 77–78
  ratings for external outputs, 76–77
  size and, 71
  software size units and, 105
  task-based estimation and, 186
  technical, see Technical complexity
  test cases, 189
  testing and, 188
  of use cases, 84–85, 87
Components, 21, 22, 196, 276–277
  breaking the project down into, 22–25, see also Work breakdown structure
  complexity of, 25–26
Composite weight factor (CWF), 62–63, 191
Concurrent testing, 175–176, 179
Configuration, 261
Configuration management plan, 185
Confirmation message, 76, 77
Construction, 33, 34, 99, 102, 103, 124, 125, 131, 144, 201, 253–254
Constructive Cost Model, see COCOMO
Contingency allowance, 100, 101, 117
Contract software development, 68
Control charts, 229, 234–235
Control data element (CDE), 98, 100, 101, 278
Control limits, 234, 235
Convergence, 241
  of experts' opinions, 56
Conversion, 32, 39, 238, 263
Conversion factor, 206
  for software-size-based estimation, 182
  for software test unit, 191

Conversion guidelines document, 39
Conversion project, 58
Cooperation, 208
Correlation, 200, 232–233
Correlation analysis, 226, 231–237, 264
Corrective action, 5, 29
Cost
  actual values, 198
  impact of change request on, 261
  price versus, 165
  reviews, 199
  testing, 180
  variance analysis, 226, 227, 228, 229, 230, 231
Cost accountants, 5, 6
Cost drivers, 121
Cost estimation, 49, 165–172, 207, 210, 260, 262, 264, 273
  cost of effort, 169–172
  detailed estimates, 52
  for functional expansion, 44–45
  gross estimates, 51, 52
  history of, 2
  maintenance of, 219
  pricing models, 165–168
  tools for, 201–202, 218–219
  traditional, 5–7
Cost of effort, 169–172
Cost-plus pricing, 6, 50, 165–166
COTS software, see Commercial off-the-shelf software
Counting Practices Manual, 53, 76, 77, 80, 84, 198
Critical examination, 264
Critical examination table, 227, 228
Critical order, 167
Critical path method, 219
CRM, see Customer relationship management
CRUD, 74, 275
Crystal Reports, 99
Currency exchange rates, 50
Customer acceptance objectives, 179
Customer relationship management (CRM), 35, 51, 58, 61, 63
Customer satisfaction, 45
Customization, 71, 127
CWF, see Composite weight factor

D

Data
  currency of, 247–248
  symmetry of, 245
Database, 46, 175
Database server tier, 45

Data collection, 182
Data element, 98, 99, 100, 104, 105, 277–278
Data element type (DET), 74, 75, 76, 77, 78, 79, 91, 92
Data file, 33, 74, 99, 109
Data manipulation, 46
Data migration, 38, 256–257, see also Migration
Data modeling, 91
Data retrieval, 77
Data warehousing, 35
Debugging, 13, 119
Declaration of variables, 112
Defect analysis, 180
Defect density, 207
Defect fixing, 32, 40–41, 42, 102, 238, 263
Defect injection, 196, 197
Defect report, 40
Defects, testing, 173, 174, 176, 178, 179, see also Testing
Degree of influence (DI), 93, 277
Deliverables, 55
Delivered software size, 99–100
Delivery, 256
  commitments, 5, 10
  schedule, 28, 29, see also Schedule
Delphi estimation, 33, 34, 37, 39, 41, 42, 43, 44, 51, 70, 210, 237, 238
Delphi technique, 54–57, 181, 186, 239–241
Density
  complexity versus, 112–113
  software size units and, 105
Deployment, 135
Deployment testing, 176
Design, 13, 16, 27, 33, 34, 68, 99, 102, 103, 118, 119, 120, 124, 125, 127, 131, 135, 143–144, 201, 248, 253, 260
Design modification, 43
DET, see Data element type
Detailed estimates, 49, 52, 60, 62
Deutsches Institut für Normung, 53
Developers, 146
Development, 135, 141–145, see also specific activities
Development cost, 3, 4, see also Cost estimation
Development effort, 3, 4, see also Effort estimation
  from software size, 115–118
Development environment, 59, 61, 62, 63
Development location, 60, 61, 63
Development methodology, influence on estimation, 118–120
Development projects, task-based estimation phases, 124–126

Development schedule, 3, 4, see also Schedule estimation
Development team, co-location of customer/ end user with, 44, 119
DI, see Degree of influence
Differences map, 36
Direct staff, 169, 170
Documentation, 44, 68, 102, 119, 120, 125, 127, 132, 144, 204, 209, 215, 249, 255–256, 260
Documenting assumptions, 128–129
DotNet, 148
Drop-down, 76
Duration, see also Schedule
  effort and, 159–161
  for estimation, 199, 203
  for preparing estimate, 214
Dynamic systems development method, 119

E

EAF, see Effort adjustment factor
ECF, see Environmental complexity factor
EF, see Environmental factor
Efficiency, 12, 136
Effort, 248
  actual values, 198
  converting software size into, 27
  cost of, 169–172
  duration and, 159–161
  expected, 128, 183, 185, 186
  reviews, 199
  testing, 180
  variance analysis, 226, 227, 228, 229, 230, 231
Effort adjustment factor (EAF), 121
Effort estimate, 21, 185
Effort estimation, 5, 16, 49, 53, 63, 64, 70, 115–133, 192–193, 260, 262, 264
  analogy-based, see Analogy-based estimation
  COCOMO, 120–123, see also COCOMO
  conversion of software size to, 53, 115–118, 201, 204
  delivered software size and, 99
  detailed estimates, 52
  for functional expansion, 44, 45
  gross estimates, 51, 52
  history of, 2
  influence of software development methodology on, 118–120
  from software size units, 100, 102–103
  task-based, 124–133, see also Task-based estimation
  calculation, 128–132
  merits and demerits of, 133

phases for development projects, 124–125
phases for testing projects, 126–127
templates for, 209
test size and, 173–193, see also Testing
  approaches to, 181–186, 187, see also specific approaches
  basics, 173–174
  methodology, 177–179
  product, 174, 175–177
  project/embedded, 174
  sizing, 186–192
  strategy, 179–180
  test estimation, 180–181
  tools for, 201–202
  variation and, 29
Effort level, 15, 16, 29, 139, 140, 141, 197
EI, see External input
EIF, see External interface file
Embedded project, 120, 121
Embedded testing, 174, 180
Empirical data, 205
Empirical methods, 274
  to determine productivity, 145–146
End milestone, 153, 154, 155, 156, 157, 158, 159
End-to-end testing, 175, 190
Engineering drawings, 113
Engineering projects, 124
Enterprise application integration, 35
Enterprise resource planning (ERP), 35, 51, 58, 126, 127
Entity, 91, 92
Environmental changes, 46
Environmental complexity factor (ECF), 85, 86, 87, 279
Environmental factor (EF), 85, 86
EO, see External output
EQ, see External inquiry
ERN, see Estimation request note
ERP, see Enterprise resource planning
Error message, 76
Estimate,
  defined, 3
  single or a range of, 207–208
  templates for, 209, 210, 213–216
Estimated values, actual values versus, 15–17, see also Variance analysis; Variation
Estimate preliminaries, 214
Estimates repository, 57, 204–205
Estimation, see also Software estimation; specific types
  defined, 2
  details, 215
  flow, 69

impact of project execution on, 29
methodology, 210, 214
norms, 15–17, 29, 210
over- or under-, 202–203
presentation, template, 265–267
process definition for, 259–264
request, 210
revision, 210
techniques, project type and, 237–238
uncertainty in, 27–28, see also Uncertainty
Estimation request note (ERN), 214, 259, 260, 262, 263, 269–271
Estimator, see Software estimators
EstimatorPal, 162
Euro conversion, 32, 39
Event-driven programming, 118
Exclusions, 215
Executable code, 68
Existing code, 88–89, 90
Expected effort, 128, 183, 185, 186
External input, (EI), 74, 75–76, 78, 79, 83, 275
External inquiry (EQ), 74, 77–78, 79, 83, 275, 276
External interface file (EIF), 74, 77, 78–79, 83, 275, 276
External output (EO), 74, 76–77, 78, 79, 83, 275
Extreme Programming, 119
Extrapolation, 200

F

Fair effort, 139
Fair skill, 139, 140
Feasibility studies, 33
Feature-driven development, 119
Feature point, 11, 52, 181, 182
FF, see Finish-to-finish relationship
File retrieval, 201
File type referenced (FTR), 74, 75, 77, 78
Finish-to-finish (FF) relationship, 156, 157, 158, 159
Finish-to-start (FS) relationship, 156, 157, 158, 159
Fixed bids, 2, 14
Fixed costs, 170
Flat file, 31, 61, 74, 75, 83
Formats, 204, 209, 210, 212
Fourth-generation language, 74
Four-tier application, 182
FP, see Function point
FPA, see Function point analysis
FPI, see Function point index
Fragmentation, 22
FS, see Finish-to-start relationship

FTR, see File type referenced
Full life cycle project, 32, 33, 44, 58, 129, 218, 237
Functional decomposition, 197
Functional expansion, 32, 38, 43–44, 238
Functionality, 43, 112, 113, 274
Mark II function point analysis and, 94
sources of detail on, 24–25
testing and, 173, 174, 178, 179, see also Testing
Functional measurement, 68–69
Functional testing, 13, 43, 175, 177, 188, 190, 192
Function point (FP), 11, 12, 26, 33, 52, 53, 69, 73–84, 97, 189, 191, 198, 233, 249, 263, 274–275
adjusted count, 82
conversion factors, 181, 182
external input, 75–76
external inquiry, 77, 78
external interface file, 78–79
external output, 76–77
internal logical file, 78, 79
merits and demerits of, 82–84
unadjusted count, 79
value adjustment factor, 80–81, 82
Function point analysis (FPA), 107, 198, 248
Function point index (FPI), 92, 94

G

Gantt chart, 161, 162
Gap analysis, 127
General system characteristic (GSC), 80–82, 84, 275
Geometric mean, 244
Going rate pricing, 166
Goodness of fit, 200
Granularity, 128, 188
Graphical user interface (GUI), 74, 75, 76, 77, 83, 84, 87, 118, 178, 218, 221
Graphics, 46, 76
for schedules, 161–165
Gross estimates, 49, 51–52, 60, 62–63, see also specific types
GSC, see General system characteristic
GUI, see Graphical user interface
Guided walk-through, 260, 262
Guidelines, 204, 209, 210, 212

H

Hardware, 1, 2, 33, 112
adding, 44
attributes, 121, 122

cost of, 169, 171
porting of software, 36
Harmonic mean, 244
Historical data, 15, 16, 34, 51, 52, 57, 205,
    see also Past projects
lack of, 198, 203
HTML pages, 46
Hunch-based analysis, 123

I

IBM, 1, 52, 73
Icons, 76
IFPUG, see International Function Point
    Users Group
ILF, see Internal logical file
ILO, see International Labor Organization
Images, 76
Implementation, 33, 237
Implementation project, 58, 71, 218
Incentive payments, 16
Inclusions, 215
Incremental costing, 6
Incremental development, 119
Independent testing, 173, 190
Independent verification and validation, 34,
    102, 135, 237
Indirect staff, 170
Industrial engineering, 5, 13, 15, 35, 103,
    205–206
Infrastructure projects, 52, 129
In-line documentation, 72, 73
Input process element (IPE), 98–99, 100, 104,
    278
Inquiry screen, 104
Inspection, 13, 14, 174
Installation, 135
Install testing, 177
Institute of Electrical and Electronics
    Engineers, 53
Integration, 43, 125, 131, 156, 254
Integration testing, 27, 35, 102, 174, 175, 177,
    179, 184, 187, 189, 190
Interfaces, 44, 74, 84, 99
Internal logical file (ILF), 74, 76, 77, 78, 79,
    83, 275, 276
Internal projects, 4, 5, 10, 22, 211, 261–262,
    see also Project approval
International Function Point Users Group
    (IFPUG), 27, 53, 73, 76, 77, 80, 84, 197,
    198
International Labor Organization (ILO), 146
International Organization for
    Standardization (ISO), 208

International Software Benchmarking
    Standards Group, 27, 64
Internet, 25, 26, 27
    disconnection, 176
Internet point, 11, 52
Interpolation, 200
Introductory pricing, 166
Intuitive testing, 177–178
IPE, see Input process element
ISO, see International Organization for
    Standardization
ISO 9000
Iteration, 44, 119
Iterative models, 119

J

JAD, see Joint Application Development
Java, 148, 233, 243
JD Edwards, 51
Joint Application Development (JAD), 119

K

Karner, Gustav, 84
Kickoff meeting, 185
KLOC, see Thousand lines of code
Knowledge repository, 26, 57, 64, 198, 199,
    203, 204–205
KPMG, 90

L

Labor, 6, 69
Lag time, 156, 157
Linear correlation, 232
Line balancing, 150
Line graph, 229, 234
Lines of code (LOC), 11, 12, 51, 52–53, 68,
    71–73, 112, 195, 243, 244, 246, 247, 248,
    263
    merits and demerits of, 73
List box, 76, 77, 104
List view, 76, 77, 104–105
Load testing, 175, 177, 178, 184, 190
LOC, see Lines of code
Logical data files, 74
Logical line, 73
Logical testing, 178
Logical transaction, 90, 91, 276
Login screen, 83, 87
Loss leader pricing, 166–167
Lower control limit, 234, 235

M

Machine reset, 176
Macro-productivity, 137

Made-to-order industry, 14
Mainframe applications, 83
Maintenance projects, 32, 39–44, 55, 64, 71, 129, 210, 218, 238, see also specific types
Maintenance work request, 40
Management, attitude of, 49
Managerial review, 60, 62, 63, 199–200, 203, 204, 260, 261, 262
Manual testing, 180
Manufacturing, 12, 13
Manugistics, 51
Marginal costing, 6
Mark II function point analysis (MK II FPA), 33, 52, 69, 90–94, 198, 249, 276–277
  conversion factors, 181, 182
  merits and demerits of, 94
Mark II function point index, 276, 277
Market opportunity, 168
Master data files, 33
Material cost, 6, 7
Materials, 69
Maynard, John, 138
Mean, 18, 56, 145, 244, 245, 246, 247, 248
Measures of central tendency, 243, 244, 247
Median, 18, 145, 244, 246, 247
Methods of working, 209
Metrics council, 264
Micro-productivity, 137
Microsoft Excel, 24, 129, 161, 201, 220 230, 233, 235, 246
Microsoft Project, 70, 133, 161, 219, 220
Microsoft Windows, 37
Middleware, 46, 59, 61, 62, 63
Migration, 32, 37–39, 58, 161, 238, 256–257, 263
Milestones, 153, 154, 155, 156, see also End milestone; Start milestone
MK II FPA, see Mark II function point analysis
Mode, 18, 56, 145, 244, 245, 246, 247, 248
Modification of software, 32, 42–43, 238
Modules, 61, 63, 128, 129, 177, 197
  adding, 43
  integration, 156, 157
  nature of, 59
Monopolistic pricing, 166, 168
Motion studies, 16, 146
Motivation, 15
Moving average, 18, 248
MS-DOS, 37
Multiple correlation, 232
Multi-tier architecture, 118
Multi-user applications, 175
Multi-vendor projects, 34

N

Naming conventions, 201
Navigation testing, 178
NDE, see Numeric data element
Negative correlation, 232
Negative testing, 176, 178, 188
Negotiation margin, 7
Network diagram, 161, 163, 284
New object point (NOP), 88–89
Nonlinear correlation, 232
Nonnumeric data, 178
NOP, see New object point
Normal-case scenario, 27, 28, 116, 117, 128, 129, 183, 185, 186, 187, 207, 208
Normal distribution, 18
Normalized test case, 274
Norms, 195, 196, 204, 205, 210, 249
  estimation, 15–17, 29, 210
  organizational, 204, 264
  productivity, see Productivity norms
  setting, 205–206
  validation of, 225, 226
Notification messages, 76, 77
Numeric data, 178
Numeric data element (NDE), 98, 100, 101, 278

O

Objectives, 55
Object-oriented analysis and design, 118, 119
Object-oriented languages, 118
Object point (OP), 11, 12, 33, 52, 69, 88–90, 107, 198, 249, 263, 277
  conversion factors, 181, 182
  merits and demerits of, 89–90
Odd behavior, 32, 42, 238
Oligopolistic pricing, 166, 168
On-line input/output, 74
OP, see Object point
OPE, see Output process element
Operating system, 37
Operational support, 32, 41, 42, 238
Operations manual, 68
Opportunity, 167, 168
Opportunity costing, 6, 7
Opportunity pricing, 50, 166
Oracle, 37
Order book position, 167
Organic project, 120, 121
Organizational norms, 204, 264
Organizational productivity standard, 248
Organizational support, 204–208
Organization size, 58, 61, 63

Output process element (OPE), 99, 100, 104, 278
Outsourcing, 1, 4
Overestimation, 16, 202–203
Overhead, 6, 7, 22, 29, 69, 103, 169, 170, 192

P

Parallel run, 33
Parallel testing, 175, 179, 190
Parametric estimation, 51
Partial correlation, 232
Partial life cycle project, 32, 33–35, 129, 230
  tool selection, 220
Partitioning, 178
Past projects, 51, 53, 58, 185, 199, see also
    Historical records
  analogy-based estimation, 57–64
  deriving productivity from, 243–249
Past records, 205
Patch, 41
Pearson's coefficient of correlation, 232
Pearson's coefficient of skewness, 245
Peer review, 41, 42, 43, 60, 62, 63, 102, 184,
    185, 199–200, 203, 204, 210, 260, 262
Penetration pricing, 166
People Soft, 51
Performance improvement, 70
Performance measurement, 83
Performance testing, 176
Periodic jobs, 41
Personal computer, 1
Person-day, 7, 12, 103, 115, 116, 128, 129,
    159, 180, 183, 185, 248
  costs, 219
Person-hour, 7, 12, 26, 115, 116, 128, 180,
    182, 183, 185, 187, 233, 247, 248
  computing cost of, 169–172
Person-month, 51, 120, 121
Person-week, 128
Personnel attributes, 121, 122
Phases, 128
  for task-based estimation, 251–257
  in testing project, 184–186, 187
Physical line, 73
Pilot run, 33
Platform, 59, 62, 198, 218, 233–234
  porting of software, 36
  task-based estimation and, 186
PMPal, 133, 161, 162
PMO, see Project management office
Point, 11, 97, 189
Porting, 32, 36–37, 38–39, 58, 238, 263
Positive correlation, 232

Positive testing, 174, 176, 177
Postdelivery, 125, 126, 127, 132, 257
Predecessor, 118, 154, 155, 156, 157, 158,
    159, 160, 161, 274
Preproject activities, 141
Presentation tier, 45
Price, 4, 202, 203
  cost versus, 165
  factors in determining, 167–168
  steps in determining, 168
Pricing, 6–7, 10, 28, 29, 273
  models, 165–168
Primavera, 70, 133, 161, 162, 219, 220
Probability distributions, 18
Probability of success, 18
Procedure description, 211
Procedure documents, 211
Procedures, 204, 208, 210, 273
Process, 273
  components of, 209–212
  defined, 208–209
  having a defined, 204
  software estimation, 208–213
  stable, 234
Process definition, for software estimation,
    259–264
Process description, 211
Process document, 209, 210, 211
Process-driven approach, 49, 50–51
Process-driven working, 208
Process element, 98, 99, 100, 104, 105, 278–279
Process flow, 234
Process improvement, 83, 117
Product, defined, 67
Product attributes, 121, 122
Product certification objectives, 179
Product costing, 6
Productive time, 149
Productivity, 15, 53, 69, 70, 83, 192, 274
  capacity versus, 273
  deriving from past projects, 243–249
  development methodology and, 119, 120
  for effort estimation, 117–120
  internal projects, 261
  paradox of, 12–14
  programmer knowledge of, 196–197, 203
  reviews and, 199, 200
  for software estimators, 135–151
    capacity versus, 149–151
    concerns with, 136–137
    defined, 135–136
    empirical methods, 145–146
    software development activities, 141–145

standard time, 137–141
  tool selection, 222
  work measurement, 146–149
task-based estimation and, 133
test-case-enumeration-based estimation and, 184
testing, 182, 186
tool selection, 218, 222
training in concepts of, 197
use case points and 87
variance analysis, 226, 227, 228, 229, 231, 233, 234, 235
Productivity factor, 192
Productivity figure, 7, 200, 205
  applying, 26–27
  deriving from past projects, 243–249
  for effort estimate using software size, 115–120
  how to obtain, 103–104
  for skill sets, 102, 103
  for testing, 181
  use of a single, 201
Productivity norms, 198, 210, 249
  erroneous, 225
  setting, 205–206
Productivity standards, 209
Product rating, 179
Product testing, 174, 175–177
Professional worker, 146
Profit, 6, 7, 69, 171, 219
Profit margin, 168
Program change request, 40
Program design, 102
Program evaluation and review technique, 219
Programmer, 15, 146, 196–197
  deriving productivity from past projects, 243–249
  senior, 196, 197
Programming language, 36, 37, 46, 59, 61, 62, 63, 232, 249
  productivity and, 147–148
  weight, 190
Program modification request, 40
Progress reporting, 180
Project
  past, see Past projects
  phases, in testing project, 184–186, 187
Project acquisition, 4–5, 200, 211, 260
  breaking the project down into components, 22–25, see also Work breakdown structure
  complexity of components, 25–26, see also Components

productivity figure, 26–27, see also Productivity figure
project execution, impact of, 28
software-sizing techniques, 26, see also specific techniques
uncertainty in estimation, 27–28
Project approval, see Project acquisition
Project attributes, 121, 122
Project-based development, 68
Project-based methodology, 6
Project closure, 103, 125, 126, 127, 130, 185, 257
Project details, 214
Project execution, 29, 195, 196, 211
Project initiation, 103, 124, 126, 127, 129, 184, 185, 251
Project initiation note, 22, 185, 261, 262
Project leader, 135, 196, 197, 203, 260, 261, 262, see also Project manager
Project management, 13, 103, 196
Project management office (PMO), 17, 26, 241, 260, 261, 262, 263, 264
Project management plan, 185
Project manager, 15, 135, 140, 141, 185, 197, 200, 260, 261, 262, 263, see also Project leader
  types of, 16–17
Project planning, 5, 18, 103, 124, 126, 127, 129, 130, 184, 185, 251–252
Project plans, 185, see also specific plans
Project postmortem, 15–16, 186, 200
Project scope, 24, 55, 199, 203, 211
Project start-up activities, 141
Project testing, 174, see also Testing
Project type, 61, 63
  estimation techniques and, 237–238
Proposals, evaluation of, 4

Q

Qualified worker, 138
Quality, 83, 119, 179, 197, 207, 234, 261
Quality assurance, 13, 22, 26, 29, 211
Quality assurance plan, 185

R

RAD, see Rapid Application Development
Radio button, 76
RAM, see Random access memory
Random access memory (RAM), 109, 112, 175
Rapid Application Development (RAD), 119
Rational Unified Process (RUP), 84, 119, 279
RDBMS, see Relational database management system

Record element type (RET), 74, 78, 79
Record keeping, 35, 64, 192
Reengineering, 263
Reestimation, 210, 259, 260–261
Reference documents, 215
Regression testing, 41, 42, 43, 126, 131, 176,
    180, 184, 188
Relational database management system,
    (RDBMS), 11, 31, 59, 61, 63, 74, 75, 78, 83
Relaxation allowance, 149
Repeat orders, 168
Reporting capability, tool selection, 222
Reports, 41, 43, 77, 88, 89, 90, 99, 102, 110,
    277, 278
Request for proposal (RFP), 5, 7, 21, 22, 24, 167
Requirements, changes in, 43
Requirements analysis, 27, 33, 34, 99, 102,
    103, 118, 119, 120, 130, 135, 143, 144
    testing, 124, 126, 201, 248, 252–253, 260
Requirements elicitation, 201
Requirements review, 144
Requirements specification, 5, 68, 124, 130
Resource allocation, 4, 140–141, 274
    work breakdown structure, 159–161
Resource request, 185
Resource requirements, 10, 185
    tool selection, 219–220
Resources, 202
    availability of, 274
    cost of, 169
    efficiency and effectiveness of, 70
    estimation of, 5, 140
    scheduling, 154
RET, see Record element type
Retrieval, 59
Reviewer, 214
Reviews, 210, 248, see also Managerial
    review; Peer review
    nonconformance to, 199–200, 203
RFP, see Request for proposal
Right-sizing, 203
Risks, 214–215
Rollout, 125, 127, 135, 142
Rounding, 102, 103, 169, 246, 247
Rules engine, 46, 59, 61, 63
RUP, see Rational Unified Process

S

Safety factory, 27
Sanity testing, 176
SAP, 51
Schedule, 202, 203
    actual values, 198

delivery, 28, 29
    impact of change request on, 261
    reviews, 199
    testing, 181
    variance analysis, 226, 227, 228, 229, 230, 231
Schedule estimation, 49, 153–163, 210, 260,
    262, 264
    detailed estimates, 52
    for functional expansion, 44–45
    graphic representation, 161–163
    gross estimates, 51, 52
    tools, 161, 201–202
    uncertainty in, 18
    work breakdown structure, 154–161
Scheduling, 274
    objectives of, 219
    tool selection, 161, 162, 219–220
SCM, see Supply chain management
Scope, 24, 55, 199, 203, 211
Scope of work, 214
Screens, 43, 88, 89, 90, 99, 104, 110, 277, 278
SCRUM, 119
Security management, 46
Security server, 45
Security testing, 176
Semi-detached project, 120, 121
Senior programmer, 196, 197
SEPG, see Software engineering process
    group
Server timeout, 176
Service costing, 6
Service fee, 2
Service industry, 9, 12
Service level agreement, 40, 41
Setup time, 148
SF, see Start-to-finish relationship
Shortlisting of past projects, 60–64
Simple average, 18
Simple correlation, 232
Simple mean, 244
Size
    complexity and, 110–112
    testing, 180, see also Testing
Size estimation, 195, 197, see also Software
    size estimation
    effort estimation and, 181–182, see also
        Effort estimation
    test, 173–193, see also Testing
    approaches to, 181–186, 187, see also
        specific approaches
    basics, 173–174
    methodology, 177–179
    product, 174, 175–177

project/embedded, 174
sizing, 186–192
strategy, 179–180
test estimation, 180–181
Size measure, 195
Sizing a testing project, 186–192
Skewness, 205
Skewness coefficient, 245, 246, 247, 248
Skill level, 15, 16, 29, 102, 138–139, 140, 169, 188, 197, 245
Skill sets, 102, 117, 118, 135, 137, 159
Skimming pricing, 166
Software design, see Design
Software developers, 146
Software development, see Development
Software development companies, 1
Software development life cycle, 31, 33–35, 102, 122, 123
Software development methodology, influence on estimation, 118–120
Software engineer, 196
Software engineering activities, 142
Software Engineering Institute of Carnegie Mellon University, 208
Software engineering process group (SEPG), 26, 261, 262
Software estimation, 273
analogy-based, see Analogy-based estimation
approaches to, 49–65, see also specific approaches
ad hoc, 49, 50
detailed estimates, 52
gross estimates, 51–52
process-driven, 49, 50–51
background, 1–2
best practices, 203–216
checklists, 209, 210, 212
defined process, 204
document, 209, 210, 211
formats, 209, 210, 212
guidelines, 209, 210, 212
knowledge repository, 204–205
organizational support, 204–208
presentation of estimates, 213–216
procedures, 209, 210, 211
process, 208–213
productivity norms, 205–206
single estimate or range of estimates, 207–208
standards, 209, 210, 212
templates, 209, 210, 212
unit of measure for software size, 206–207

complexity versus density, 107–114, see also Complexity; Density
cost, see Cost estimation
defined, 2–4
deliverables from, 3–4
effort, see Effort estimation
importance of, 4
organizational support for, 204–208
paradoxes of, 9–19
actual versus estimated values, 15–17
offering fixed bids, 14
software productivity, 12–14
software size, 11–12
uncertainty, 17–18
why it is performed, 10
pitfalls, 195, 196–203
absence of software estimation tools, 201–202
inadequate duration for estimation, 199
inexperienced estimators, 196–197
lack of causal analysis of variances, 200
lack of historical data, 198
lack of training, 197–198
nonconformance to reviews, 199–200
not measuring the software size of the product delivered, 200
over- or underestimation, 202–203
use of a single productivity figure, 201
presentation of estimates, 213–216
process definition for, 259–264
at project acquisition stage, 21–30, see also Project acquisition
by project type, 31–47, see also Project type; specific types of projects
schedule, see Schedule estimation
size, see Size estimation; Software size
tools, see Tools
when it is carried out, 4–5
Software estimators, productivity, 135–151, 214
capacity versus, 149–151
concerns with, 136–137
defined, 135–136
empirical methods, 145–146
experience of, 196–197, 203
productivity tool selection and, 222
software development activities, 141–145
standard time, 137–141
training of, 197–198, 199, 203
work measurement, 146–149
Software maintenance projects, see Maintenance projects
Software modification, 32, 42–43, 238
Software Process Improvement Network, 27

Software product, defined, 67
Software productivity, see Productivity
Software Project Managers Network, 27
Software size, 3, 4, 197, 198, 248
   for agile projects, 45
   agreement on, 4
   conversion to effort, 53, 201, 204
   converting effort into, 27
   deriving test units from, 34
   detailed estimates, 52
   development methodology and, 119, 120
   effort and, 49
   effort estimation using, 115–118
      COCOMO, 120–123
   estimated versus actual, 5, 29, see also
      Variance analysis
   estimation of, 6, 7, see also Size estimation;
      Software size estimation
   gross estimates, 51
   not measuring the product delivered, 200, 203
   paradoxes of, 11–12
   partial life cycle projects and, 34–35
   testing and, see Software-size-based
      estimation; Testing
   tool selection, 217–218
   unit of measure for, 52, 206–207, 274–279,
      see also specific units of measure
   variance analysis, 226, 227, 228, 229, 231, 233
   for Web application, 46
Software-size-based estimation, 181–182, 237
Software size estimation, 49, 52–53, 67–95,
      97–106, 237, 238, 260, 262, 264, see also
      Size estimation; Software size; specific
      units of measure
   approaches to measurement, 68–70
   complexity versus density, 107–114, see also
      Complexity; Density
   concerns with, 70–71
   function points, 73–84
   for internal projects, 262
   lines of code, 71–73
   Mark II function point analysis, 90–94
   object points, 88–90
   software size units, 97–106
   templates for, 209
   tools for, 201–202, 221
   use case points, 84–87
   using software size units, 99–100, 101, see
      also Software size unit
   what is measured, 67–68
Software size measures, 34, 67–95, 97–106,
      210, 211, 260, 263–264, see also specific
      measures

Software size unit (SSU), 33, 52, 69, 97–106,
      198, 248, 249, 263, 277–279
   actual values, 198
   conversion factors, 181, 182
   definition of, 98–100
   effort estimation from, 100, 102–103
   FAQs, 104–105
   how to obtain productivity figures, 103–104
   merits and demerits of, 105
   procedure for size estimation using, 99–100,
      101
   reviews, 199
Software sizing, 39
   for functional expansion, 44, 45
   techniques, 26
Software testing project, 263
Software test unit (STU), 11, 189–192, 237,
      249, 263, 274
Software tools, see Tools
Sound bytes, 76
Source code, 68, 73
Specifications, 7, 14, 21, 22–23, 49, 54, 69, 197
   testing and, 173, see also Testing
Spiral models, 119
Spreadsheet, 24, 129, 161, 201–202
Sprints, 119
Spyware, 176, 179, 192
SS, see Start-to-start relationship
SSU, see Software size unit
Stable process, 234
Stand-alone application, 182, 187
Standard costing, 6
Standard deviation, 232, 234, 246, 247
Standards, 208, 209, 210, 212
Standard time, 12, 16, 137–141, 149, 274, see
      also Productivity
Standard unit of measure, 206–207
Standard value, 234, 235
Start milestone, 153, 154, 155, 157, 158
Start-to-finish (SF) relationship, 156
Start-to-start (SS) relationship, 118, 156, 157,
      158, 159
State transitions, 175
Statistical mean, 18, 145
Statistical median, 18
Statistical mode, 18, 56, 145, 146, 246, 247,
      248
Statutory requirements, 43
Storage, 24, 59, 99
Story point, 11, 45, 52
Stress testing, 176, 178, 190
STU, see Software test unit
Subcontracting, 202

Successor, 118, 155, 156, 157
Super effort, 139
Super-performer, 16, 70
Super skill, 138, 139, 140, 141
Supply chain management (SCM), 35, 51, 58
Symmetry of data, 245
Symons, Charles, 90
Synthesis, 16, 146, 206
System, defined, 99
System implementation, 33
Systems analysis, 13
System software, 33, 112
System testing, 27, 102, 125, 131, 132, 174, 179, 184, 187, 188, 189, 190, 192, 254–255

T

Tape drives, 109, 112
Task (activity)-based estimation, 26, 33, 34, 37, 39, 41, 42, 43, 44, 45, 53, 70, 181, 184–186, 187, 210, 237, 238, 263
  effort estimation, 124–133
  suggested phases and tasks for, 251–257
Tasks, 128, 153, 154, 161
  for task-based estimation, 251–257
  in testing project, 185–186
TCAF, see Technical complexity adjustment factor
TCF, see Technical complexity factor
TDE, see Total data elements
Technical complexity, 93
Technical complexity adjustment factor (TCAF), 93, 277
Technical complexity factor (TCF), 85, 86, 87, 279
Technical factor (TF), 85, 86
Templates, 204, 209, 210, 212
  for estimation presentation, 265–267
  for estimation request note, 269–271
Test-case-enumeration-based estimation, 34, 181, 183–184, 237
Test cases, 34, 178–179, 187, 189, 274
  coverage, 188
  design, 184, 187
Test-cases-based testing, 177, 180
Test-driven development, 119
Test effort estimation, 210, 274
Test environment, 184
Test estimation, 180–181
Testing, 27, 33, 34, 38, 99, 102, 103, 118, 119, 120, 126, 127, 144, 173–193, 201, 248, 249, 254–255, 263, see also specific types
  basics, 173–174
  cost, 180, 274

effort, 180, 274
  environment, 188
  methodology, 177–179
  objectives, 179
  scenarios, 174–177
  schedule, 181, 274
  size, 180, 274
  sizing testing projects, 186–192
  strategy, 179–180
  test effort estimation, approaches to, 181–186, see also specific approaches
  test estimation, 180–181
  tools, 190
Testing projects, 129, 218, 237
  task-based estimation phases, 124–126
Test logs, 68
Test plan, 178, 187, 189
Test-plan-based testing, 180
Test planning, 125, 131, 184, 187
Test point, 52
Test report preparation, 185
Test result logging and reporting, 184
Test strategy, 179–180
Test units, 34
TF, see Technical factor
Therbligs, 146
Third-generation language (3GL), 52, 72, 74, 88, 89, 263, 277, 278
Thousand lines of code (KLOC), 120, 121
3GL, see Third-generation language
Three-tier application, 182
Tiers, 45, 59, 61, 62, 63, 99
Time and material contract, 2
Timesheets, 145, 182, 192
Time study, 16, 146, 149
Tool-based testing, 180
Tools, 16, 64, 129, 133, 161, 162, 175, 186, 188, 200, 210
  absence of, 201–202, 204
  conversion factors, 206
  cost of, 169, 171
  criteria for selecting, 217–223
  testing, 190
Top-down approach, 24
Total data elements (TDE), 100, 101
Tradematrix, 51
Training
  cost of, 171
  estimators, 197–198, 199, 203
Transaction, see Components
Transfer pricing, 166
Travel cost, 169, 171
Trend analysis, 200, 226, 229–231, 264

Troubleshooting guide, 68
Two-bid system, 166

U

UCP, see Use case point
UKSMA, see U.K. Software Metrics Association
U.K. Software Metrics Association (UKSMA), 90, 91, 94, 276
UML, see Unified Modeling Language
Unadjusted actor weight, 85
Unadjusted function point count, 79
Unadjusted use case points (UUCP), 85, 87
Unadjusted use case weight, 84
Uncertainty, 17–18, 22, 27–28, 133, 197
Underestimation, 17, 202–203
Unified Modeling Language (UML), 84, 87, 263, 279
Uninstall testing, 177
Unit, 11, 97, 98, 186, 189
Units of measure, 67–95, 274–279, see also specific units of measure
   for software size, tools selection, 217–218
   standard, 206–207
Unit testing, 13, 27, 34, 35, 39, 102, 135, 174, 175, 179, 187, 190
Unit of work, 138
Upgrades, 37, 46
Upper control limit, 234, 235
Usability, 179
   of tools, 220–221
Usability testing, 176
Use case point (UCP), 11, 12, 33, 52, 69, 84–87, 107, 189, 198, 249, 263, 279
   conversion factors, 181, 182
   merits and demerits of, 87
User acceptance testing, 27, 35, 37, 38, 39, 125, 132, 174, 175, 176, 177, 179, 189, 190, 192
User accounts, 41
User documentation/guide, 68, 176, 177
User interface, 102, 221
User management, 41
User requirements analysis, 33, see also Requirements analysis
User specifications, 69
User training, 33, 125, 127, 132
UUCP, see Unadjusted use case points

V

VAF, see Value adjustment factor
Vaknin, Sam, 108

Validation, 34, 135, 237
Value adjustment factor (VAF), 75, 80–82, 84, 275
Variable declarations, 72, 73
Variance, 200, 202, see also Causal analysis; Variance analysis
Variance analysis, 5, 50, 57, 123, 190, 195, 196, 198, 199, 200, 204, 205, 210, 211, 225–235, 249, 264
   control charts, 234–235
   correlation analysis, 231–234
   project, 226–229
   trend analysis, 229–231
   types of variation, 225
Variation, 15–17, 29. see also Variance analysis
Vendor proposals, 4
Verification, 34, 102, 135, 237
Viruses, 176, 179, 192
Visual Basic, 37, 233
Volume testing, 175

W

Walk-through, 13, 34, 39, 188, 260, 262
Warranty phase, 257
WBS, see Work breakdown structure
Web applications, 83, 87, 99, 175, 187
Web projects, 32, 45–46, 88
Web server, 45, 59, 61, 63
Web site, 52, 83
Weighted average, 18
Weighted mean, 244
Weights, for converting size estimate, 189–192
White box testing, 173–174, 180, 187, 190
Wideband Delphi estimation, 55
Work breakdown structure (WBS), 22–25, 274
   initial, 154–155
   with predecessors defined, 155–157
   with resource allocation, 159–161
Working, methods of, 15, 16, 209
Working environment, 16
Work measurement, 146–149, 274
Work norms, 16
Work-sampling technique, 16, 103, 146, 149, 206
Worst-case scenario, 27, 28, 29, 116, 117, 128, 129, 171, 183, 185, 186, 187, 208

Y

Y2K, 32, 39